NEGOTIATING TRANSITIONAL JUSTICE

The recent Colombian peace negotiations took the art and science of negotiating transitional justice to unprecedented levels of complexity. For decades, the Colombian government fought a bitter insurgency war against FARC guerrilla forces. After protracted negotiations, the two parties reached a peace deal that took account of the rights of victims. As first-hand participants in the talks, and principal advisers to the Colombia government, Mark Freeman and Iván Orozco offer a unique account of the mechanics through which accountability issues were addressed. Drawing from this case study and other global experiences, Freeman and Orozco offer a comprehensive theoretical and practical conception of what makes the 'devil's dilemma' of negotiating peace with justice implausible but feasible.

Mark Freeman is the founder and executive director of the Institute for Integrated Transitions (IFIT). He is the author of *Necessary Evils: Amnesties and the Search for Justice* (Cambridge, 2010) and *Truth Commissions and Procedural Fairness* (Cambridge, 2006), which received the American Society of International Law's Certificate of Merit.

Iván Orozco is Associate Professor in the Department of Political Science at the Universidad de los Andes (Bogotá). He is the author of several books – all published in Spanish – including *Justica Transicional en tiempos del deber de memoria* (2009), *Sobre los Límites de la Conciencia Humanitaria* (2005) and *Combatientes, Rebeldes y Terroristas* (1st edition, 1992).

Negotiating Transitional Justice

FIRSTHAND LESSONS FROM COLOMBIA
AND BEYOND

MARK FREEMAN

Institute for Integrated Transitions

IVÁN OROZCO

Universidad de los Andes

CAMBRIDGE
UNIVERSITY PRESS

University Printing House, Cambridge CB2 8BS, United Kingdom

One Liberty Plaza, 20th Floor, New York, NY 10006, USA

477 Williamstown Road, Port Melbourne, VIC 3207, Australia

314–321, 3rd Floor, Plot 3, Splendor Forum, Jasola District Centre, New Delhi – 110025, India

79 Anson Road, #06–04/06, Singapore 079906

Cambridge University Press is part of the University of Cambridge.

It furthers the University's mission by disseminating knowledge in the pursuit of education, learning, and research at the highest international levels of excellence.

www.cambridge.org
Information on this title: www.cambridge.org/9781107187566
DOI: 10.1017/9781316941485

© Mark Freeman and Iván Orozco 2020

This publication is in copyright. Subject to statutory exception and to the provisions of relevant collective licensing agreements, no reproduction of any part may take place without the written permission of Cambridge University Press.

First published 2020

Printed in the United Kingdom by TJ International Ltd, Padstow Cornwall

A catalogue record for this publication is available from the British Library.

Library of Congress Cataloging-in-Publication Data
NAMES: Freeman, Mark, 1968– author. | Orozco, Iván, author.
TITLE: Negotiating transitional justice : firsthand lessons from Colombia and beyond / Mark Freeman, Institute for Integrated Transitions; Iván Orozco, Universidad de los Andes.
DESCRIPTION: Cambridge, United Kingdom ; New York, NY, USA : Cambridge University Press, 2020.
IDENTIFIERS: LCCN 2019017891| ISBN 9781107187566 (hardback) | ISBN 9781316638156 (pbk.)
SUBJECTS: LCSH: Peace-building–Law and legislation. | Transitional justice. | Peace-building– Law and legislation–Colombia. | Transitional justice–Colombia. | Colombia. Marco Juridico para la Paz. | Colombia–Politics and government–1974-
CLASSIFICATION: LCC KZ6787 .F74 2020 | DDC 340/.115–DC23
LC record available at https://lccn.loc.gov/2019017891

ISBN 978-1-107-18756-6 Hardback
ISBN 978-1-316-63815-6 Paperback

Cambridge University Press has no responsibility for the persistence or accuracy of URLs for external or third-party internet websites referred to in this publication and does not guarantee that any content on such websites is, or will remain, accurate or appropriate.

Contents

Preface	page vii
Acknowledgements	ix

PART I: NEGOTIATING TRANSITIONAL JUSTICE:
A CONCEPTUAL FRAMEWORK   1
    Introduction   1

1. **General Considerations**   3
   a. Safeland, Transitionland, and Negotiationland   6
   b. A Balanced Approach   13
   c. Determinative Choices   14

2. **The Role of International Law**   22
   a. Making the Case for New Law   24

3. **Elements of Practice**   37
   a. Process Design   37
   b. Tactical Considerations   40
   c. Justice Considerations within the Negotiation   48

4. **Conclusions**   56

PART II: NEGOTIATING TRANSITIONAL JUSTICE:
THE CASE OF COLOMBIA   57
    Introduction   57

1. **The Context**   59
   a. The Havana Talks in Perspective   59
   b. Victims and the Politics of Transitional Justice   74

2. **The Experience** 105
   a. Victims versus Victimisers 105
   b. Ordinary versus Extraordinary Justice 160
   c. Dignity versus Legal Security 203

3. **Conclusions** 243

Annex 1: Basic Information about the Havana Negotiation 247

Annex 2: The Legal Framework for Peace (2012) 249

Index 253

Preface

It is frequently remarked that negotiating peace with justice is a great challenge. Indeed, few would argue otherwise. Yet, the causes of the challenge are rarely interrogated honestly or fully, and the practical means for surmounting it even less so.

This book fills that gap. In part, it is inspired by our firsthand experience of the Colombian government's negotiations with the FARC rebel group, when the negotiating parties made the counterintuitive decision to put the issue of 'victims' at the centre of the negotiating agenda. Although the parties took the decision on the basis of very different political, legal, and moral premises, it was made in full knowledge that the issue would prove an extraordinarily difficult hurdle to climb.

As we discovered through our experience of the talks, the parties' expectations about the meaning and scope of the issue were surprisingly non-overlapping. This manifested itself in the great difficulty each side experienced in deciphering and deconstructing the adversary's distinctive presumptions, and in identifying realistic pathways to achieve an overlapping consensus.

Being independent advisers to the government delegation throughout the negotiation of the 'victims' issue in Havana – which began in June 2014 and lasted until December 2015, when a complete agreement on the issue was published – we had the privilege of being insiders and outsiders at the same time. We were present at most internal deliberations of the government delegation, and at the negotiation table itself, but without the burden of representing particular views or taking formal decisions. This constituted a unique perch, allowing us to be 'participant-observers' inside the process.

Yet, while the book is inspired by our firsthand experience of the negotiation – and the luxury of hindsight – it is not written as a chronicle of what transpired. Instead, it offers an intellectual exploration of the how and why of key aspects of the agreements reached in Havana on the subject of criminal justice and the related themes of truth, reparation, and non-repetition. In doing so, the book also draws upon our previous scholarship and experience working on issues of peace, war, negotiation, and justice elsewhere.

Throughout the text we pay close attention to questions of law and legal theory, as these are intrinsic to the exercise of negotiating transitional justice. Yet, by necessity, we endeavour to pay equal attention to the theory and practice of negotiation. In a *negotiation* of justice, there is no adequate or responsible way to divorce the two themes.

The book has two main parts that draw upon nearly five years of in-depth conversation between the authors. Part I, written by Mark with Iván's feedback, offers a general conception of what makes negotiating peace with justice implausible but feasible. Part II, written by Iván with Mark's feedback, goes into the specifics of the Colombian experience, beginning with a contextual overview and continuing with three personal essays.

Being in Havana was a rare experience. In the following pages we transmit some of the knowledge we were privileged to acquire while there, and the broader understanding it allowed us to have of the devil's dilemma of foisting justice on peace.

Acknowledgements

Mark is sincerely grateful to Iván for his friendship and collaboration throughout the writing of this book. He would like to thank the Board and staff of IFIT for their support, as well as the many expert colleagues in IFIT's practice groups and brain trusts. Mark also wishes to acknowledge and thank Sergio Jaramillo for the opportunity to serve as an advisor in the Havana peace talks, and for the chance to work alongside the many other remarkable members of the government delegation. Above all, Mark thanks his wife, Annamie, for her extraordinary patience and constant support throughout the talks and the writing that followed.

Iván would like to express his thanks to Mark in reciprocal terms. Additionally, he wishes to thank his friends and colleagues Pablo Kalmanovitz, Alejandro Reyes, Rodrigo Uprimny, Eduardo Pizarro, and Carlo Nasi, who read one or more chapters and helped improve them through their feedback. He is also grateful to Sergio Jaramillo for his wisdom and friendship; the many colleagues from the government negotiating team; María Victoria Llorente; and the members of the Fondo de Capital Humano for helping him reconstruct important episodes from the negotiations. Iván expresses his deepest appreciation to his wife, Alma Clara.

Both Mark and Iván extend their gratitude to John Berger and the full team at Cambridge University Press, and to the Universidad de los Andes for having allowed Mateo Reyes to translate, with great skill, the majority of Iván's first draft from Spanish to English. A very special thank-you is also due to Vivian Newman Pont, who accompanied the authors for two full days of discussion in the summer of 2016, at the start of the work on this book.

PART I

Negotiating Transitional Justice
A Conceptual Framework

INTRODUCTION

It is tautological to say that the Colombian experience of negotiating peace with justice was unique. How could it be otherwise? Yet, the uniqueness of the experience was limited, not absolute. Some aspects of the experience were context-specific, while others were intrinsic to the choice to negotiate peace with justice in the first place. Separating out these aspects is a sine qua non for making sense of the Colombian experience, or indeed any experience, of negotiating peace with justice.

As such, Part I is devoted to this endeavour. It is divided into three main sections.

First, there is an examination of what makes ensuring justice for atrocity crimes more difficult, both normatively and practically, than for non-atrocity crimes. In terms of practical difficulties, the analysis distinguishes three types of situations: one in which there is neither negotiation nor transition out of war; one in which there is transition without negotiation; and one in which there is negotiation without transition. Subsequently, the analysis focuses on the unique structural complications of seeking justice in the latter situation.

The second section of Part I examines a surprising gap in international law when it comes to the negotiation of peace with justice. It is the absence of a body of law that could provide incentives, guidance, and support to states such that they could become both more inclined to choose and better able to achieve negotiated rather than military solutions to prevent and resolve internal armed conflict.

The third and final section enumerates some conceptual and practical rules of thumb to guide future efforts at negotiating peace with justice. These draw from the Colombian experience as well as other country contexts.

1

General Considerations

The term 'atrocity crime', as used here, refers to the international crimes of genocide, crimes against humanity, and war crimes – and could reasonably be extended to include gross human rights violations. Such crimes destroy human dignity, life, or both, and on levels that are usually irreparable. That is because no amount of justice against the perpetrator of such crimes, and no amount of reparation in favour of the victim, can be adequate to redress the harm caused. Morally speaking, every remedy is second best. Restoring the status quo ante is not an option.

Nevertheless, international law obliges states to make a good-faith effort to ensure national-level justice for atrocity crimes. Thus, the normative and practical impossibility does not exonerate the legal responsibility.

In a state in which there is neither negotiation nor transition out of war, the fulfilment of this legal responsibility involves what we may designate **first-order** difficulties. These are the kinds of unavoidable challenges that may be expected in any case of serious crime for which the perpetrator does not admit guilt, such as the high burden of proof that must be met; the limited amount of direct, inculpatory evidence; the exorbitant time and cost of investigation; the lack of willing and reliable eyewitnesses; and so forth.

These difficulties will be familiar to any prosecutor or judge in a country that enjoys the rule of law. Trying serious crimes is, with rare exception, an uncertain and complex undertaking in the absence of a guilty plea.

In a state in which a transition out of war or dictatorship is under way, a set of **second-order** structural difficulties exists on top of the first ones. First, wars and dictatorships tend to produce an unmanageable number of perpetrators, and equally unmanageable number of victims, in relation to the capacity of the justice system. Second, the independence and effectiveness of legal institutions themselves are typically low. Third, the destruction of evidence is often widespread. Fourth, the fears of witnesses will be deep-seated, as threats and intimidation will remain prevalent. Fifth, legal obstacles to justice – such as lapsed prescription periods, earlier amnesties that remain in force, and lacunae in the criminal code vis-à-vis atrocity crimes – are common. Sixth, less money tends to be available for retroactive justice efforts, since so much has to be allocated to national reconstruction, institution building, and processing of new crimes. Finally, with the exception of trials against dispensable enemies, transitional governments tend to be reluctant to prosecute the past, as they are understandably wary about jeopardising a fragile or hard-won stability.

Let us now imagine a third state in which there is negotiation without transition (i.e., a state that remains at war politically, militarily, or both). Here, each of the first- and second-order difficulties of achieving justice must be taken into account, but also a **third-order** set.

What are these? First, prior to signing any political settlement or peace accord, the parties to a negotiation need and want to understand the legal risks their signature might entail inside the borders of the country. As such, if there is going to be justice as a formal part of the settlement, it will have to be the subject of explicit, consensual agreement. Second, in a negotiation, consent will normally have to come from the persons presumed to bear greatest responsibility for past atrocity crimes, as they will almost always be among those sitting at the negotiating table. The prospect of retroactive justice is something such persons most certainly perceive as contrary to their interests. Third, as any negotiated settlement involves multiple and competing agenda items, the issue of justice cannot be hived off but must instead be form-fitted with the other issues. These may include complex security, political, economic, and other decisions that move in the opposite direction of justice.

This being the case, it is not surprising to observe that affirmative national-level justice commitments rarely appear in negotiated political and peace settlements (unless foisted by third-party mediators upon weak parties, as in South Sudan 2015). Instead, the parties to a negotiation typically resolve the issue in one of the following ways:

- With guarantees of neither justice nor truth-seeking against those presumed to bear greatest responsibility for past atrocity crimes (e.g., Lebanon 1991, Bosnia 1995, Afghanistan 2001, Angola 2002),
- With guarantees of truth-seeking but explicit deferral or conditioning of the prospect of justice to another time or process (e.g., El Salvador 1992, Burundi 2000, Kenya 2008, Philippines 2015), or
- With guarantees of truth-seeking but neither explicit deferral of justice nor explicit promises of it (e.g., Haiti 1993, Guatemala 1994, Sierra Leone 1999, Nepal 2006, Mali 2015).

The reason for this pattern should be self-evident. The combination of first-, second-, and third-order difficulties radically reduces the bandwidth for guaranteeing justice in any form. As such, the default outcome is either one of those described above or a breakdown in the overall talks (as occurred in Uganda where, from 2003 to 2008, the government sought to negotiate national-level justice as part of a larger agreement with the Lord's Resistance Army meant, in fact, to avert the threat of international justice).

It was only in Colombia that the parties succeeded, in the central negotiation process, to reach agreement on the establishment of a national-level, post-conflict justice mechanism and corresponding set of criminal sanctions (all of which was part of a comprehensive transitional justice system). The result, though messy, is unprecedented – and, for that reason alone, worth understanding in detail.

Yet, before examining the factors that made Colombia's agreement possible, it is first important to understand two key implications of the *non*-context-specific difficulties of negotiating justice for atrocity crimes.

First, the combined effect of (1) the requirement of consensus, (2) the decision-making role of those bearing greatest responsibility, and (3) the imperative to align justice with other agenda items obligates the negotiating parties to be far more **flexible** in legal, tactical, and other terms. That is because the force of these three variables militates massively against agreements on justice.

Second, the combined effect of these same variables also compels the parties to adopt an **integrated** concept of justice that (1) takes account of the original insight of transitional justice, which conceives justice as something broader than mere criminal justice, (2) interlocks the mechanisms and rhythms of justice with those pertaining to disarmament, political participation, institutional reform, and more, and (3) understands the imperative of ending armed conflict or repressive rule as superior, rather than subordinate, to that of justice.

In turn, these structural needs – for flexibility on the one hand, and integrated methodology on the other – produce yet more consequences in the context of an effort to negotiate peace with justice.

First, a wide range of *negotiation-specific* techniques must be learned and deployed. Three of these we examine in some depth in this book: recourse to constructive ambiguities, use of confidence-building measures, and the separation of controllable and uncontrollable risks. Second, a parallel set of *justice-specific* techniques must be canvassed and utilised. These include a variety of creative options for reconciling competing expectations of dignity and legal security; choosing between ordinary and extraordinary mechanisms; agreeing on who is victim and who is victimiser; distinguishing causes and consequences of the conflict; resolving the interplay of truth-seeking and justice; parsing retributive, restorative, and distributive forms of justice; and balancing national sovereignty and international standards.

What must be understood is that these techniques and choice points cannot be avoided in any setting in which a deliberate decision is made to negotiate peace with justice. That is because, without them, there is no way to be sufficiently flexible and integrated so as to consummate an agreement. Indeed, we can see this with particular clarity in the case of Colombia's negotiation because the negotiating parties made the unprecedented and radical choice to put victims 'at the centre' of the negotiation agenda, and because the government was emphatic that it would not sign a deal that risked breaching its international legal obligations.

But before we come to all of this (in Part II of the book), we present the reader with the following, more general theory of negotiating peace with justice.

A. SAFELAND, TRANSITIONLAND, AND NEGOTIATIONLAND

In any context of dictatorship or armed conflict, there is a strong likelihood, if not guarantee, that atrocities will be committed. Even a conflict actor that is broadly committed to upholding international human rights and humanitarian law will have difficulty preventing excesses across the entirety of its political or military structures.

However, under international law, positive intentions are all but irrelevant to the question of state responsibility. They will not excuse a government from its duties to investigate, prosecute, and punish those responsible for atrocities.

Nevertheless, the kind of damage wrought by atrocity crimes is fundamentally unfixable. A group killed in the course of a genocidal campaign cannot be restored to life by the courts. Neither can an individual, enslaved and tortured as part of a systematic attack directed against a civilian population, be made whole again. This is so regardless of how severely the torturers are sanctioned, how much compensation is paid, and how much rehabilitation is offered. Physically, one can survive; morally and emotionally, the only true justice would be to have never suffered corporal and psychological desecration in the first place.

With this in mind, we offer the reader a thought experiment. Let us imagine a peaceful and democratic place called **Safeland**, in which grave violations (whether committed by state or non-state actors) very rarely occur. Rights prevail, and crime is the exception not the rule.

Now let us imagine the occurrence of an individual atrocity in Safeland. Beyond the immediate shock, what would be the official response in such a place? The answer is obvious: investigations would be conducted, trial procedures undertaken, and sanctions and other remedies imposed should criminal culpability be established. A prosecutor or investigating judge in Safeland would have no choice but to prioritise such a case, as a failure to investigate would constitute a public scandal.

Yet, even in Safeland, finding the right evidence, persuading the witnesses, and proving the case beyond a reasonable doubt – while the defendant receives counsel from the country's top criminal lawyer – would be anything but easy. In the absence of an admission of guilt, the case could last for years; and even if proven in the first instance, it could involve many years of motions and appeals. As such, even in Safeland, a single serious case could consume considerable time and resources of the legal system, without any guaranteed outcomes.

Let us now imagine a very different country: one that is in the midst of a transition out of genocide, civil war, or prolonged and violent dictatorship. We will call it **Transitionland** and will presume that a new political dispensation is under way as the result of a public uprising, external intervention, leadership death, military victory, electoral win, or some combination thereof.

Among its many challenges, Transitionland's new government faces the question of whether or how to confront the legacy of mass violence that occurred during the prior period of repression or tumult. For purposes of illustration, we can be generous in our premises: we can assume that the new government is willing to adopt the boilerplate elements of transitional justice (i.e., truth, justice, reparation, and guarantees of non-recurrence).

However, even with good intentions, it is all but certain that the government of Transitionland will be stymied by a combination of unpleasant realities affecting the pursuit of justice.

For example, tens or hundreds of thousands of atrocity crimes may have been committed, producing untold numbers of victims who suffered at the hands of untold numbers of perpetrators – far more than even the world's best justice system could cope with. The country may also be wholly or partially impoverished after years of repression, looting, and more. In addition, much of the evidence has likely been destroyed or gone missing; and in any case, prosecutors and judges, not to mention the court facilities themselves, are ill equipped to offer fair trial standards. The country may be experiencing a spike in current crime as well, with remnants of the former militia and the old guard applying their criminal skills to new targets.

Thus, in the pursuit of justice, not only would the government of Transitionland face the first-order difficulties of Safeland; it would also face the aforementioned second-order difficulties, guaranteeing inadequate justice vis-à-vis all those responsible for past atrocities.

The government could thus choose an alternative path. It could opt, for example, to establish a truth commission to gather evidence that could be used for follow-on efforts at prosecution and for the development of a victim reparations programme. Yet, even such a commission could be expected to fall short because of the lack of time or resources to conduct an in-depth investigation of anything more than a fraction of the total universe of atrocity crimes. Likewise, even a generous reparations programme could be expected to prove inadequate, as it would be unable to offer compensation, restitution, and rehabilitation measures commensurate with the real scale of physical, psychological, and economic costs inflicted on the country's thousands of victims.

As for criminal trials, the government may discover it has to reconsider its initial (already modest) ambitions, as judicial pursuits could risk diverting precious financial and political capital away from other urgent priorities of reconstruction, economic growth, institutional reform, and much else. Having recently overcome war or tyranny, the prospect of retroactive justice likewise could risk triggering new cycles of violence. Besides, the country's court system is likely unable to guarantee due process except in the long term, leaving only the option of politically sensitive international trials in the short and midterm. Legal obstacles such as earlier amnesties may give yet more reason to defer or delegate the task of criminal justice.

Consequently, despite its good will, the government of Transitionland (especially but not only in a postwar environment) can be expected to struggle greatly in the face of the legacy of atrocities and abuse it inherited.

Let us finally imagine a third country: **Negotiationland**. Like Transitionland, it has experienced a long history of violence, which has produced vast numbers of atrocity crimes. Yet, unlike Transitionland, it is not a country in transition; instead, its conflict persists, making problematic the very invocation of the term *'transitional* justice'.

To add colour to the thought experiment, let us presume in particular that Negotiationland is experiencing a civil war that pits state forces against rebel forces, and that there is no serious prospect of total victory for either side. The only way out appears to be through negotiation – a fact that, independently, both parties to the conflict eventually come to accept. Exploratory talks get under way, allowing the leaders of each side to assess if there is scope for a bona fide peace negotiation.

After multiple forays over many months, the parties manage to agree to an agenda for formal peace talks. The agenda includes vague references to human rights and accountability (as opposed to a specific mention of criminal trials) and a set of rules and protocols to guide the overall process.

Yet, questions immediately arise with the public: Does the agenda imply that judicial accountability will be part of the deal? If so, what will each side have to concede to make that happen? Will the victims receive compensation? Won't the mere prospect of accountability get in the way of a final settlement, and thus discourage an end to the conflict?

In order to answer these questions, an immediate impulse many will have is to reach for the standard toolkit of transitional justice. After all, although we are in Negotiationland, and notwithstanding the absence of transition, the situation has the aura of a Transitionland challenge.

Two realities explain this impulse; together, they constitute the raison d'être of transitional justice. The first is the mass scale of violence in the war scenario in question. *Quantitatively speaking*, this guarantees a very incomplete form of *collective redress*, taking account of the number of violations. The second is the extraordinary depravity of the war violations themselves. *Qualitatively speaking*, this guarantees a profoundly unsatisfying form of *individual redress*, even for those who one day may be fortunate enough to have their cases included in a transitional justice policy.

Because of these two realities, it is understandable that many tend to 'default' in their minds (and actions) to the logic and methods of transitional justice. After all, the same impediments to individual and collective redress exist in Negotiationland.

Yet, this is deeply mistaken. Transitional justice is decidedly *not* the right analytic starting point for Negotiationland. Instead, the proper starting point is the *fact of negotiation* – and *its* intrinsic constraints.

There are three cumulative, differentiating factors (which we have called third-order difficulties) that illuminate why this is so.

Factor 1: The generic difference between bilateral negotiation and unilateral decision-making

Outside the confines of a formal negotiation, a government can take unilateral decisions on anything within its legal and political authority. While it may be prudent for it to *consult* political opponents or the public about its transitional justice plans (or anything else), it is under no obligation to obtain anyone's formal consent unless there is an independent legal obligation to do so.

In a negotiation, by contrast, formal consent is always required. Compromise and mutual concessions are intrinsic to the very choice of negotiation.

Structurally, they offer the *only* pathway to agreement, whether on questions of transitional justice or whatever else.

Naturally, the balance of power at times can shift in a negotiation, making one side better able to secure concessions than the other. However, ultimately neither side can impose its will and vision on the other. Otherwise, it would not be a negotiation.

Intellectually and practically, the impact of this 'fact of negotiation' is hard to overstate. It affects the *moral* playing field profoundly, inasmuch as opposing interests and worldviews (some of them strongly illiberal) must be reconciled. It controls the *legal* playing field, inasmuch as the ability of the state to meet its constitutional and international legal obligations in the realm of human rights and humanitarian and criminal law becomes much more constrained. And on a *practical* level, it undercuts the speed at which decisions can be made, not merely because the parties must go through a process of identifying common ground on disputed issues, but also because anything they agree must be meticulously reduced to a detailed joint text.

These moral, legal, and practical constraints are especially pronounced in the case of a Negotiationland scenario of internal armed conflict. Negotiations in such contexts tend to have a high level of formality, rigour, and density of agenda. By design, they require a 'fiction of equality' between the parties that intrinsically favours the weaker side, as the image and reality of the negotiation must be one of procedural equality. Indeed, the parties must be seen to come to an agreement through an exercise of mutual consent, in which neither side is a clear loser or winner – hardly an environment that incentivises the negotiation of criminal accountability.

Even in a different model of Negotiationland – in which a civilian or military government is negotiating with opposition parties on the terms of a political settlement to restore democracy or instate power-sharing – the fact of negotiation has a determining influence on what may or may not be viable in the realm of justice. While such negotiations are more likely to be secret, loosely structured, and more narrowly focused on political power than those between parties to a civil war, it is the mere fact of negotiation that, once again, compels mutual concessions of a sort no transitional government would recognise. Indeed, this fact is the central reason why a broad amnesty (or extended absence of national-level justice) is far more likely in *either* version of Negotiationland than in *any* version of Transitionland.

In brief, in Negotiationland it will never be sufficient, as it might be in Transitionland, to consult and accommodate the views of opponents before ultimately making one's own decision on how to proceed. Instead, neither side gets the final say in Negotiationland. Just ask those who negotiated transitions in contexts as diverse as Spain, Chile, Guatemala, Bosnia and Herzegovina, Ivory Coast, Mozambique, Lebanon, Tajikistan, Northern Ireland, and Nepal.

Factor 2: Negotiations take place at the leadership level

In Transitionland, government leaders can establish the transitional justice policy they want, constrained only by what the law requires and wise policy dictates. In Negotiationland, by contrast, not only are explicit mutual concessions necessary; they must also be formally agreed upon by the *leaders* of one's military or political adversaries.

For justice, this is a colossal hurdle. Especially in a civil war or dictatorship, the leaders of one or multiple sides of the negotiation process are the persons *least* likely to agree to any robust form of transitional justice, because of the implications any judicial threat could have for them personally. As such, any potential concessions in the area of transitional justice are going to be viewed by them as existential and personal threats, and not merely as institutional risks. The mere evocation of justice may be impossible to get onto the *agenda* of a negotiation, let alone into a final accord.

Factor 3: The inseparability of transitional justice and the larger agreement

The first job of peace agreements is to bring about the formal end of armed conflict. At a minimum, this implies finding consensus on a set of conditions under which the particular non-state armed group is willing to disarm. In the normal scheme of things, such conditions will include special measures to guarantee their physical security, economic reintegration, and political participation following disarmament.

Inevitably, the conditions the armed group's leaders will consider minimally acceptable also encompass expectations about broader national measures (e.g., institutional reforms and resource redistribution arrangements) that help validate their purported cause and initial choice to take up arms.

Hence, if there is to be transitional justice amidst these many other agenda items, it will have to fit with all of them – and not the other way around. To misunderstand this reality is to misunderstand everything. Peace, not accountability, is the supreme objective in a peace negotiation. Questions of transitional justice are no more than a potential subcomponent. As such, transitional justice must be made to fit within the larger pact or, as often happens, reveal itself as discordant with the exigencies of the larger pact.

Things would not be materially different in the case of a government and opposition negotiating the terms to restore democracy or share power. The parties would face the same structural necessity for transitional justice to fit with the larger settlement. All that may vary is the scope of such imperative, not its existence.

***

Before passing to the next stage of analysis, it is important to note the limits of our Safeland, Transitionland, and Negotiationland archetypes.

First, each reflects particular understandings of what a 'transition' or 'negotiation' is. For example, it is evident that a transition out of a decades-long civil war in a state lacking basic institutions and a formal economy does not present the same issues and challenges as one arising in a democratic country overcoming a years-long violent insurgency but possessing functional public institutions. Likewise, the transition out of an entrenched semi-authoritarian regime in an industrialised and cohesive country does not present the same issues and challenges as one arising in the aftermath of a violent but short-lived dictatorship in an impoverished country with low social cohesion.

With negotiations, the spectrum of potential scenarios is likewise intrinsically diverse. An internationally facilitated, highly structured negotiation to bring about the end of a civil war that involved atrocity crimes on all sides constitutes a very different scenario than an ad hoc, direct and secret negotiation involving civilian and military authorities discussing the terms for democratic restoration in the context of overwhelmingly state-sponsored violence. The procedural dynamics and policy options that arise in these types of settings are, ex ante, of a distinct nature.

Second, we use archetypes not for their realism but for their approximation of reality, in order to illuminate a larger point. In this case, it is to highlight the *structural* implications that different scenarios present for securing transitional justice. It has been noted how these constraints unfold as a kind of inverted triangle, with Safeland involving only first-order difficulties associated with any attempt to try a single atrocity; Transitionland entailing the additional difficulties that arise at the end of a dictatorship or civil war in which state capacity is lower and the scale of past atrocities massive; and Negotiationland involving the same difficulties as the other two, *plus* the constraints created by negotiation's requirements of consensus with leaders of an enemy group, and the alignment of justice with everything else on the negotiation agenda.

The point is that *any* version of Negotiationland presents third-order difficulties that are not structurally present in either Transitionland or Safeland. No matter how complex and constrained the nature of the transition in any version of Transitionland, the government will not confront the additional challenges of Negotiationland – challenges that make it far harder to incorporate judicial accountability of any kind.

It is only once this structural reality is recognised that one can properly understand the *non*-context-specific differences that make the negotiation of transitional justice solutions – especially, but not only, in the midst of armed conflict – something altogether different (and harder) than the declaration of such solutions by transitional governments that, at most, need to consult opponents and citizens before finalising their policies.

B. A BALANCED APPROACH

Up to now we have said that what makes the framework for transitional justice hardest in Negotiationland is an agglomeration of three principal variables: (1) the fact of negotiation, (2) the need for leadership consent, and (3) the inability to handle transitional justice in isolation from the larger compact. To this, one must add the intrinsic limitations of transitional justice itself, namely (1) the extraordinary scale of past violence, which guarantees a high level of overall impunity, and (2) the extraordinary depravity of the violations, which guarantees that even individual forms of redress will be inadequate.

Combined, these five factors make it inevitable that, in a negotiation, the objectives of peace and justice will be in dramatic tension with one another. Armed groups and political and military leaders simply do not want to negotiate agreements that land them in courts or prisons. Understandably, they want to negotiate a pathway to legal safety. As such, if justice is meant to form part of a negotiated agreement, the only serious question is how the tension between peace and justice can be managed and, ultimately, resolved. Seeking to avoid it is a fool's errand.

It is all the more distressing, therefore, to see so many leaders in the human rights field (and beyond) choose to ignore or deny this, often taking positions that are ideologically incoherent, intellectually dishonest, or both. Especially counterproductive is when such actors claim to be in favour of negotiated solutions, but when asked whether this implies the inevitability of mutual concessions, insist that there can be zero concessions on certain human rights issues.

This is a position that offends both negotiation and justice. In the context of an ongoing armed conflict or dictatorship, one who claims to be pro-negotiation yet insists on human rights 'red lines' is, a priori, in favour of the continuation of war and repression. It amounts to a preference to continue with violent conflict until such time as one side (i.e., the one you like) dominates the other to such a point that all that remains to negotiate are the terms of surrender.

The position is fatuous. Naturally, the hardest negotiations are the ones in which there is a delicate balance of bargaining power between the different sides. It is not one in which side A is simply working out the terms of the subjugation or surrender of side B. As already noted, real negotiations involve hard bargaining and formal equality at the negotiation table. That is not a circumstance compatible with red lines – least of all on existential and personal threats such as justice.

International law is a further source of confusion and dishonesty. Certain types of amnesties are now widely considered to violate international law, causing the prospect of international, foreign, or domestic court interventions to loom larger in the minds of those at any negotiating table. However, international law and practice allow for significant legal leeway on the issue, as comprehensive examinations such as the Belfast Guidelines on Amnesty and Accountability attest. It is simply false to assert that armed groups and political and military leaders responsible for certain kinds of crimes must accept the prospect of jail as part of a modern negotiation process.

The problem is that, by misunderstanding or misrepresenting the true room of legal manoeuvre, unnecessary harm is done. In particular, the application of the wrong standards makes it more likely that negotiation processes will collapse, or conversely, that well-intentioned parties will inadequately explore the scope for creative justice options. Worse still, applying the wrong standards will prevent some peace talks and political dialogues from even getting off the ground, because unless and until parties have some basic sense that there are reasonable legal guarantees they could obtain in the process, they will not acquiesce to formal negotiations in the first place.

This is something Colombia understood from the start, prompting the government of former President Santos to promote the Legal Framework for Peace (*Marco Jurídico para la Paz*): a constitutional amendment to reflect its understanding of international legal standards applicable to a peace negotiation. To a large degree, the Framework highlights an awareness of the previously discussed third-level difficulties of negotiating peace with justice, most notably the need for sufficient legal flexibility to ensure justice can be fitted with the larger peace agenda and the constraints of negotiation itself. Such an approach does not reveal any dilution of legal standards. To the contrary, it reflects a matching of the leeway that law already allows, with the exigencies (and independent value) of peace negotiation. In the absence of such matching, law is nothing more than an obstacle, serving neither peace nor justice.

C. DETERMINATIVE CHOICES

Despite the challenges intrinsic to negotiating peace with justice, once the inception choice is made, a host of consequent issues and method choices arise. In this section, we mention the most important of these: three negotiation-specific ones and seven justice-specific ones. These arise in the context of two interdependent 'pulls' that are unavoidable in Negotiationland: one toward leniency in the area of criminal justice and the other toward non-judicial measures to compensate for such leniency.

Negotiation-Specific Techniques

- Controlling Risks

In any sophisticated negotiation, the parties will be constantly assessing risks of all sorts, and making choices on the basis of those assessments. In general, the risks take two forms: ones that can be controlled, whether fully or partly, and ones that cannot. In few areas is this more evident than justice.

In the course of any negotiation, there is an understandable desire by parties to exploit the talks to eliminate any future risk they might see for their side. For example, the FARC wanted to have a truth commission in place to conduct investigations and make findings while the negotiation was still under way, rather than as part of a future peace agreement implementation phase. For them, it was not enough to control the design of the commission (i.e., by agreeing on a text about its mandate, composition, and so forth); initially, they wanted to control the outcome as well.

The FARC also wanted to have a legislative drafting commission within the negotiation space, rather than leaving it up to the Colombian Congress to draft the statute for mechanisms like the agreed post-conflict tribunal. Again, this was an attempt to 'control contingencies'.

These are but two examples. The point is that the instinct to exert control of future risks is a structural inevitability of the inception choice to negotiate. It applies to justice issues, and everything else that may be on the agenda; and is especially acute when the backdrop is one of an active democratic state.

- Constructive Ambiguities

Some differences in a negotiation cannot be resolved in explicit terms. Instead, they must be agreed with a certain amount of conscious, or unconscious, ambiguity in order for the talks to advance. These are called 'constructive ambiguities'.

Put simply, constructive ambiguities are devices to resolve a matter indirectly that cannot be resolved directly. On justice issues, recourse to such ambiguities is particularly rife, as the subject is so intrinsically sensitive.

Constructive ambiguities help expand the range of interim solutions on the thorniest questions, as explained later in Part I.

- Confidence-Building Measures

In any peace negotiation or political dialogue, efforts at confidence-building will be necessary. These can include measures across, but also within, delegations.

Examples of confidence-building measures (CBMs) are countless. They can include anything from ceasefires to joint declarations of intent, individual amnesties, release of hostages, and 'ice-breaking' social events. CBMs can also be geared at building the confidence of influential third parties or the public at large.

Without CBMs, negotiations cannot advance and cannot culminate. Ipso facto, the same is true for the negotiation of questions of individual criminal accountability. Whether unilaterally offered or bilaterally agreed, CBMs grease the wheel of negotiation.

Justice-Specific Choice Points

In addition to the negotiation-specific choices mentioned above, there are scores of justice-specific ones that can be expected to arise in parallel. Below we touch upon seven of them, the first three of which are examined in extended essays in Part II of the book (using the lens of Colombia's negotiation with the FARC). The other four are discussed in more detail in the final section of Part I.

- Reconciling Competing Expectations of Dignity and Legal Security

Of the many justice-specific choice points in a negotiation, the least obvious one is in fact the most important: namely, how to reconcile competing expectations of *dignity* on the one hand, and *legal security* (i.e., legal guarantees) on the other.

The concept of legal security – more familiar in the civil law tradition than the common law – can have a host of meanings. For the ordinary person, it may only refer to the notion that law is meant to be known and enforceable; but for a person at risk of prosecution, it may be an indirect way to describe the expectation of receiving amnesty or a comparable form of legal leniency in relation to past wrongs. In a peace negotiation, this is precisely what many will expect, and they will want it to be as iron clad as possible vis-à-vis domestic or foreign courts.

Yet, such understandings of legal security involve an excess of wishful thinking. In fact, legal security depends primarily on the perceived legitimacy of the overall peace agreement. If the accord has little legitimacy – among other things, by failing to reflect an effort to incorporate justice – then no matter how much impunity the accord explicitly offers, the amount of legal security will in reality be minimal. That is because it will make future governments and foreign tribunals more, not less, likely to attack it.

But even if one accepts this premise, there is a further obstacle to be overcome: namely, that negotiating parties are likely to resist post-conflict judicial accountability because it represents an attack on their sense of self-dignity and their understanding of the balance of blame they bear for past violence. For them, the prospect of being subjected to an investigation or trial conjures more than just a loss of liberty. It is also sure to be viewed by many leaders – whether rebels or state agents – as humiliating and at odds with their rightful place in history. In the former's case, it will also be seen as a threat to their movement's future electoral prospects, including of their leaders.

The point is that expectations of legal security and dignity will not only arise but also compete. As such, negotiators and mediators will need to draw on a wide range of creative concepts and devices. These might include the use of a single legal regime applicable to all sides; recourse to the tradition of 'political offences' for politically motivated armed groups; guarantees of impartiality and independence for any special justice mechanisms; participation in appointment processes for the judges, prosecutors, and investigators; exceptional legal incentives, such as reduced or commuted sentences for voluntary recognition of individual responsibility; and special conditions of detention that avoid offending either negotiating party or the public.

- Choosing between Ordinary and Extraordinary Mechanisms

Once the inception choice to negotiate peace with justice has been made, another inevitable challenge concerns the tension between ordinary and extraordinary mechanisms.

As noted earlier, the government side of a negotiation may naturally seek to vindicate the institutions of justice that already exist, whereas the non-state armed group may naturally do the opposite, considering them biased and thus unacceptable. By contrast, both parties may be attracted to the idea of establishing a truth commission – by definition, an extraordinary mechanism – even if their expectations about its investigative mandate and its relation to criminal investigations may be vastly different.

Such choices will reflect deep beliefs about whether the conflict constitutes an unacceptable and violent aberration in an otherwise stable legal order, or a deep national trauma requiring transformative measures that address exclusionary root causes. The former type of belief leads to arguments favouring recourse to ordinary (i.e., existing) mechanisms, the latter to extraordinary.

A peace negotiation encompassing questions of accountability cannot avoid this debate.

- Agreeing on Who Is Victim and Who Is Victimiser

The apportionment of victimhood is another inevitable controversy in the negotiation of peace with justice. The issue obviously has enormous implications for each party, extending beyond the judicial sphere to the political, economic, social, and reputational.

In all likelihood, each side sees the other as the primary victimiser, and itself – and those it represents – as the primary victim. In addition, each side is likely to consider the types of crimes committed by the other as morally and legally worse than its own, and the victims of such crimes thus deserving of greater attention and consideration.

As such, the issue of victimhood is bound to be deeply contested terrain inside the negotiation. However, it is not an issue the parties can (or need to) resolve at the table. Instead, it is usually enough for them to agree on future impartial mechanisms that will make specific, subsequent determinations about violations, victims, and victimisers. Ultimately, neither side will countenance the negotiation space converting into a moral or legal judgement space.

- Distinguishing Causes and Consequences of the Conflict

A related justice-specific choice point is how to negotiate questions around a conflict's causes (origins) and consequences (symptoms). The issue is crucial in the arena of justice because of the role that intent and justification play in the determination of historic as well as criminal responsibility.

An original sin, or *casus belli*, may not exonerate individuals or groups from criminal responsibility. However, in the eyes of the conflict actors, the reasons certain crimes were committed is a matter of vital interest since it provides the context that shapes public opinion – and thus the perceived weight of responsibility. No negotiation of peace with justice can avoid confronting this issue. It is decisive for the nature and reach of the mechanisms that can be agreed.

- Resolving the Interplay of Truth-Seeking and Justice

Another justice choice to be faced in negotiations relates to South Africa, and in particular, the trade-off it is understood to have made in favour of truth and against justice, in the aftermath of the political settlement that averted civil war.

The country's Truth and Reconciliation Commission (TRC) was empowered to offer full individual amnesties on condition of full disclosure by the perpetrators of politically motivated gross human rights violations who applied for amnesty. But by design, criminal trials were also meant to take place: both concurrently with the commission's investigations (to incentivise amnesty applications and thus disclosures of past crime) and afterward (against rejected applicants as well as non-applicants alleged by the truth commission to have committed gross human rights violations).

Because of these innovations (and despite the fact that few post-TRC prosecutions occurred), South Africa remains the top global reference on transitional justice. As such, invocations of the South African 'model' by parties who like the idea of swapping truth for justice is inevitable. Yet, even bad-faith invocations of South Africa's transitional justice experience are useful because they can highlight the wide diversity of choices parties have to structure the interrelation and sequencing of truth and justice devices within a larger transitional justice system. This diversity is critical to negotiating peace with justice.

- Parsing Retributive, Restorative, and Distributive Forms of Justice

Another justice choice point in negotiations is primarily rhetorical, but no less important on that account. Parties to a negotiation in which accountability is on the agenda will have fierce debates about the respective merits of so-called retributive, restorative, and distributive forms of justice. Criminal justice will be associated with the first, reparations with the second, and inclusive growth and development with the third.

The 'retributive' label is, of course, meant to make criminal justice sound petty and vengeful, rather than honourable. Its primary invocation is typically made by parties seeking to *avoid* national-level justice. The second and third labels, by contrast, promise something gentler – in the case of restorative justice, a kind of middle ground requiring reparations for victims but not necessarily any sanction, sentence, or jail time for perpetrators; and in the case of distributive justice, an attractive slogan for a non-state armed group to justify its ostensible struggle against inequality or discrimination.

Parsing through these labels, and through the interests underlying them, is laborious but unavoidable in any negotiation of peace with justice.

- Balancing National Sovereignty and International Standards

A final justice choice point relates to the challenge of balancing national sovereignty concerns (i.e., the particular) and international legal standards (i.e., the universal).

Parties amenable to justice will tend to emphasise the latter, while detractors will tend to insist on the former. To resolve the difference, concepts such as the 'margin of appreciation' – inspired by the European Court of Human Rights – will usually arise.

In practice, however, this can be resolved only in small details, not big concepts. In that respect, determining the precise room of manoeuvre that national and international law, respectively, allow in matters of justice is more science than art. Such determinations are a sine qua non for successfully negotiating peace with justice, because they establish the scope that exists for innovation, without which no settlement could ever be reached.

Summary

Our intention in presenting this basic theory of negotiating peace with justice has been to highlight all that is *non*-context-dependent (i.e., structurally unavoidable) from the moment the choice is made, or the intention announced, to negotiate peace with justice.

Only by understanding what is unavoidable can one effectively separate out symbolic and substantive issues in the negotiation; increase capacity for identifying creative solutions to seemingly impossible problems or irreconcilable interests; and augment conceptual and tactical rigour. In particular we have emphasised the need for a structured understanding of:

1. *Three intrinsic types of difficulties:*
    a. First-order ones associated with any national-level attempt to try serious crimes for which perpetrators do not admit guilt. These can arise even in the most stable and rights-respecting societies.
    b. Second-order difficulties attendant on settings of post-conflict or democratic transition, in which the scale and severity of violations have been especially extreme.

c. Third-order difficulties tied to the specific constraints of negotiation settings, namely: (1) the requirement of formal consensus; (2) the decision-making role of those bearing greatest responsibility; and (3) the imperative to align justice-related agreements with the other issues under negotiation.
2. *Three cumulative practical consequences of these intrinsic difficulties*:
   a. Dramatic reduction of the bandwidth for guaranteeing justice in any form as part of a peace deal or political settlement.
   b. Requirement for the parties to be unusually flexible in legal, tactical and other terms.
   c. Obligation to adopt a broad but nevertheless subsidiary concept of justice that bends it to the superior imperatives of peace or political settlement.
3. *The techniques and choice points that arise as a result of the above:*
   a. Three negotiation-specific techniques: (1) separating out controllable and uncontrollable risks, (2) recourse to constructive ambiguities, and (3) usage of confidence-building measures.
   b. Justice-specific choice points: (1) reconciling competing expectations of dignity and legal security; (2) choosing between ordinary and extraordinary mechanisms; (3) agreeing on who is victim and who is victimiser; (4) distinguishing between the causes and consequences of armed conflict; (5) resolving the choices in, and between, truth and justice; (6) parsing retributive, restorative, and distributive forms of justice; and (7) balancing national sovereignty with international standards.

2

The Role of International Law

As we have noted, the challenge of negotiating peace with justice extends far beyond – and has more to do with – the intrinsic constraints of negotiation than those of transitional justice. Put simply, one cannot reach a proper understanding of the bandwidth for negotiating transitional justice if the analytic starting point is something other than the fact of negotiation.

However, what bearing does international law have on the matter? Is it a help or a hindrance for the negotiated resolution, in particular, of internal armed conflicts?

Astonishingly, it is absent. *There is no international law whatsoever on the topic of negotiation* as a means for preventing or ending internal armed conflict. Instead, there are only non-negotiation-specific (i.e., general) norms about war and justice.

In the domain of international humanitarian law (IHL), there are three relevant strands: first, a cluster of rules that armed actors need to adduce to justify entering into war (*jus ad bellum*); second, an extensive set of rules to be applied once hostilities are under way (*jus in bello*); and third, a patchwork of rules to be applied once a war has concluded (*jus post bellum*).

However, on the crucial question about the international law for transiting *from* jus in bello *to* jus post bellum, there is absolutely nothing. For all intents and purposes, IHL is a bystander, offering no contribution to the choices that states make on whether a civil war ends vertically (by militarily triumph) or horizontally (by negotiated settlement). There is no *jus e bellum*.

International human rights law is even less helpful. It offers norms and guidance on substantive matters such as restitution, refugee protection, minority rights, and self-determination, but nothing whatsoever on the nature, relevance, scope, or design of negotiations or anything analogous thereto.

As for international criminal law, there are only two indirectly relevant provisions, both of them in the Rome Statute of the International Criminal

Court (ICC). The first is Article 53, which gives the prosecutor the responsibility to decide whether to initiate an investigation, allowing her the possibility to refrain from initiating one when, among other things, it would threaten 'the interests of justice'. The second is Article 16; under certain conditions (including when there exists a threat to international peace and security), it allows the UN Security Council to obligate the Court to defer investigations or prosecutions for renewable twelve-month periods. Yet, neither Article 53 nor Article 16 says a word about – nor has been interpreted by the Court as being directly related to – peace negotiations.

Yet, while negotiation is not a subject that is formally addressed in international law, conflict clearly is – primarily but not exclusively through IHL.

Public international law distinguishes between four types of conflict situations, allowing varying levels of flexibility about the standards for evaluating state compliance in each:

- *Situations of Internal Tensions and Disturbances.* This refers to situations that fall short of armed conflict, but involve the use of force and other repressive measures by a government to maintain or restore public order or public safety. In such situations – which can include 'riots, isolated and sporadic acts of violence and other acts of a similar nature' (Protocol II) – governments are permitted to (1) derogate from a controlled list of obligations under international human rights law and (2) place limits on the scope of other human rights.
- *International Armed Conflict.* This refers to situations that involve two or more states engaged in armed conflict. The central provisions of IHL become operative in such situations, particularly those contained in the four Geneva Conventions and Protocol I thereto. In addition, most human rights guarantees remain applicable during such conflicts, albeit subject to the same derogations and limitations that states can impose in situations of internal tensions and disturbances.
- *Wars of National Liberation.* This refers to armed conflicts in which 'peoples are fighting against colonial domination and alien occupation and against racist regimes in the exercise of their right to self-determination'. In practice, this is a concept of the past, but on paper it still exists as a category of IHL.
- *Internal Armed Conflict.* This refers to situations that involve armed conflict (thus exceeding situations of mere 'internal disturbance') but that cannot be characterised as international armed conflicts or as wars of national liberation. Common Article 3 of the Geneva Conventions defines such conflicts as ones that are 'not of an international character

occurring in the territory of one of the High Contracting Parties', while Article 1 of Protocol II to the Geneva Conventions goes further by providing that such conflicts 'must take place in the territory of a High Contracting Party between its armed forces and dissident armed forces or other organised armed groups which, under responsible command, exercise such control over a part of its territory as to enable them to carry out sustained and concerted military operations and to implement this Protocol'. As with other forms of armed conflict, most human rights guarantees remain applicable. However, IHL imposes a more limited set of obligations on states in respect of situations of internal armed conflict, as compared to other situations of conflict.

But despite so much law in place on matters of conflict, neither the word 'negotiation' nor anything analogous appears in IHL. Simply put, the fact of negotiation is nowhere to be found – whether as a critical tool for preventing or resolving armed conflict, or as a legal basis for states to exercise greater flexibility in the interpretation and application of their obligations. Instead, by omission, international law treats identically a state that has chosen the path of negotiation to prevent or end a violent internal conflict, and one that is stable and free from the need to negotiate with powerful armed groups.

Thus, we return to ask the obvious question: why is there is no treaty, no body of jurisprudence, and not even tailor-made soft law to encourage and assist states (and non-state armed actors) to choose negotiated rather than military solutions to internal strife? Why does international law provide so much guidance on conflict types and the norms applicable therein, yet none on the crucial challenge of negotiating the prevention or resolution of a civil war?

Unfortunately, law and literature offer no clear answer to the question. As such, in what follows we examine how to fill the gap, offering arguments for and against. We do so under the reasonable but rebuttable premise that, unless the gap is filled with something fit for purpose, fewer negotiations will arise or culminate in accords.

A. MAKING THE CASE FOR NEW LAW

Since the establishment of the UN Charter system at the end of the Second World War, atrocity prevention and conflict resolution have become universal goals. Indeed, the system was principally conceived to prevent war from happening at all, and to facilitate resolution should it nevertheless arise.

Yet, the UN Charter system's norms and procedures (e.g., Chapters VI and VII) are designed to address wars occurring between states, rather than those occurring within states. The same is true for the major regional systems that exist for Europe, the Americas, and Africa.

It is certainly true that the UN Security Council, UN Secretary-General, and their regional equivalents often facilitate or promote dialogue or negotiation in respect of internal armed conflicts that may arise. However, none of these institutions (nor their member states) is in a position to plead sources of international law in order to compel, encourage, or support states in making the choice of dialogue and negotiation that they call for. The matter is simply left to the realm of politics, and thus sovereign discretion.

What is clearly missing is an international legal framework that (1) offers incentives to help 'nudge' conflict actors toward dialogue and negotiated solutions as a preferred option for preventing atrocities and resolving internal armed conflict, (2) provides effective guidance on vital questions of substantive and procedural law in a way that accommodates the intrinsic possibilities and constraints of negotiation, (3) provides conflict actors a 'choice architecture' and set of guiding principles on key questions such as how to balance peace and justice imperatives, and (4) allows interested states to affirm their symbolic and political commitment to negotiation as a tool for preventing atrocities and resolving internal conflicts.[1]

Remarkably, the idea of creating a treaty or body of law on peace negotiations for internal armed conflicts seems never to have been seriously considered. We have scoured the literature and found no evidence to suggest otherwise.

But rather than asking why that is so, we instead examine a set of foreseeable objections likely to arise in response to the prospect of a first-ever international legal instrument on peace negotiations. Most of these are concerns or dangers that states, in particular, might raise:

- Diminution of the flexibility states currently enjoy to make war, as and when they want at the national level
- Negotiation becoming an obligation rather than remaining a discretionary option
- Legal-political recognition of non-state armed groups

---

[1] The concepts of 'nudge' and 'choice architecture' are taken from Richard H. Thaler and Cass R. Sunstein, *Nudge: Improving Decisions about Health, Wealth, and Happiness* (New Haven, Conn.: Yale University Press, 2008).

- Bad-faith invocation of the treaty by such groups, in order to weaken or distract the government
- Loss of confidentiality inside the negotiation process
- The introduction of legalism into a process that is fundamentally political in nature
- The increased chance of formulaic approaches ousting creative approaches in the negotiation
- Reduced control over the terms of any negotiated settlement, including on questions of transitional justice
- Policy adventurism that is disconnected from legal precedents.

Below we examine each of these.

Diminution of the Flexibility States Enjoy to Choose War-War over Jaw-Jaw

As already observed, states can do as they please when it comes to exiting from internal armed conflict. If they want to fight to the death, they can; if instead they want to negotiate, that's their prerogative as well. As long as they respect international human rights and humanitarian and criminal law, there is no 'extra' law that makes negotiation a better option.

If we assume that states enjoy having such unfettered discretion, the question arises: why would they want to give this up? The answer is that it is possible to design a fit-for-purpose legal framework on peace negotiations that offers benefits without unduly diminishing state discretion.

For one thing, the legal instrument we imagine – hereafter referred to as the 'resolution treaty' – would bind only states parties (i.e., those that voluntarily enter the treaty's system). Those not wishing to join the system would not be bound. In addition, the treaty could use a sliding scale of obligations, according to which states parties could increase or decrease their obligations under certain conditions. Moreover, the enforcement mechanism for the treaty could be designed flexibly for the first years of any state's participation, incorporating a transitional provision (much like Article 124 of the Rome Statute) that allows opt outs for a fixed number of years in regard to selected obligations or provisions.

Beyond this, it is important to make a more general point: the resolution treaty, like all treaties, would not represent a zero-sum proposition in which states parties would take on costs without acquiring benefits. Instead, upon entering the treaty's regime, a state would cede some control but also gain a series of important advantages, ones not available (in full) except by virtue of being a state party. For example, the treaty could offer states parties greater flexibility in the interpretation of existing international law, especially on critical issues of amnesty and accountability, which rank high in the minds of armed actors. The treaty could also offer a support structure for states parties – perhaps in the form of a treaty-based advisory committee, plus a built-in mechanism for states to sign up as guarantors, observers, or facilitators – that would likewise be available only to states parties. In addition, the specific norms of the treaty (and their progressive implementation and ongoing interpretation) would give all affected parties a degree of additional legal security about the durability of any final settlement that would otherwise be unattainable.

In brief, even a robust version of the resolution treaty should involve only a fraction of the sovereignty adjustments that states have already made, voluntarily, in scores of other areas. In that respect, the acceptance of an obligation to negotiate with armed enemies, under a limited set of circumstances, would constitute a low cost compared to the much greater risks and burdens states have signed up for in other realms, not least international human rights and humanitarian and criminal law.

The Undesirable Recognition of Non-state Armed Groups

Another hypothetical concern states may have is that the resolution treaty would give undue political recognition to the illegal armed groups they are fighting against in contexts of civil war. They may fear it could establish an undue moral and legal equivalence between the two sides. Yet, such a concern would be unwarranted. Already, over 168 states are party to Protocol II to the Geneva Conventions, the main treaty regulating internal armed conflicts, which explicitly recognises the existence of such groups (albeit against a high definitional bar) for purposes of international law. In that regard, the resolution treaty would have no cause to stretch recognition further.

However, the resolution treaty could go an extra step in a different direction – namely, by giving states parties the authority to determine which armed actors to recognise (or not) for purposes of negotiations. This would offer an additional assurance against unwarranted or undesirable acts of recognition, while also generating the opportunity to bring any recognised group into the treaty's organised system of procedures, norms and accompaniment, thus increasing the cost of bad-faith actions in the negotiation and incentivising good-faith ones. As non-state armed groups may be fearful of entering into negotiations with governments they do not trust, the resolution treaty could help them overcome such fears.

In any case, independent of the resolution treaty, Common Article 3 of the Geneva Conventions stipulates that the application of IHL norms in a non-international armed conflict 'shall not affect the legal status of any party'. The resolution treaty would not change this.

The Risk of Bad-Faith Appeals to Negotiation

Currently, states do not face the risk that illegal armed groups will invoke the relevance or applicability of any treaty-based duty to negotiate. Thus, while such groups may use the media to pressure the state in question to negotiate, there is no treaty they can cite – in good or bad faith – to argue: 'We and you are obligated by law to end to this internal armed conflict by means of negotiation'.

The resolution treaty would not affect this. Only states would have the right to ratify the treaty; non-state actors could not. Also, only states would have independent standing to file pleadings before any treaty-based enforcement body. Finally, the treaty could include a case-specific opt-in system, such that the triggering mechanism for the obligation – as a matter of law – would remain under the particular state's control. As such, there would be no risk that governments could be sideswiped diplomatically by clever armed groups, merely as a result of the treaty's adoption.

The Risk That Negotiation Becomes an Obligation Rather Than a Discretionary Option

Since there is no duty to negotiate under international law, it is reasonable to assume that states would prefer such a status quo to hold.

Yet, the nature and scope of any treaty-based obligation to negotiate could take many potentially appealing forms. For example, the materialisation of the obligation could require an affirmative, case-specific governmental declaration in respect of particular armed groups. The resolution treaty could also put in place a scheme by which states willing to take on higher levels of obligation and supervision would be eligible for corresponding increases in their legal room of manoeuvre as well as in the technical and political support available from states parties.

The enforcement scheme for the treaty could also take many forms, possibly erring on the 'light' side of state accountability initially, in order to maximise ratifications and early adoption. Likewise, the resolution treaty could explicitly enshrine the principle that the obligation to negotiate would never, as such, affect the right of states parties to use force simultaneously. To the contrary, the obligation to negotiate could explicitly coexist with the use of force, enabling negotiations to take place in the absence of a bilateral ceasefire (as was done in Colombia).

These are just some of the possible forms that the core obligation to negotiate could take in the resolution treaty. Regardless, it bears repeating that the treaty would create obligations only for states parties (i.e., for voluntary joiners). Other states would remain outside the system, thus allowing them to preserve a desired status quo but making them ineligible to enjoy the benefits the treaty would offer.

Fear of Loss of Confidentiality Inside the Negotiation Process

For negotiations to consummate in agreements, a high degree of confidentiality is of utmost importance. Governments and third-party facilitators would not want to put that at risk for any process.

Yet, the resolution treaty need not introduce any risks on the matter of confidentiality. Indeed, a central purpose of the treaty would be to establish a legal framework that deliberately facilitates, not complicates, the effective practice of negotiation. Any negotiation obligations for states parties would be premised (and if necessary conditioned) on the absolute non-disturbance of the confidentiality levels set by the parties to the talks. The creation of the treaty could even offer the opportunity to elevate standards and mechanisms for needed levels of confidentiality, abuses of which are currently unprotected at international law.

The Risk of Introducing Legalism into a Process That Is Political in Nature

It is trite to observe that the solutions to armed conflicts are political in nature. The claim is that all such conflicts are about power contestation and consequently require significant legal flexibility for deal-making to occur. If a treaty caused negotiations to become too legalistic in nature, the risk is that the bandwidth for resolving underlying political causes of the conflict could be jeopardised.

Yet, this risk is miscast on multiple levels. First, even if armed conflicts require political solutions, the law cannot simply be cast aside. It is always there, both discursively (through the parties' competing interpretations of applicable legal norms) and structurally (inasmuch as a peace accord or political settlement is, in essence, just a contract). Second, because it is a more technical domain, law can lend itself to more technical discussions that politics often cannot. In that regard, rather than shrinking the space for politics, law can instead help illuminate the scope of the playing field, helping bring clarity to issues where there is presently incorrect or inconsistent guidance that undermines progress in the negotiation. Indeed, this is precisely one of the ambitions of the resolution treaty: to provide the negotiation-sensitive guidance, on procedural and substantive matters alike, that is absent in prevailing international law.

It is also worth considering the possible advantages of the resolution treaty for the successful implementation and long-term sustainability of any peace accord or political settlement that is reached. For example, the treaty could create an optional mechanism for parties to 'embed' the negotiation process and 'lock down' the final agreement at the international level. In particular, the treaty could give states parties the option of formal accompaniment, guidance, and support from the period of negotiation through to implementation. This would provide a unique 'certainty benefit' to law and politics alike, and could include expedited advisory opinions on key legal questions, fast-track devices for a final agreement's recognition, and mechanisms through which other states parties could formally pledge support in enforcement. All of this would facilitate, rather than complicate, political solutions to prevent or end armed conflict.

Concern That Recourse to Formulaic Approaches Will Increase

Some may cite Colombia's negotiations with the FARC as an example of why a resolution treaty would be counterproductive, claiming that a treaty will impose or encourage boilerplate standards that reduce, rather than expand, the drive and scope for creative and contextually tailored solutions.

However, by design, the resolution treaty can easily avoid this risk. First, by clarifying the in-built flexibility of the law – not least on crucial questions of amnesty and transitional justice – it will trigger the opposite of formulas. It will highlight how much room of manoeuvre law and policy truly allow, thus enabling greater customisation and innovation according to context, rather than the formulaic approaches that dominate today. Second, far from creating a straightjacket, the resolution treaty can offer a choice architecture on substantive and procedural issues alike, so that creativity is expanded to cover a more comprehensive checklist of considerations than is presently the case. Third, by attaching an expert body to the treaty and giving it an upon-request mandate to support context-specific explorations and solutions, the negotiating parties will be better positioned to innovate with confidence.

Fear of Reduced Control over the Final Terms of Any Negotiated Settlement

No state would be willing to cede its authority for deciding the terms of a final settlement meant to avert or resolve an internal armed conflict. So why risk entering a legal regime that might put that authority in jeopardy?

This is another misplaced concern, and one that inverts the true value proposition of the resolution treaty. One of the main motivations for ratifying such a treaty would be to stretch, not curtail, the parameters of what can be agreed in a negotiation. Indeed, the fundamental quid pro quo of the treaty would be to exchange the burden of a new obligation for a series of countervailing benefits, such as greater legal flexibility and clarity in regard to the dozens of hard choices that any negotiation imposes.

In any case, the resolution treaty is not meant to promulgate a supranational tribunal nor to commit states parties to a review regime in which final settlements would risk being overturned. Such jurisdiction belongs with the courts of the country in question.

Concern about Inventing a Body of Law Out of Thin Air

If there is no law of peace negotiations for internal armed conflicts, where will the appropriate legal standards be found and how will they be justified? Isn't the enterprise of the resolution treaty ripe for abuse by activist members of the legal and human rights communities, given the absence of existing doctrine?

These concerns are logical but surmountable. First, the preparation of the resolution treaty would necessarily involve the same careful process of expert consultation, study, and research that goes into any new legal instrument. This would include scouring all areas of relevant international law and practice, including obvious ones (such as human rights, the laws of war, and international criminal law) and less obvious ones (such as international arbitration law, UN Security Council resolutions, and national jurisprudence). Likewise, there are scores of relevant official documents associated with peace processes and political settlements that would merit review, in addition to a vast literature on key topics ranging from conflict prevention to mediation support, transitional justice, and peace accord implementation.

In short, there will be every opportunity for the resolution treaty to draw upon a vast supply of relevant law, ideas, and knowledge. A set of commissioned research papers can be reproduced as an interpretive 'commentary' to the eventual treaty, much as was done in the development of concepts like genocide and crimes against humanity – both of which lacked meaningful precedents in law.

* * *

Taking this exercise of imagination one step further, we now consider what the resolution treaty could look like in concrete form.

To begin, we recall the minimal benefits the resolution treaty must offer. It should help (1) incorporate existing knowledge, innovations and standards from the decades-long experience of design and practice in the realm of negotiation and conflict resolution, (2) legally incentivise a preference for dialogue and negotiation, (3) allow a state to affirm its symbolic and practical commitment to such a preference, (4) provide a comprehensive framework and set of choice points for states parties to make wiser decisions, in terms of both process design and substantive law and policy, and (5) offer an independent, advisory support system for successful dialogue and negotiation to occur.

Other benefits of the resolution treaty could include to (1) help improve the depth of understanding and quality of debate in society and in the international community on issues of negotiation and (2) provide more stability to the trajectory and outcome of specific negotiations that a state party brings into the treaty's system.

In this regard, it is important to consider the treaty's potential utility at three potential stages: (1) pre-negotiation, by helping validate and incentivise the choice of negotiation in the first place; (2) mid-negotiation, by assisting negotiations to consummate wisely and effectively; and (3) post-negotiation, by helping resolve technical implementation challenges in order to prevent the recurrence of conflict.

Will the resolution treaty apply only to internal armed conflicts (and their negotiated aftermath), or to political conflicts as well? That is something we do not need to determine here. It is enough to posit that an ambitious version would cover both forms of conflict, while a more conservative version would cover only internal ones.

Will the treaty incorporate detailed treaty enforcement mechanisms? This too is an issue that need not be determined here. It is a threshold decision that the promoters of the treaty must make – knowing that the softer the enforcement mechanisms, the greater the number of likely ratifications during the early years; and the stronger the enforcement mechanisms, the lower that number.

Yet, these questions aside, it is not difficult to envisage the basic potential outline of the resolution treaty. Key elements would likely include:

- First, a **preamble** that
  1. Affirms a commitment to state sovereignty and the purposes and principles of the UN Charter,
  2. Emphasises the universal value of peace and conflict prevention for countries and peoples around the world,
  3. Makes special mention of victims, whose interests should be taken into account as a primary motivation for negotiation, and for whom more beneficial things can be done in times of peace than in times of war,
  4. Acknowledges the special structural constraints that accompany negotiation processes, and the corresponding need for flexibility toward states that make such a choice, and
  5. Explains the key objectives of the treaty (as mentioned above).
- Second, a presentation about the **scope** of the treaty, with an accompanying set of **definitions** for key terms like 'internal armed conflict' and 'negotiation'. For the former, there is an existing IHL framework; but if the treaty were to take a more expansive notion of conflict (e.g., to encompass certain types of social and political conflict), another definition would be needed. As for the term 'negotiation', it has not been codified as such in international law. The resolution treaty would provide the overdue opportunity to produce a succinct definition that can encompass diverse forms of practice (e.g., distinguishing negotiation from dialogue, facilitation, mediation, and arbitration). Other key terms, such as 'non-state armed group', would also require a definition.
- Third, a set of **general principles** reflecting the structural constraints at the heart of negotiation, and according to which the treaty must be interpreted. These might include, for example:
  1. A flexibility principle, which explicitly allows states parties a 'margin of appreciation' in interpreting and implementing their treaty obligations – not least on the topics of amnesty and accountability;
  2. A use-of-force principle, making clear that nothing in the treaty may be read as prejudicing the existing (but limited) right of states to exercise armed force, bearing in mind that negotiation and the use of such force are not mutually exclusive choices;
  3. An inclusion principle, which emphasises values of consultation and participation for directly affected constituencies;
  4. A national ownership principle, which underlines the need for nationally led negotiation processes that, only if necessary and if requested, can involve an international role; and

5. A harmonisation principle, providing that in the event of potential conflicts between the obligations of the resolution treaty and those of other treaties, the conflicting provisions shall, to the greatest extent possible, be interpreted in a manner that is mutually compatible.
- Fourth, a core **commitment** to make use of dialogue and negotiation as primary tools of national conflict prevention and resolution. This obligation would be owed *inter se* between states parties to the treaty, rather than being imposed by a supranational body; and it would set out the categories of situations in which the obligation would arise (fundamentally to prevent or resolve internal armed conflict). Under no circumstances would the core commitment allow for the imposition of negotiation on an unwilling party. To the contrary, the **predefined obligations and benefits system** of the resolution treaty would be triggered only in relation to a specific situation, as and when the affected state party formally opts to have a situation brought under the provisions of the treaty. Once activated, the **opt-in system** would include (1) a good-faith obligation to apply the principles, standards, and practices designated in the treaty in the case at hand for the explicit purpose of reaching settlement, and (2) a series of practical benefits, including greater flexibility in the application of substantive international law, organised support mechanisms afforded by other states parties, access to the specialised guidance of a treaty-based technical advisory group, and greater legitimacy and legal certainty for any eventual accord.
- Fifth, a choice architecture of **process design** considerations, covering the full range of options about structure, rules, participation, agenda, procedures, and so on. Key concepts and terms – such as 'confidence-building measures', 'mediation support', and more – would be set out. Being a source of law, this section of the resolution treaty would help create a common framework and terminology on comprehensive process design, one which could inspire non-states parties to structure negotiations better as well.
- Sixth, a corresponding choice architecture on questions of **substantive law and policy**, offering guidance on the hardest substantive challenges of negotiation.
  1. One of these would certainly be the question of amnesty, given the structural constraints that negotiation imposes on the scope for transitional justice agendas (particularly the criminal justice element). A negotiation-sensitive approach to amnesty involves recognising that it is a topic for which there is no treaty-based prohibition or discouragement of any kind, but about which there is a perception of

increased prohibition and international opprobrium. The kind of negotiation-sensitive guidance the 2013 Belfast Guidelines on Amnesty and Accountability offers could be a good starting point. But in addition, consideration must be given to the fact that, within and across many human rights and IHL treaties, there are specific references to both prosecution obligations and prevention and suppression obligations (in relation to the same sets of violations). What negotiation requires is a general rule in favour of the balancing of these obligations, taking into account (1) the objective structural constraints of negotiating peace with justice, and (2) the lack of a hierarchy between prevention and punishment obligations under international law.
2. The resolution treaty must also offer general guidance on more specific questions, such as the scope of a prosecutor's discretion to make plea bargains, indict for lesser offenses in respect of serious international crimes, conduct selective prosecutions of those bearing greatest responsibility, and so forth. All of these would be interpreted in light of the general principles set out in the first part of the treaty.
3. An additional area of needed substantive guidance in the resolution treaty concerns the relationship between the different potential components of a comprehensive agreement. Indeed, transitional justice is only one of a plethora of issues that may form part of any peace accord or political settlement. Others may include rules for elections and the expansion of political participation; a system of disarmament, demobilisation, and reintegration; reforms to institutions involved in the provision of public security, justice, and land registration; and so on. Understanding the relevant parameters of international law on these issues – to the degree it is relevant – would be important.
4. A further area of substantive guidance should focus on commitment mechanisms aimed at advancing implementation of the accords the negotiating parties may reach. For example, the treaty might make reference to the use of two types of conditionalities: front-end ones (i.e., preconditions to accede to a legal benefit) and back-end ones (i.e., conditions to be met in order to retain the conferred benefit). These are often the glue that holds obligations in place and convert security, justice and reform commitments from a wish list into an integrated system.

- Seventh, the creation of a treaty-specific **expert advisory body** that would be available to offer support to states parties in the effective application of the treaty, by helping structure issues, share lessons, and provide feedback

on challenges of negotiation and implementation that may arise. The body could also potentially be mandated to give rapid-response advisory opinions on technical matters, at the request of the negotiating parties.
- Eighth, a treaty-based mechanism through which states parties can **roster** themselves to serve in a facilitator, observer, mediator, or guarantor role to other states parties.
- Ninth, **signature** and ratification procedures, including rules on whether reservations or treaty amendments are permitted.

***

Can the resolution treaty can go from an idea to a reality? Though ambitious, the idea is feasible; and if it materialised, a huge legal gap would be filled. Indeed, it remains an astonishing fact that, despite centuries of global experience in negotiating the end of wars – both interstate and intrastate – there is no corresponding body of international law setting out both general principles and specific norms of negotiation to help encourage and guide such efforts to a principled and effective conclusion. Today, with dozens of private and multilateral organisations dedicated to fields such as peace mediation support, how is it that such a legal regime has not been explored?

Whatever the explanation, we believe that international law should not remain indifferent to the choices states make on questions as crucial as dialogue and negotiation in the midst of crisis or conflict. The option of negotiation should be more than a 'take it or leave it' proposition. International law should give incentives – 'nudges', in the expression of Thaler and Sunstein – so that states become more likely to choose negotiation whenever that choice is likely to bring more peace and justice, and less war and injustice.

However, because the resolution treaty is not yet a reality, in the next section we offer a checklist of practice-oriented ideas and recommendations – drawn from our experiences in Colombia and elsewhere – regarding how to advance negotiations in general, and justice issues within that.

3

Elements of Practice

As we have argued, without understanding what makes negotiations difficult in general, one cannot understand what makes peace negotiations difficult in particular. Likewise, without understanding what makes peace negotiations difficult, one cannot understand what makes negotiating transitional justice an especially difficult component thereof.

With this in mind, the following section provides elements of practical guidance focused on the intersection of negotiation, peace, and justice. It includes ideas and lessons that amplify our overall conception of negotiating peace with justice (section 1), while also taking into account the current gap in international law (section 2). Many of the ideas discussed below could be components of the eventual resolution treaty.

A. PROCESS DESIGN

It is common for people to have the wrong image of how a negotiation comes about, how it is run, and what helps it move forward. Often, attention focuses on the substantive issues on the agenda, and comparatively little on the design of the process.

This inattention constitutes the downfall of many processes. In practice, the chances of success or failure in a negotiation are profoundly affected by how it is conceived and designed. Indeed, just as the quality of the playing field, fairness of the rules, and impartiality of the referees are major determinants of the dynamics and outcomes of a football match, so too the design of a negotiation is a critical factor in determining the results that are within reach.

In the best cases, process design helps reduce distrust between the negotiating parties, manage crises, increase public engagement, and improve the odds of implementation of any accord that is struck. By contrast, bad process design can undo a negotiation almost before it gets started. If the format is unbalanced, the impartiality of facilitators questioned, the rules unclear, and the agenda vague, the chances that a negotiation can reach a happy conclusion are close to zero.

For starters, with the **structure** of the negotiation, it can be important to (1) reach clear and early agreement on the end-objective, (2) have a well-defined agenda of substantive issues, linked to the end-objective and bolstered by a set of procedural rules concerning the who, how, when and where of the negotiation, and (3) make all of this a matter of public record, once agreed. The latter, in particular, builds legitimacy and accountability for the process on three levels at once: within the negotiating blocks, across them, and between the participants and the public.

Naturally, some negotiations (or early phases thereof) won't be able to take such a public and detailed shape, as any publicity would doom them. Yet, when possible, it makes an immense and positive difference to the process (and thus the result) if the three mentioned elements can be established.

Regarding rules about **communications**, it is evidently important for there to be strict guidelines on the confidentiality of what is discussed. It must be impermissible for anyone involved to reveal anything to the public, except when explicitly and mutually agreed. Likewise, it is advisable that each side designates one spokesperson, to avoid confusing or conflicting accounts about the vision, rules, and intended results of the process. In this regard, simple actions – such as establishing an official negotiation website and a system for periodic joint statements – can ensure the availability of accurate and objective information for outside stakeholders. There are few things more damaging to the legitimacy of a negotiation than a 'war of microphones' in which the different parties involved are regularly contradicting each other's account of basic facts about the process.

Expert input mechanisms can also be vital to the success of a negotiation. For example, it can be important for each side of a negotiation to have a secretariat or technical team (possibly supplemented by external advisors) in order to do research, prepare options papers, support the main negotiators, and more. In the absence of a technical team, it is very difficult for the principals to be sufficiently organised to achieve good results in the talks.

It can also be important to allow periodic expert input by third parties, especially on topics that are highly sensitive or technically complex. In such cases, the sides can jointly invite independent experts to give technical briefings – or integrate them into special working groups or committees that may be established. The presence of such third parties can sometimes be crucial to depoliticise issues and offer neutral pathways for resolving tensions and roadblocks on particular subjects.

The negotiation can also be designed in a way that allows for even broader forms of input. In particular, there can be a mechanism by which civic groups and others in society are able to present ideas, suggestions, and technical proposals to the parties. This can be permitted, for example, through electronic forms, in-person visits, and purpose-built conferences and assemblies.

However, greater participation *inside* a process is double-edged. For example, while the visits of delegations of victims, women's groups, and others to the Colombian talks in Havana helped to bolster the process's legitimacy, they also had the effect of slowing down the negotiation; such visits consume an immense amount of time and energy – before, during, and after they take place. Thus, the question of public participation should not be treated as an absolute good, as it may involve diminishing returns that are not offset by the greater legitimacy such participation can add. This is especially important to bear in mind if speed is a key criterion of the talks – as, for example, when the parties are trying to negotiate a short framework accord, as opposed to a comprehensive point-by-point agreement.

The presence of **process-facilitation actors** at the negotiating table – a trend that expanded in the aftermath of the Cold War, and remains strong today – is another issue for consideration. Facilitation can take the form of third-party mediators, observers, guarantors, special envoys, contact groups, or combinations of all of these. Such actors may issue from foreign governments or specialised organisations (whether multilateral or non-governmental), or they may be eminent individuals unattached to a particular institution or government. Colombia offers a good example of just this: the Havana talks were not mediated, but they involved two guarantor countries (Cuba and Norway), two accompanying countries (Chile and Venezuela), and the periodic involvement of other third parties at key junctures, either directly (e.g., the UN joined for part of the final phase of the talks on the issue of disarmament) or indirectly (e.g., the US government and the EU both appointed special envoys who periodically met the negotiating parties in the latter stages of the talks).

The integration of such actors is meant, above all, to advance the legitimacy and the flow of the negotiation process. Their role may encompass anything from facilitating confidence building, to monitoring compliance with the rules, serving as repositories for key documents, announcing agreements when the parties so request, assisting to overcome blockages, helping resolve disputes of interpretation about commitments made, and much more.

But these many elements of process design – including public input mechanisms, process facilitation, communication rules, and so on – represent only a sampling of the many options available. There are scores of additional choices about the 'how' of the negotiation, ranging from procedures for the drafting of agreements, to the design of failsafe mechanisms, selection of the negotiation site, monitoring of ceasefires, and the establishment of deadlines. The possible use of cross-cutting principles (e.g., the principle that 'Nothing is agreed until everything agreed', which was first used in Northern Ireland) or special rules (such as 'sufficient consensus', which was developed in South Africa) is likewise part of comprehensive process design.

When done well, choices of process design can convert the negotiation space into a dynamic centre of gravity for solving problems and reaching political agreements that would otherwise be unattainable.

B. TACTICAL CONSIDERATIONS

The design of the negotiation process is a critical determinant of its potential to succeed. However, beyond that come an array of tactical decisions by the negotiating parties. These are 'games within the rules' that the established 'rules of the game' permit. They, too, are part of the toolbox of negotiation practice.

Three of these techniques we have already mentioned, as they are unavoidable parts of any peace negotiation: constructive ambiguities, confidence-building measures, and contingency calculations. We will say a word about each of these – with some reference to the experience of Colombia's negotiations – before examining other techniques.

The technique of **constructive ambiguity** is an inevitable part of any negotiation. Ipso facto, the concept involves two working parts: the deliberate use of *ambiguity*, and its application toward a *constructive* end (i.e., to help avoid or solve a problem).

Constructive ambiguities are primarily used in a negotiation when clarity is not possible except at a potentially great risk or cost (such as a breakdown of trust or a massive delay in the talks). In that respect, they can offer temporary solutions that allow a negotiation to move forward and key relationships to be preserved, on the conscious understanding that the ambiguity may carry the seeds of problems for the future.

Yet, sometimes the nature of the ambiguity is not fully understood by one or more of the parties (or by one or more future implementation bodies). When this happens, what began life as a constructive ambiguity may become a destructive one. For example, in the Colombian talks, the negotiating agenda did not use the word 'justice' anywhere. Instead, as a constructive ambiguity, the item on victims referred only to 'the human rights of victims' and 'truth'. Yet, in mid-2014, when it came time to negotiate the item on victims, the same ambiguity proved a bone of contention. The FARC insisted that they had never agreed to negotiate any form of criminal justice, citing the literal wording of the agenda item in which no mention of justice appears; whereas the government – which had reformed the constitution in 2012 to enable a justice accord to be reached, and had spoken repeatedly in public about its commitment to ensure peace with justice in the negotiations – insisted that justice had always formed an implicit part of the agenda item.

In this regard, as a matter of practice, it is usually desirable in a negotiation to signal the ambiguity – in the moment it is proposed – and explain one's understanding of what is being agreed and why. This can help to make the ambiguity a 'known known', thus preventing the ambiguity from becoming the object of a future, nasty surprise for one or both sides. Having said that, such openness will not always be desirable; sometimes silence about one's understanding of an expression is a necessary condition of the constructive ambiguity's survival.

What matters is to avoid an excess of constructive ambiguities on any one issue, especially if that issue is essential to the viability of the overall accord – as was the case of justice in the context of the Colombian peace deal. The destabilising nature of the issue generated a wide range of ambiguous expressions midway through the process, such as 'restriction of liberty' (*restricción de libertad*) instead of incarceration, 'room' (*sala*) instead of tribunal, and many others. As explained in Part II of the book, the ambiguous status of an initial seventy-five-point partial agreement on justice almost destroyed the whole negotiation.

In brief, while constructive ambiguities are inevitable – and useful – the key is to keep the ambiguity to a minimum so that it (1) avoids hosting too many seeds of future destruction, and (2) ensures the constructive benefit, in terms of relationship preservation or agreement making, outweighs the risks.

The usage of **confidence-building measures** (CBMs) is another critical negotiation device. These are voluntary actions which, as the term suggests, increase confidence. Yet the expression masks as much as it reveals. For example, a CBM can be jointly agreed or unilaterally undertaken; deliberately intended to build confidence or accidentally have that effect; directed at one's negotiation opponent or alternatively at a myriad of other actors, such as one's own delegation, the public, or the international community.

The classic CBM has a deliberate signalling function to adversaries. For example, it is common for a ceasefire to be offered as a gesture of good faith at the start of a negotiation, as a signal of commitment. The same might be said of an initial handshake ceremony or joint press conference. Once the negotiation is under way, however, the process of offering or agreeing new CBMs can take on a life of its own that sometimes competes for time with the principal negotiation. In Colombia's talks with the FARC, it took the parties months of back and forth to reach agreement on a mid-negotiation demining project in order to increase confidence in each other, affected communities, and the public at large. Despite its eventual benefits, the discussion of the project took much time away from the main negotiation, which was already in a worrying logjam.

Thus, as a general rule, one has to be confident that any elaborate CBM is going to be worth the effort. If it is unlikely to deliver on high-priority objectives – such as strengthening the pace and quality of the negotiation, or bolstering the legitimacy of the process at a critical juncture – then it is probably not worth doing.

As for the forms that a CBM can take, the range extends as far as one's imagination. Examples from Colombia include, on the part of the FARC, everything from their public acknowledgement of wrongdoing in communities like Bojayá to officially ceasing the recruitment of minors and delivering personalised holiday cards to members of the government delegation. On the part of the government, CBMs included everything from conditional pardons for selected FARC prisoners in advance of the final accord to military de-escalation measures and respectful responses to deliberately provocative submissions at the negotiation table.

As for bilaterally agreed CBMs, these included the organisation of victim hearings, a special panel with women's groups, agreement on the establishment of an interim task force on missing persons, the issuance of periodic joint declarations, and much more. The negotiation's guarantors – Cuba and Norway – also played a part in this. For example, they organised periodic social encounters, from piano concerts to evening cocktails at the ambassador's residence, meant to facilitate interpersonal CBMs.

But the value of CBMs ought to be seen in a long-term perspective, as the process of building confidence continues long past pre-negotiation and negotiation, running deep into the implementation phase when the mass of stored-up confidence may be critical to overcome unexpected crises. In this regard, CBMs should be understood not as ends, but rather as means to build the confidence without which trust erodes, relations rupture and the larger objective of settlement falls out of reach.

A third element of negotiation practice – something we call **calculations of contingency** – concerns tactical calculations about those risks that can be controlled, and those that cannot.

There are two different ways of thinking about such risks within the negotiation: either one seeks to resolve all the details of an accord and all the eventualities of future implementation at the negotiating table (including to situate oneself at the centre of any future interpretation mechanism); or one takes a more indirect approach, focusing on the establishment of a framework of rules and commitments but leaving the details of implementation to be worked out over time.

In the Colombian negotiation, the tension between these poles – one of greater control, one of lesser – was a constant. For example, the FARC frequently insisted that the truth commission would need to begin work during the negotiation, in order to establish the 'Truth' up front. This was likely motivated by the desire to exert maximum control over the findings, something the FARC was more likely to achieve in the tight structure of the negotiation than in a peacebuilding phase with its dozens of centres of gravity.

On the government's side, the decision to pursue a comprehensive agreement (rather than a framework accord akin to Northern Ireland's Good Friday Agreement) was also largely about control. It wanted to leave the FARC as little wiggle room as possible to elude its undertakings in Havana. However, this proved to be a choice with dramatic consequences in terms of the speed at which accords could be reached.

However, none of this is meant to be judgemental. Trade-offs between pace and depth are intrinsic to the exercise of negotiation, and one simply has to choose a preferred weighting. In general, though, it is often best to avoid overly programmatic texts, details, and nuances, and instead focus in a minimalistic fashion on agreeing the objectives, principles, and implementation bodies for the future peacebuilding phase. This is especially the case in the area of transitional justice, where investigations, findings, and recommendations should be left in the hands of future commissioners, judges, and investigators, rather than attempting to be resolved within the talks themselves. A negotiation cannot and should not operate as a grand jury.

Another key tactical consideration in peace negotiations is the tension between a **holistic or incremental methodology**. This is an issue that exposes the depth of preparation of each side.

Under optimal circumstances, a peace agreement will express the vision of a self-contained system for ending war and building peace, encompassing:

- A clear justification for each element within the overall system, such that everything – from political participation to disarmament, economic reconstruction, constitutional reform, prisoner exchanges, amnesty, suspension of arrest warrants, return of displaced persons, and searches for missing persons – has its valid place;
- A convincing but simple narrative about the why, what, when, and how of the system's operation;

- Independent verification, failsafe mechanisms, and organised spaces for ongoing dialogue in order to manage implementation disputes and crises effectively;
- An overarching set of principles (e.g., inclusion, conditionality, good faith, transparency) to guide choices within the system and minimise the risk of debilitating mistakes; and
- Benchmarks for progress and results, in order to have realistic outcome goals for the short, medium, and long term.

Naturally, it is unrealistic at the start of a negotiation for any of the sides to have such a complete vision. The process is inescapably iterative. Yet, it is advisable for each party to have at least a general concept about what an ideal outcome looks like – a 'plan A' – in order to avoid agreeing things on a piecemeal basis that end up creating problems later in the negotiation, or reducing the space to solve other substantive issues along the way.

In this regard, conversations between the sides regarding end-visions should ideally happen early and often, provided those conversations are about exchanging ideas and not reaching accords. This can serve as a critical, mutual learning process about the premises, assumptions, and expectations of the other side, enabling greater possibilities for incrementally reaching accords thereafter.

A related element of good negotiation practice involves having a plan and set of rules for the **internal negotiation within one's own delegation**.

To a surprising degree, peace negotiations involve a relatively small amount of time spent with the other side, as compared to the amount spent with one's own side. Understandably, many imagine that the parties to a negotiation work day and night with their sleeves rolled up, tackling one issue after the next, across from each other at a table. The reality is very much the opposite. The large majority of a negotiation is spent with one's own side, working through ideas, strategies, and disagreements. This is particularly the case for a government delegation, because of the larger number and diversity of internal stakeholders that need to be consulted (and convinced) in the formulation of negotiating positions.

As such, the internal negotiation needs a process design of its own. The better that design is, the better the process of internal consensus-building will be; and with it, the better the chance of a rapid and effective negotiation with the external adversary. Indeed, it is trite to observe that a precondition to any successful negotiation between enemies is the internal cohesion of each side. This denotes much more than the promotion of congenial interpersonal relations; it implies a deliberate, ongoing process for forging unity about the contours of a final agreement and the team strategy for getting there.

But even when the internal negotiation is well organised, it can be confusing for those on the outside who may fail to appreciate that positions expressed at the negotiation table sometimes have more to do with appeasing internal allies and overcoming internal divisions, than anything to do with the external adversary. Failing to appreciate this can easily lead to crises in the talks – as occurred more than once in Havana, when the reason behind the adoption of certain positions was driven primarily by internal rather than external considerations.

A further tactical issue concerns the formation of **negotiation rituals** inside a peace process. Often, from a very early stage, a 'way of working' consolidates itself – only part of which can be traced back to the agreed rules. For example, in Havana, the parties established a whole set of routines that worked well for quite some time, but at moments became obstacles. These included the routine of eleven-day meeting cycles, a standard walk-in ceremony before the press gallery, rules about days off, and much more. All of these rituals created endowment effects that the parties struggled to overcome even when they needed to expedite discussions, extend the length of negotiation cycles, and re-brand the image of the process with new public relations measures that could overcome the talks' flagging legitimacy.

This inability was most pronounced during the negotiation of criminal accountability issues. Because of the unusual sensitivity and complexity of the topic, radical changes in format (e.g., periodically walling off the process from outside visitors, or organising special sessions with a core group in order to have more free-flowing exchanges) were required. Yet, the negotiations continued by and large unchanged, resulting in months of lost time and repeated deferral of the issue of justice (and its substitution with all kinds of lower priorities). This ultimately produced a crisis that led President Santos to hire a team of legal consultants who put speed above all other considerations. As a result, the government's 'plan A' on justice – painstakingly crafted, and endorsed by all key levels of power after months of internal consultations and revisions – was never really tested.

The application of **leverage** is another critical ingredient of effective negotiation practice.

The concept of leverage is above all one of advantage or superiority. Its form may be geographic-territorial (e.g., one party owns or control most of the relevant territory in dispute), political (e.g., one side holds the reins of electoral power), military (e.g., one party has superior strength of arms), socio-cultural (e.g., one side enjoys the balance of public support), administrative (e.g., one faction has far greater representation in national institutions), constitutional-legal (e.g., the constitution favours one party's political ideology more than the others), or economic-financial (e.g., the business sector depends primarily on one faction for most of its profits).

These forms of superiority create structural pressures on declared adversaries in a negotiation, and can be reinforced by the use of threats ('sticks') and incentives ('carrots'). Regarding the latter, these can take one of two basic forms – the offer of a benefit, or the withdrawal of a burden or cost – and may relate to different spheres of interest. These include political (e.g., offering a place in government), economic (e.g., ending sanctions), security (e.g., offering a ceasefire), socio-cultural (e.g., increasing access to public media), or legal (e.g., dangling an amnesty). Such incentives can also vary as a function of whether they (1) are fully within one's control (e.g., a unilateral ceasefire) or not (e.g., a foreign boycott); (2) involve fixed capital (e.g., an offer of statehood) or fungible (e.g., offering a seat at the negotiation table); (3) are conditional (e.g., political participation rights that require prior disarmament) or not (e.g., an unconditional offer of safe haven); (4) affect existential interests or expedient ones; and (5) are credible or unconvincing.

By corollary, threats can involve the imposition of a cost or burden, or the withdrawal of a benefit. The threats can of course relate to different spheres of interest, including political (e.g., threatening to walk away from the negotiation), economic (e.g., engineering new sanctions), security (e.g., threatening new violence), socio-cultural (e.g., organising public protests), or legal (e.g., threatening investigation and prosecution). Likewise, they can vary as to whether they (1) are fully within one's control (e.g., withdrawal of a power-sharing offer) or not (e.g., applying for an arrest warrant); (2) involve fixed capital (e.g., threatening to poison a water source) or fungible (e.g., threatening to cancel a reintegration programme); (3) affect existential interests or expedient ones; and (4) are credible or unconvincing.

In brief, any negotiating party must understand – and apply – its existing and potential sources of outside leverage if it wants to optimise outcomes inside the negotiation.

Yet, if leverage is the most powerful determinant of negotiating power, it is not the only one. Tactics within the negotiation – and **perceptions about the other side's interests and intentions** – are likewise critical. This is almost a realm of psychology more than politics, as it is replete with all the unconscious biases (loss aversion, availability heuristics, optimism bias, etc.) associated with the field of behavioural economics.

In the realm of perception, what is needed is the will and the skill to see the negotiation through the eyes of one's adversary. In the case of Colombia's talks, the government delegation spent much of the transitional justice negotiation presenting *its* vision of the principle of individual and collective accountability. To do so, it often cited reasons of international law and public opinion, arguing that accountability was required, not optional.

However, in hindsight, a more effective method of persuasion might have involved application of John Rawls's concept of 'overlapping consensus'. The FARC perceived that the government was trying to impose its worldview, as it rarely tried to situate its arguments within the ideological and doctrinal world of the rebels. Had it done so, the parties may have come to a faster or deeper consensus, creating the possibility of accountability being perceived by the FARC as a first-best option in line with its core beliefs (an ideal outcome for the stability of future peace implementation) and not a second-best compromise in the face of superior power.

To be sure, some opponents are unreasonable interlocutors, and need to be treated as such. Indeed, sometimes a negotiating party adopts the view that tactical gains are achievable only by being as extreme and unreasonable as possible. This can lead to a lot of 'bluff', which can complicate the task of identifying the underlying interests, intentions, and settlement possibilities. Yet, there is no excuse for failing to probe the self-perceived identity, doctrines, and methods of the adversary – seeking to frame arguments in ways that on occasion may allow for win-win results. After all, regardless of the adversary, negotiation outcomes are not zero-sum events: in the end, both sides may be correct in perceiving that they obtained most of what they were seeking.

Nonetheless, each side in a negotiation at some point may feel it is owed a **debt** by the other, on account of some prior act of (self-assessed) generosity. More than once, this dynamic manifested itself during the discussion of victims and justice in the Havana talks. For example, the government delegation felt it had been comparatively generous to the FARC on the first three chapters of the negotiation (drugs, political participation, and rural reform), with the expectation that the FARC would reciprocate on the subject of transitional justice. This was an unstated feeling that, unsurprisingly, proved hazardous, as the FARC clearly did not feel it owed any debt to the government.

Examples of such misunderstandings were ample, underscoring how calculations of debt in a negotiation tend to be illusory and counterproductive. The party 'owing the debt' often rejects the very existence of any debt. Meanwhile, the party supposedly 'owed the debt' tends to become resentful, even incredulous, at the other side's perceived bad faith.

In Havana, the government delegation was scandalised by the FARC's lack of generosity on the issue of reparation, not only because of what they objectively owe victims, but also because of how demonstrably generous the state had been for years through its national reparations scheme. As advisers, we shared their feelings. However, such sentiments have no place in a negotiation, which more often requires sangfroid than indignation to inch forward.

C. JUSTICE CONSIDERATIONS WITHIN THE NEGOTIATION

We have discussed the need for good process design vis-à-vis the negotiation, so that the 'rules of the game' are clear and the parties formally committed to them. We have also discussed tactical 'games within the rules' that negotiating parties tend to use, in good faith or bad. We now turn to the attendant, more specific challenge of negotiating accords on justice.

A first important task negotiators face is to identify and articulate the **legal playing field** in which justice questions are meant to be resolved. Unlike most other areas of a negotiation (e.g., disarmament and land reform), there is no way to address the topic of justice without a heavy dose of law: at a minimum, constitutional and international law, but undoubtedly domestic criminal law as well. The challenge is that different parties will disagree about the legal floor and ceiling within which solutions can be explored.

We have already noted that on critical topics – such as amnesty and negotiation – international law is unhelpful or simply absent. This creates the pretext for every kind of argument – most prominently, in the case of amnesty, of exaggerated claims of impermissibility. The consequence is that international law unduly loses both accuracy and utility.

Another justice-specific choice in peace negotiations concerns the **blending measures** needed to overcome inherent imperfections that any settlement on international crimes necessarily involves. There are three aspects to this.

First, the more any component of judicial accountability tends toward leniency (e.g., by suspending its application, reducing or foregoing punishment, limiting the number of cases, etc.), the greater the need to compensate by increasing the quality and reach of the accompanying package of truth-seeking, reparation, and reform measures. In Havana, it was thus inevitable that the issue of 'victims' would involve a full transitional justice agenda. Otherwise, the criminal justice component of the final settlement, which was already controversial, would have met even more opposition by victims and the public.

Second, special incentives and conditions are necessary in respect of any judicial leniency or accountability that forms part of a negotiated peace deal.

In the case of the Colombian process, it was clear from an early stage that the envisaged post-conflict tribunal would need to incorporate devices such as: (1) conditioning legal leniency on a series of prior or accompanying actions, such as disarmament in the case of the FARC, or acknowledgment in the case of all actors; (2) offering greater leniency to those offering greater levels of acknowledgment of past crimes; (3) including deadlines in order to encourage widespread participation in the transitional justice system; (4) creating a multi-track system to reward earlier acts of recognition over later ones; (5) creating an indirect cap on the number of trials by delimiting prosecutorial discretion in various sensible ways; (6) avoiding the risk of double jeopardy by ensuring all conflict-related cases pass through a single jurisdiction; and (7) establishing a common legal standard of conflict-related culpability (e.g., international humanitarian law).

Third, the use of legal presumptions can also compensate for the intrinsic defects of negotiated accountability. Justice systems cannot cope with individual assessment and verification procedures when there is a massive universe of cases involved. As such, rather than futilely attempting to verify that tens of thousands of persons have complied with an agreed condition of legal leniency – such as the requirement of individual acts of truth-telling or reparation – there can be a rebuttable presumption of compliance. This presumption can in turn be subject to an agreed mechanism of randomised control trials, partial third-party verification, or something similar, thus avoiding case-by-case verification by the overburdened judicial implementer.

Another justice consideration in a peace negotiation concerns the distinction between **pacted conditions and voluntary undertakings**. The latter are collective or institutional commitments, freely undertaken in the context of a negotiated settlement, to promote or execute certain measures or actions upon the accord's implementation. For example, one or more of the negotiating parties may commit to carrying out acts of public acknowledgment of past wrongs, or to returning stolen assets, without tying the commitment to any corresponding or reciprocal benefit. This has the effect of lifting the undertaking to a higher moral plane, but the disadvantage that it is not legally enforceable by the intended beneficiary, since non-performance of the undertaking is non-justiciable in that it lacks the element of 'consideration' (i.e., the exchange of one thing of value for another).

Such voluntary undertakings contrast with the backbone of any peace agreement: pacted conditions. Most of an agreement's benefits involve formal exchanges of value, meaning that the benefits are conditional on performing certain actions – whether as a means of access to the benefit, or of after-the-fact retention. Such conditions are arguably more important in the area of justice than in any other area of a peace negotiation. That is because they help fill the legitimacy gap that ensues from inevitable concessions in the area of justice, and likewise serve as an adhesive that holds all of the commitments and accords together in an interdependent system of risks and guarantees – precisely as it should be for a comprehensive peace settlement in which the non-implementation of any one component undermines the system as a whole.

An additional justice consideration in the context of a peace negotiation concerns the **choices in – and between – truth and justice**. Some of these we have already mentioned, such as the incorporation of truth-telling as a precondition for judicial leniency. However, the most complex question concerns the structuring of the relationship between a potential truth commission and post-conflict court system.

Truth commissions and tribunals pursue many common objectives. Both do fact-finding, both can advance victim reparations, both can contribute to public debate and acknowledgement, both may validate victim experiences, and both can deliver meaningful accountability for a range of individual and collective wrongs. Depending on their design, truth commissions and tribunals may also have overlapping powers and functions, as both tend to conduct statement taking, wield powers of investigation, and hold a mix of public and private hearings.

However, if tribunals had identical functions and advantages to truth commissions, the two types of mechanism would not exist. As such, it is important to understand their chief differences, which include the following:

- Truth commissions are primarily or exclusively non-judicial (providing greater flexibility in evidence), whereas tribunals are exclusively judicial (requiring greater rigour in evidence).
- Truth commissions' primary focus is on victims (displacing the focus away from perpetrators and emphasising trauma over accountability), whereas tribunals' primary focus is on perpetrators (emphasising accountability above all else).
- Truth commissions' primary purpose is historical clarification and public understanding (ensuring that broader truths are discussed rather than crowded out by legalistic quibbling), whereas tribunals' primary purpose is making determinations of individual criminal culpability (ensuring punishment for established wrongdoing above all else).
- A truth commission's final product is a non-binding report containing findings of fact and recommendations for redress and reform, whereas a tribunal's is a binding, written judgement.

These differences were parsed in detail in the Havana talks. First, it was only after months of FARC resistance – during which the rebels pushed for a super-empowered truth commission – that the parties eventually agreed that there would be a truth commission *and* a post-conflict tribunal. But even then, the parties still would have to negotiate (1) the respective mandates and powers of each mechanism, and (2) the interrelationship and sequencing of them.

For the sake of brevity, we can describe the competing positions as follows: (1) the government believed that a non-judicial truth commission should begin operating only after a special prosecutor selected a limited number of individuals to answer before a special tribunal for war-related crimes, and (2) the FARC believed that any judicial action should be suspended until after the truth commission concluded its work and made recommendations, or binding decisions, about who should receive special legal treatment (including pardons) for war-related crimes.

In the end, the negotiated solution came closer to the government's position – but at a cost. First, as the truth commission's mandate was negotiated in the absence of a concurrent negotiation of justice, this produced large delays – less because the government and FARC had different visions about the commission, and more because they had different visions about its relationship with the sensitive issue of justice. The same was true in respect of the armed forces, which appeared to view the proposed commission as a Trojan horse that might sully the reputation of the institution and harm the careers of its leaders, and thus produce negative follow-on consequences for them in the courts.

Ultimately, only parts of the interrelationship between the truth commission and the tribunal were clarified in the final accord and in the subsequent implementing legislation. As such, it was left to the implementation period to determine key aspects of the relationship, thus limiting the level of legal certainty that any of the parties could have about the risks and opportunities of the comprehensive transitional justice system.

Arguably, the better approach for any accountability-oriented negotiator is to invest time in the development of an in-house **global vision of transitional justice**, and to present the contours of that to one's counterpart before negotiating any individual components thereof.

In the Colombian context, despite a very impressive level of internal preparation – and a commendable 'Legal Framework for Peace' that had been adopted as early as 2012 – the government delegation did not have a sufficiently clear transitional justice strategy at the start of the negotiation of agenda item 5 ('Victims'). It knew that it wanted a comprehensive scheme, but it lacked internal clarity in terms of (1) how the moving parts of transitional justice (i.e., justice, truth, reparation and guarantees of non-repetition) might ideally fit with each other, and (2) how the transitional justice system might ideally fit with the other issues on the negotiation agenda (i.e., disarmament, political participation, rural reform, and the problem of drugs). As a result, the delegation was unable to present a global picture of its vision of agenda item 5. Instead, more by default than by design, it opted for a piecemeal approach that back-ended the controversial question of criminal accountability, arguably producing more elevated fears that in turn produced extra delays and increased distrust.

In this regard, it is worth underlining the importance of the distinction between existential and non-existential interests in any negotiation process. Such interests should never be handled or negotiated in the same way, as the former are tied up with a set of fears that put them on a different emotional plane. Anyone who has ever tried to negotiate leadership-level criminal accountability as part of a peace negotiation understands this intuitively.

Counterintuitively, there is good cause to address the existential threat of justice *early*, not late, in a negotiation – knowing it will be painful, but also potentially liberating. However, it is worth repeating that the potential benefits of such an approach can materialise only if the party in question has a clear vision about where criminal accountability fits into the whole of its transitional justice strategy. Otherwise, the tendency will be to defer the issue, ostensibly under the popular logic of leaving the hardest issues until the end, but at the foreseeable cost of decelerating the pace – and capacity – of negotiating everything else.

In short, on some topics it may be advantageous for the overall cause of the negotiation to do the hardest things first – and quickly – rather than postponing them to a later date. The same logic can apply to the implementation of the final accord itself. If justice is part of any comprehensive settlement, it should ideally be addressed somewhere in the first stage of implementation; providing an early, solid dosage of legal certainty for everyone, so that good-faith implementation of all other commitments stands a greater chance. The faster legal certainty is achieved for all, the smoother the implementation of the other elements of the peace accord can be.

Yet, in any negotiation, certain substantive **trade-offs** cannot be avoided. For example, in most cases, there will be strong public demand for legal vengeance against the leaders of any non-state armed group that has carried out attacks against civilians. At the same time, in order for there to be an effective disarmament process following negotiations, the cooperation of the leaders of that group will be necessary. As such, they cannot be in jail while facilitating the demobilisation and disarmament of their forces; and it would be wishful thinking to expect that any group leader would negotiate on that basis.

Thus, a way must be found of balancing such competing prerogatives, bearing in mind the magnitude of existential threat that criminal accountability represents (to insurgent leaders and state agents alike). In brief, if justice will be part of the final deal, a priori, trade-offs will arise. As such, a wise negotiator will make a point of identifying and leveraging the concept of justice held by the adversary (and the factual premises that may underlie it) since there could be points of convergence that help avoid the need for certain trade-offs. Over time, this proved essential for concluding the negotiation of transitional justice in Havana, as the parties gradually discovered that, to varying degrees, they both held the following minimal convictions: (1) it is honourable to recognise one's responsibility for serious crimes; (2) both sides of the conflict produced victims; (3) certain types of crimes can never be justified by the ends; (4) public opinion is relevant to the justice solution that may be reached; (5) both sides deserve as much legal certainty as possible; (6) any post-conflict justice will have to apply to all conflict actors; (7) more favourable legal treatment should be given to those who accept responsibility; and (8) in the case of the FARC, any model of justice must be articulated with the disarmament process on the one hand, and the transformation of the FARC into an unarmed political group on the other.

Once these and other shared premises became clear, two things happened: (1) certain kinds of trade-offs were mitigated or avoided (not least, that justice needed to be sacrificed for peace), and (2) many creative and realistic options came to the fore. The lesson is that, in a negotiation, early and broad exchange between the parties about what 'justice' and other hard issues signify to each side can help to uncover surprising layers of shared premises, thus expanding the bandwidth for reaching substantive accords.

A final consideration in the negotiation of peace with justice concerns the distinction between **legitimacy** on the one hand, and **legal security** (*seguridad jurídica* in Spanish) on the other. The latter refers to the reasonable expectation of negotiating parties that the scope of personal and institutional legal risks arising on account of a settlement should be as precise and knowable as possible.

The concept has at least three dimensions, the first of which is contractual. Each party is responsible for completing, in good faith, every action it undertakes in the agreement. If parties cannot rely on each other to deliver on promises entirely within their control, legal security cannot even begin to materialise. While some of the promised actions will be joint (e.g., the state and the FARC agree to work jointly against drug traffickers), others will be individual (e.g., the FARC agrees to disarm). What matters is that promises made are promises kept; only then can the minimal form of legal security be met.

The second dimension of legal security is akin to force majeure. It concerns a category of events that threaten legal security but cannot be prevented. Examples include incidents like the following: a future elected government accedes to a request for extradition of a former guerrilla leader, despite his having delivered on first-dimension promises; an international prosecutor issues an arrest warrant against a military leader, despite good-faith fulfilment of the conditions of his special legal treatment; or a future case-specific challenge by an aggrieved victim results in a constitutional court decision that reconfigures a fundamental element of the peace accord. Such eventualities remain beyond the control of the negotiating parties no matter how legitimate the overall peace deal.

The third dimension of legal security is subtler and more overarching. It involves identifying which decisions and actions – apart from the satisfaction of first-dimension promises – can help reduce the likelihood of second-dimension problems, so that an aura of 'untouchability' is created in relation to the overall peace package. This aura can act as a shield, putting future governments and independent national, foreign, and international courts in a position in which they dare not disturb implementation.

The creation of this aura of untouchability depends, in turn, on the perceived legitimacy of four interlocked variables of the peacemaking process:

- *The peace negotiations:* Every statement, action, and gesture by the conflict actors in the lead-up to an accord either fortifies or weakens everyone's legal security to the extent it reinforces – or undermines – the external legitimacy of the overall deal. Stated differently, the content of the future final agreement does not, alone, define the parameters of legal security.
- *The peace accord's content*: The impression the accord must generate is that 'the parties went as far as morally and politically possible in negotiating the justice elements of the accord'. In the case of Colombia, some notable indicators of this included the agreement's universality (the parties reached a deal that has everyone pass through a common transitional justice system), its respect for precedent (the agreement met the baseline standard of negotiated justice in Colombia, established under the 2005 Justice and Peace Law), and its balance of truth and justice (the accord avoids creating a truth commission that looks like a surrogate for justice).

- *The peace accord's approval:* Over the lifetime of a peace agreement, governments will change and prosecutors and judges will come and go. Therefore, peace deals – including their judicial components – can eventually be thwarted. All that can limit such an eventuality is the creation of a kind of supreme national consensus that future governments and courts would dare not contradict. Ideally, the peace deal's terms (or agreed modifications thereof) come to be seen as unassailable; something that can occur through a combination of formal endorsement (by plebiscite, parliament, a supreme court, etc.) and continuous public debate and consensus-building.
- *The peace accord's implementation:* For legal security to exist in the manner contemplated in a final agreement, the implementation process must look sound. Thus, effective implementation is yet a further guarantee of legal security.

4

Conclusions

While negotiating peace with justice requires the skills of an artist, some science is nevertheless involved. Part I demonstrated how that is so.

First, we examined what makes ensuring justice for atrocity crimes more difficult, both normatively and practically, than for other crimes. Three imaginary country situations were presented: one in which there is neither negotiation nor transition out of war; one in which there is transition without negotiation; and one in which there is negotiation without transition. We explained how and why the latter presents the greatest structural constraints of all, in terms of ensuring justice.

Subsequently, we identified the striking indifference (or insensitivity) of international law to the value and practice of negotiation as a tool for preventing or ending internal armed conflict. We observed that there is no law of peace negotiation, nor anything close to it. As such, we analysed the possibilities for creating a 'resolution treaty' that could fill the gap and offer incentives, guidance, and support to states parties, in order to increase recourse to negotiation as a means to avert or end conflict, and to facilitate the taking of wiser decisions and creation of more lasting settlements.

The final section involved the review of a wide range of practical lessons and strategic considerations for effectively negotiating peace with justice.

The next part of the book will delve more deeply into the specific experience of Colombia's negotiations with the FARC, offering contextual description, as well as detailed analytic essays on three crucial issues: (1) reconciling competing expectations of dignity and legal security, (2) choosing between ordinary and extraordinary mechanisms, and (3) sorting out contending claims about who is victim and who is victimiser.

PART II

Negotiating Transitional Justice
The Case of Colombia

INTRODUCTION

On the subject of negotiating peace with justice, Colombia stands out. Three factors explain why. First, the parties to the Havana talks made the radical and counterintuitive choice to put victims 'at the centre' of the negotiation agenda. Second, the government publicly promised to ensure a justice solution (within the larger political solution) that respects its international human rights and humanitarian and criminal law commitments, including under the Rome Statute. Third, because it actively drew lessons from scores of peace processes elsewhere, the Havana negotiation functioned as a modern laboratory for the theory and practice of peacemaking. As such, the case has unusually powerful lessons to teach about pathways for peace in general, and negotiating transitional justice in particular.

In the next part of the book, we highlight the complexity of what took place by reflecting critically, and with the benefit of hindsight, on (1) the larger meaning of the results that were achieved, (2) the arduous process by which they were reached, and (3) the structural constraints under which everyone laboured. It is only by understanding this complexity that the Colombian experience can be understood in its proper light, and consequently offer meaningful lessons for peace negotiations in other parts of the world.

The first section of Part II sets the overall context: first, by offering a historical perspective on how the Havana talks came about and the environment in which they unfolded; and second, by providing a reflection about the place of victims in Colombia and the 'politics of transitional justice' in general. The second section of Part II encompasses three essays, dealing with essential dividing lines that revealed themselves inside the talks: one about 'victims versus victimisers', another about 'ordinary versus extraordinary' concepts of justice, and a final one about 'dignity versus legal security'.

1

The Context

A. THE HAVANA TALKS IN PERSPECTIVE

To understand the nature of the Havana talks, a brief description of the context is owed – albeit with three caveats. First, the explanatory factors we outline below had both convergent and divergent effects. In some cases, they reinforced each other; in others, they gave rise to tensions that plagued the entire negotiation. Second, the relationship between context and activity is analogous to that of fabric and embroidery; context is not an external force but something that is interwoven into the many threads of the story. Third, the parties conducted the talks under the figment of sitting as equals at the table; this too had a direct effect in shaping the trajectory and outcomes of the negotiation.

Because there is no way to summarise the full context adequately, our account does not pretend to be exhaustive. Nor does it purport to be scientific in the conventional sense. Instead, the intention is to draw out some of the most obvious conditions of the talks, viewed from the inside out. This includes the formal ground rules established for the very difficult political game the parties would subsequently play out, and a range of other variables that will reappear time and again in the longer essays that will follow.

The Factors That Most Obviously Influenced the Talks

1. The FARC was a pro-Soviet guerrilla group, just like other leftist guerrillas that emerged in Colombia in the 1960s and 1980s under the guise of the various models of socialism prevailing in the aftermath of the Cuban (1959) and Nicaraguan (1979) revolutions. The FARC was born in the midst of the Cold War on the fertile soil of a society possessing an abysmal fracture between the urban centre and the rural peripheries, and one of the highest

Gini coefficients in the world. In spite of its eventual dependence on drug trafficking and other illicit economies, the FARC justified and represented itself as the agent of a social and political revolution. Its members entered the Havana talks with the expectation that, following domestic political and constitutional traditions dating back over 150 years, they would be treated with the privileged status of political offenders. As for serious crimes, including violations of international humanitarian law (IHL), they expected to receive the leniency typically accorded rebels. At the same time, given the enormous international weight attached to the crime of drug trafficking, domestic law looked like a slightly safer option than IHL. Yet, this preference was not merely borne of an interest in impunity; the domestic legal category of 'political offender' was also deeply tied to their self-understanding and sense of dignity as a rebel group with a political agenda.

2. ETA in Spain and the IRA in Northern Ireland maintained strong links with nationalist and separatist political parties: Batasuna with ETA and Sinn Féin with IRA. The groups did so while remaining independent and keeping a significant social base in the Basque region and Catholic community of Northern Ireland, respectively. By contrast, the FARC had long ago dropped any tangible connection to the Colombian Communist Party (PCC), due to a slow and painful process of reciprocal distancing that culminated in the FARC abandoning electoral avenues after their eighth conference in 1993. In fact, the adherence of both the PCC and the FARC to a thesis of 'combining all forms of struggle' had proven deadly for both. The Patriotic Union (UP) – a movement that emerged in 1985 during the peace negotiations between the FARC and the government of Belisario Betancur – consisted of cadres from the FARC and the PCC, and intellectuals from the left, among others. However, the UP was perceived by the country's anti-communist far right as the political vanguard of a triumphant armed revolution (or as the insurrection's rear guard) rather than as the guerrillas' landing pad onto mainstream democratic legality. In addition, many regional and local political bosses saw the UP as a threat to their electoral interests. The result: around three thousand of the UP's members were assassinated during its first three years of existence.

Subsequently, the PCC limited itself to calling for a negotiated solution to the armed conflict, without any formal link to the FARC or any of its subsequent peace talks with government. For its part, the FARC created the so-called Clandestine Communist Party (PC3): a subordinate structure created in the 1990s that portrayed itself as a unified political-military organisation, under peasant leadership and with a nationalist post–Cold War communist ideology. But while the PC3, as an intermediary, could not be part of the peace talks, this did not preclude the FARC and the government from concluding a negotiation agenda – in the 2012 General Agreement – which encompassed a number of social justice issues. However, the inclusion of such issues was initially rejected by certain sectors of Colombian society. In their idealised view, only political parties and interest groups acting within the law could legitimately negotiate social justice matters.

3. The armed conflict with the FARC was the longest in Colombia's modern history. Spanning over five decades – or longer, if one includes the closely linked liberal-conservative political bloodbath of the 1950s – the war has left an extraordinary toll of victims and damages, and a fierce public hatred of the FARC. Approximately one of every five Colombians is a victim of the war in one form or another, and political parties have channelled and manipulated the reservoir of negative feelings primarily against the guerrillas. This is not only because many of the parties' leaders are victims themselves, but also because it advances their electoral (and sometimes personal) interests. In that sense, today, as was the case during much of the nineteenth and twentieth centuries, Colombia's political parties remain geared as much to the promotion of political ideals as to the mobilisation of 'inherited hatreds' (as former president Miguel Antonio Caro famously called them). As such, during the intense public debates on transitional justice during the Havana process, it was often difficult to know when and to what extent certain opposition party arguments were genuine, and when they were merely the conscious or unconscious guise of a thirst for vengeance, an electoral interest, or a bid for impunity.

4. Alongside Colombia's fragmented and highly 'narcoticised' war with the FARC, successive governments since the 1980s have negotiated with various armed groups from the left and the right. This has produced what some have called 'peace by instalments', with each one mapping neatly onto successive presidential terms. In aggregate, this piecemeal approach has lowered overall rates of violence, however it has left power vacuums in several regions, which have been filled by 'recycled' demobilised combatants – and by more war. As such, it was only natural that the Santos administration's Havana process was conceived as an improvement or adjustment from prior talks. In particular, the design of the Havana talks sought to overcome defects in the Pastrana administration's failed San Vicente del Caguán (1999–2001) negotiations with the FARC, as well as drawing lessons from the Uribe administration's 2003 deal with the paramilitary United Self-Defence Groups of Colombia (AUC). Unlike the Caguán process, the Havana talks were deliberately set up with a

clear and limited agenda, strict confidentiality, a foreign location, international guarantors and accompaniment, and the absence of territorial concessions or a bilateral ceasefire. And unlike the AUC process, the Havana talks sought not merely the surrender of common criminals to justice, but rather a combination of political reintegration and transitional justice for a revolutionary, communist, rebel organisation. This approach, however, was rejected by the *Centro Democrático* opposition party, which focused its criticism only on the justice element, insisting that the politically motivated FARC should receive the same treatment as the non–politically motivated AUC paramilitaries. The FARC disagreed categorically with this argument, and made it a 'red line' from the outset that they would not submit to the same standard that was applied to the AUC. Ultimately, the matter resolved itself judicially: in their application of the 2005 Justice and Peace Law designed for the AUC, the high courts of the country insisted on the need for differential treatment of the AUC and the FARC, judging the former as common criminals and the latter as political offenders.

5. During the Caguán negotiations undertaken by the Pastrana government, the FARC's military capacity kept growing as the corresponding capacity of the state weakened. The backdrop to the Havana talks was the exact opposite: the FARC's military capacity had become significantly inferior to that of the state. As of 2008, militarily maimed, the FARC abandoned its project of taking power by force and moved towards the goal of negotiating peace and acceding to power through the electoral process. The FARC understood that it was not in a position to demand the kind of broad negotiation agenda used in Caguán, nor to obtain a demilitarised zone within Colombia's borders as a precondition for talks. The state's military superiority had also forced a turnover in the guerrillas' leadership structure: Raul Reyes, Alfonso Cano, el Mono Jojoy, and many commanders were killed during special operations carried out during Uribe's second term and Santos's first. They were replaced by a more urban and educated leadership that was better prepared to reinvent itself in the political arena of a predominantly urban country, and less willing to spend retirement as caged trophies, facing near-certain death. This more pragmatic leadership understood that a settlement of the group's debt to society would somehow need to figure in the deal, as a prerequisite for any of them to be allowed to stand as political candidates in Colombia's modern-day democracy.

6. From the moment the Havana talks were made public, it was evident that there existed a deep rift in Colombian public opinion about how to interpret the country's political violence. On an ideological level, this was mostly a disagreement between those who did not perceive an armed conflict

but only an attack against a legitimate and functional democracy by a narcoterrorist organisation that had to be reined in by force; and those who, instead, saw an armed conflict between a long-standing but weak democracy and a rebel group with ideals of social and political change, which deserved to be part of a negotiation despite a litany of serious crimes. On a factual level, the disagreement turned on whether the Santos government was negotiating with a defeated or undefeated adversary. On one side were those who believed in a negotiated solution, arguing that the FARC were weakened but not defeated, and that they had managed to adapt their tactics to the military pressures of Uribe's successful 'democratic security' policy. Under this view, it was neither plausible for the FARC to seize power militarily, nor for the state to win the war at a reasonable human and financial cost. On the other side of the debate were those who considered the defeat of the FARC a fait accompli, requiring nothing more than a final and modest push. In their view, sitting as equals at a negotiation table with the 'defeated' FARC would be tantamount to treason, not only to Uribe's legacy and loyalty to Santos (which was critical to the latter's 2010 presidential victory), but also to the 'homeland' as such.

All of this had a devastating effect on the legitimacy of the negotiations. The political right in Colombia never made peace with the FARC.

7. Following the failure of the Caguán negotiations between the Pastrana government and the FARC, the massive involvement of the United States (via Plan Colombia) shifted the military and political scales against the rebels: a trend that consolidated during Uribe's administration. Thanks to the greater tactical mobility of an upgraded air force, an increasingly powerful military made the war ever more asymmetric. Under military pressure, the FARC were obliged to abandon the positional warfare that had dominated the 1990s, returning instead to pure guerrilla warfare and forsaking their dream of overthrowing the government by force.

Nonetheless, the Santos government was aware that it was not in a position to dictate the terms of the FARC's surrender and defeat. As such, and notwithstanding its superior military position, the Santos administration's gambit to negotiate the end of the war was a rational act. At the same time, it was one that entailed the problematic but necessary fiction of sitting as equals at the negotiation table. The FARC never would have countenanced less, as they did not enter the Havana talks as an act of surrender. Yet, for those who believed that the FARC were defeated and that it was simply a matter of bringing them to justice, negotiating under the premise that the rebels were equals in the negotiation room resembled a form of treason.

During the negotiations between the FMLN and the government of Alfredo Cristiani in El Salvador, and also during Colombia's Caguán negotiations, there were heated debates about the possibility of a 'mutually hurting stalemate' as the key explanatory variable of when warring parties choose the path of negotiation.[1] This concept was used actively by the FARC in the Havana talks, where the group never ceased to remind everyone present that it was sitting as an equal because it had not been defeated; it had proven itself, if not a winning force, at least an insurmountable one. As such, it was natural for the FARC to insist on equal (and dignified) treatment under any transitional justice package that might be agreed. Likewise, the talks' fiction of equality led the FARC to decry certain actions and decisions as 'unilateral', and thus invalid, such as the Legal Framework for Peace created by the government and approved by Congress as a constitutional reform in 2012 during the negotiation's early and secret phase. At the same time, the fiction of equality enabled IHL to become the common standard used to judge the conduct of all parties in the conflict, creating a kind of positive legal symmetry to help justify and regulate a reasonable distribution of burdens and benefits stemming from the final agreement.

8. The Havana talks took place against the backdrop of the 1991 Constitution: a non-negotiable topic for the government. This had at least two major implications: first, it meant that the guerrillas would be subject to a system of separate and independent powers that the government could not control; and second, it gave a presumptive stamp of constitutional adherence and legitimacy to the government's decisions in Havana.

Regarding the first point, this made it necessary for both parties, but especially the FARC, to live with a certain amount of legal uncertainty. Any final agreement would need to pass – at different moments and on different issues – through forms of validation, approval, and oversight by independent third parties such as the Congress, the superior courts, and the voters themselves (not only in the plebiscite but also, indirectly, in every new national election). As such, the decisions taken by the government and the FARC in Havana were contractually binding between them, yet in constitutional terms, they could only ever be provisionally binding. This factor slowed down and

---

[1] I. William Zartman, 'Ripeness: The Hurting Stalemate and Beyond', in *International Conflict Resolution after the Cold War*, ed. Paul C. Stern and Daniel Druckman (Washington, D.C.: National Academy Press, 2000).

complicated the Havana talks, particularly on the legally dense issue of transitional justice, since there could be no iron-clad guarantees of future adherence.

At the same time, the appeal of the argument of constitutional adherence and continuity depended on more than mere recognition of the Constitution's validity. It also depended on a set of factual beliefs about the magnitude and scale of the war that the negotiation was meant to end. The 'cinematographic view' is that the Constitution existed on the books but not in action, incapable of affecting a fifty-year-long, large-scale war between a socially, ethnically, and regionally fractured state and a rebel group that more than once showed itself capable of being a real threat to power. The 'photographic view', by contrast, takes a snapshot of the war only in its most recent phase, when the state looked more powerful than ever and the war (which for ideological reasons some refused to acknowledge existed) had become a kind of abstract sideshow limited to a few rural peripheries. Under this view, the insistence on constitutional continuity is understandable and the suggestion that the war's termination implied the need for a new constitution laughable.

In practice, the government delegation adopted the photographic view in Havana: any agreement reached there would be subject to the 1991 Constitution in its fullness, including all of the democratic, judicial and institutional checks and balances that implied. Naturally, this bothered the FARC, which sought the control of procedures and outcomes that only a re-founding narrative of constitutional overhaul could offer. It was in the name of such control that the FARC, while negotiating agenda item 5 (victims), urged – unsuccessfully – that the members of every post-conflict body be selected directly by the parties, accountable only unto them, and insurmountable by Congress, the high courts, and future governments.

9. Another dimension of constitutional backdrop is related to political culture in Colombia. Referring to the lack of continuity of government policies – which, therefore, fail to become state policies – Eduardo Pizarro notes that governments in Colombia act under the conviction that none of what their predecessor did is worth anything and, thus, under the perpetual assumption of failure.[2] Others speak of the 'Adam syndrome': the first day of an administration is usually portrayed in Colombia as the first day of creation. This reality was a further source of FARC angst during the Havana talks, ultimately leading it to accept the trade-off of a plebiscite on the final deal: a

---

[2] Eduardo Pizarro, *Cambiar el futuro: historia de los procesos de paz en Colombia (1981–2016)* (Bogotá: Penguin Random House, 2017), 28–31.

kind of political insurance against future Adams. As a consequence, when the accord was defeated in the plebiscite, the crisis for the FARC was doubly hard. By contrast, the plebiscite's victors interpreted the result as a triumph of political wisdom and constitutional continuity and routine over a presumptuous and illegitimate project to re-found the nation.

10. The question of weapons, and how it interacted with political culture and constitutionalism, also informed the context of the Havana process. During the negotiations, the FARC's leaders insisted repeatedly that they could only ensure the state's implementation of the accord by keeping their weapons – especially bearing in mind the Adam tradition of Colombian politics. This demand was obviously unacceptable for the Santos government and for Colombian society as a whole, for whom the overriding purpose of the negotiation was the rebels' disarmament and incorporation into normal politics and the rule of law. Yet, until the very end of the negotiations, there were discussions as to whether the FARC would 'turn in' or merely 'lay down' their arms: a terminological debate that was presented as one of dignity but was doubtlessly one of guaranteeing compliance as well. The FARC leadership needed to signal to its rank-and-file that, once disarmed, Colombia's democracy would, with the pressure of international backers, honour the promises (not least in the realm of transitional justice) made by the Santos government in Havana.

In this regard, the approach of constitutional continuity favoured the military through its comparatively privileged status. It was one thing to indict those who acted on behalf and in defence of the Constitution, and an altogether different thing to indict those who, like the FARC, acted outside it. Presupposing that legal action translates – automatically – to legitimate action leads to the assumption that any actions by law enforcement are in accordance with the Constitution (with the exception of 'a few rotten apples' who may violate it). For the guerrillas, by contrast, the default assumption was that their conduct was intrinsically criminal. As such, when negotiating peace with justice in Havana, the military's principal priority was to avoid losing their existing, collective legal security, whereas for the guerrillas it was to obtain the legal security they lacked (and for a forthcoming time in which they would no longer be armed).

11. In contrast to what often happens in transitions out of civil war, transitions out of dictatorship focus on vertical victimisation models, as violence is deployed predominantly from above. Under the premise that victims acquire their status by virtue of their helplessness rather than their innocence, dictatorial states and their supporters tend to monopolise the condition of

victimiser; and the population, the condition of victimhood. Consequently, during transitions out of dictatorship, it is usually easier to determine who are the good guys and the bad, and thus attribute responsibilities. This helps explain why in transitions out of dictatorship the retributive impulse tends to be more powerful than the reconciliatory one.

However, the Colombian transition was from war to peace, and involved a more horizontal violence in which the roles of victim and victimiser largely collapsed and the identity of the good guys and the bad blurred. Nevertheless, it was morally and politically impossible for the Santos government to agree to a model of transitional justice in which reconciliation took precedence over punishment. That is principally because of the lack of national consensus as to whether what happened was a moral tragedy that manifested itself as war, or merely a terrorist aggression against a legitimate and functional democracy. This ideological chasm made it difficult to call for reconciliation, as the country was still too divided over how to interpret basic facts. Whether the chasm can begin to be overcome through the work of the national truth commission, among others, remains to be seen.

12. In negotiated transitions out of dictatorship, the legal guarantees and benefits granted to the former regime's elites – if they agree to leave power – are often, and rightly, understood as concessions made by good people to bad. This is one reason why such negotiations tend to be closed and surrounded by an aura of shame. Since they are perceived as useful but immoral, it is preferable to hold them in secret. By contrast, when a country has become consumed by civil war and humanitarian catastrophe, there is less shame in deprioritising justice: the moral imperative is to put an end to the war. As such, there is no need to make a secret of the fact that talks are under way. To the contrary, there is everything to be celebrated in the fact that the warring parties are sitting down to talk. This is why it was perfectly logical for the Colombian negotiation to have a public, solemn, and internationally supported character.

13. The Havana talks took place against the backdrop of an international human rights framework that emphasises state over individual (or private) responsibility. This fact has a tendency to lead, uncritically, to a default anti-state emphasis even in the context of a civil war, leading many to treat post-conflict transitions as though they were post-authoritarian ones. In Colombia, this made it difficult to avoid political battles between different categories of victims in the context of the armed conflict, especially with the country's main NGOs being associated with an (over)emphasis on state crimes. This fact put sectors of the political right sharply against the human rights movement, which was regarded as an ally of the communist rebellion. All told, this made

it difficult, if not impossible, to take politics out of the question of what should be done for the victims of the conflict.

14. In some respects, IHL is the diametric opposite of international human rights law. Initially created in the middle of the seventeenth century to regulate wars and relations among states in continental Europe, it was never intended to order relations between the state and its own population. Post–World War II IHL has partially extended its regulatory capacity, by adding coverage of non-international armed conflicts and by changing its main focus of interest from combatants to civilian populations. Yet, these changes only really have full meaning and application in symmetrical wars with a relatively proportionate balance of power.

In highly asymmetrical wars – such as those between the United States and Iraq, those involving violent jihadist groups like al-Qaeda or Islamic State, or those fought by Israel in the occupied Palestinian territories – the stronger party derives more benefits from IHL than the weaker one. For example, the combination of air power (including reasonably precise, high-altitude bombing), satellite intelligence, and drones can sharply reduce exposure to lethal risk for the stronger party's combatants, while simultaneously improving its capacity to distinguish between combatants and civilians. For the weaker party, such attacks greatly increase exposure to lethal risks (by regular and irregular combatants alike), thus weakening their capacity to respond in ways that respect the IHL principle of distinguishing civilians from combatants. Advised by legal teams well versed in IHL, the stronger party can plan legally impeccable yet devastating operations, designed to guarantee that military advantages are proportional to the expected collateral damage, turning IHL into an instrument that authorises and legitimises their actions. The weaker party, in contrast, is pushed – especially in the case of irregular combatants – toward systematic violations of the rules of war. To them, IHL isn't a statute that authorises certain actions but rather a straitjacket that asphyxiates their capacity for action and delegitimises it.

Under conditions of extreme asymmetry, the application of IHL favours almost exclusively the stronger party. In Colombia, this was especially the case against the FARC. During its military heyday, the guerrilla group followed the Maoist 'great march' model and – in contrast with the ELN – slept in encampments and aimed to confront the military directly, as an army, making it highly vulnerable to attacks from the air. As such, it came as no surprise when, in 2009, the Colombian military published its first operations manual using IHL as the legal foundation. Since then, humanitarian law appears to have favoured, in the aggregate, the authorisation and legal justification of its actions, rendering its responsibility almost invisible. This being the case, in the realm of transitional justice, the FARC had every reason to suspect IHL was a weapon that would harm it and beatify the military, and especially the air force.

15. At times in the negotiation, the International Criminal Court (ICC) gravitated as a sword of Damocles over the parties. Like the early decision to submit any agreements to popular endorsement, the court's shadow helped the government to convince the FARC to moderate its demands (e.g., in terms of amnesty expectations). As for the military, its fears of the ICC were initially high, but diminished rather than increased over time – especially much later, when the 'No' side won the plebiscite, which sectors of the military interpreted as public rejection of the government's excessive deference towards international courts and their standards of justice. The military would always be more comfortable with the domestic court system.

16. The Havana negotiations took place in a very favourable regional context. The Uribe government, allied with the Bush administration in the global war on terror after 9/11, was perceived as a threat by many of the left and centre-left governments in the subcontinent – particularly those of neighbouring Ecuador and Venezuela – as its 'democratic security' policy, which focused on eliminating the guerrillas by force, failed to garner their support. Upon assuming the presidency, Santos took distance from the Uribe government, redefined its foreign policy agenda, and reinstated diplomatic relations with the governments of Hugo Chávez and Rafael Correa. By the time the Santos administration made public its intention to negotiate a peace deal with the FARC, it could count on support not only from important Western powers like the United States, the United Kingdom, Germany, and France, but also from multilaterals such as the UN and the EU, and various governments in the subcontinent, most crucially Venezuela. As such, the FARC, contrary to its own expectations, found itself isolated in an environment that was akin to them ideologically – as much of Latin America had undergone a significant turn to the left by early in President Santos's second term – but resolutely in favour of electoral democracy, not armed political struggle.

17. Political realists often suppose that the balance of power in a peace negotiation is an exact mirror of the balance of power in the battlefield. As such, they likely believe that in order to improve one's negotiating power, it is best to hit the enemy hard, both before and during the negotiations. However, enemies can easily enter into a 'tit-for-tat' game such that, over time, armed confrontation between the two sides undermines the

willingness to negotiate and erodes the legitimacy of the process as a whole. Indeed, negotiating in the absence of a ceasefire – which was the important but unusual choice made in Colombia – involves the inherent risk that serious military incidents will force one or both sides simply to leave the table. In this respect, the Santos government was making a dangerous gamble in its insistence on the *absence* of a bilateral ceasefire as a condition for the Havana talks. A priori, such an approach could be effective only in a short negotiation, because in a protracted one it could easily lead to disaster. However, the rule against a mid-negotiation bilateral ceasefire suited the Santos government's strategic goals, helping it to pressure the FARC to reach a peace agreement.

The government initially wagered that the pressure of the ongoing war, and its superiority within that, would produce a negotiation that would last months rather than years, thus averting the possible impact of serious military incidents that could arise. President Santos was fond of paraphrasing Yitzhak Rabin, the former Israeli prime minister who famously quipped that Israel would 'negotiate as though not at war, and wage war as though not negotiating' in the context of the Oslo process.

For some time, Santos's strategy worked well, inasmuch as the negotiation battlefront in Havana proved resilient enough to survive episodic incidents and attacks occurring on the military battlefront in Colombia. However, on 16 November 2014, in the jungles of Chocó, General Ruben Dario Alzate was kidnapped by members of the FARC's Front 34. Out of respect for the military, the government had to temporarily suspend the Havana talks, despite the official rule that the talks would run 'without interruption'. After many weeks of tension, it was finally deemed to be an ordinary incident, typical of any armed confrontation, that shouldn't affect the course of the negotiations. After the kidnapped general was returned to the ICRC, the affair was absorbed into the normal course of war.

Yet, there would be another serious crisis in April of 2015, when the FARC attacked an army detachment in the department of Cauca, resulting in the death of eleven virtually defenceless soldiers. This led to a brutal but brief escalation in the conflict. Once again, however, the negotiations managed to go on. In order to save the negotiation as a whole, as well as the progress made, the parties agreed to 'accelerate Havana and de-escalate Colombia'. This new concept altered some of the old routines in Havana, and the FARC declared a second unilateral ceasefire to which the government responded by suspending the bombardment of guerrilla camps. Thus it was that the rhythm of war finally ebbed, as the talks came closer to their finish.

18. In forcing a strict conceptual separation between 'the end of conflict' and the follow-on 'peacebuilding' phase, the government was able to structure the Havana agenda effectively and to prevent the many problems engendered by the elastic agenda seen in the San Vicente del Caguán talks. A highly precise, five-point agenda – plus a sixth point on implementing the agreement – allowed government negotiators to successfully resist pressures from the FARC to drift off course. This manifested itself more than once – including at the start of the process in Oslo, when the chief FARC negotiator, Iván Márquez, in his inaugural speech, sought to expand the agenda by drawing on the preamble to the 2012 General Agreement.

19. Confidentiality was, naturally, the rule of the negotiation. It created conditions under which the FARC was at liberty to make proposals without the fear of causing public indignation and rejection. While this sometimes led the rebel negotiators to make wholly unrealistic proposals, there were sufficient checks against any mischief. Knowing that the eventual deal would be subject to popular ratification was one such check.

20. The government understood that any concessions offered to the FARC in matters of justice or political participation could be justified only once the rebels had disarmed, as any partial agreement reached while FARC combatants were still in arms was liable to be interpreted as the fruit of blackmail. The FARC, on the other hand, insisted on keeping their weapons until the end of the negotiations and even beyond the signature of the final deal, as a guarantee that the government would honour its commitments. Thus, the government demanded, and the guerrillas reluctantly accepted, the principle adopted from the 1998 Good Friday talks in Northern Ireland: namely, that 'nothing is agreed until everything is agreed'. This is one of the factors that explains why, for example, despite FARC urging, the government refused to operationalise the truth commission or begin implementing the agreement on drugs and illicit crops before the end of negotiations.

In terms of negative effects, the combination of confidentiality and the 'nothing is agreed until everything is agreed' principle made it difficult for the parties to publish issue-specific agreements being reached in Havana, and thus difficult to win public support for the process. All such agreements had to be treated as mere drafts and couldn't be made public or declared as binding commitments. The joint press releases issued periodically by the parties only indirectly alluded to the substance of the agreements being reached. As a result, Colombians were under the impression that the truth was being hidden from them. Enemies of the government exploited this purported lack of transparency by spreading adverse speculation about what was under discussion. Only in 2014, when the parties decided to begin publishing the partial agreements as they were reached, was it possible to alleviate this communications trap.

21. The government had a high interest in putting an end to the war with the whole of the revolutionary political left. This naturally led it to try finding a way to bring to the negotiating table the National Liberation Army (ELN): the other large guerrilla group, part of the first generation of insurgencies born in the wake of the Cuban Revolution. Facing a sceptical public, an implacable opposition, and a vigilant human rights community vis-à-vis the FARC talks, it is small wonder that an ELN deal was considered a necessary adjunct to sell the idea of a total end to war in Colombia. Time and again, the government sought to have the ELN join the negotiations as 'another wagon on the train', either through a separate negotiation or an integrated one. It even sponsored a secret meeting between the leaders of the FARC and ELN. However, the 'last wagon' idea failed, as the ELN resisted for too long to reach a deal in synch with the FARC process.

22. The government and the FARC had radically different ideologies and views on the dynamics of Colombian society and its political system, as well as the measures needed to move forward. Their views on the nature and distribution of blame for events during the war were just as different.

The underlying split stemmed from a dual divide – ideological and epistemological – making it practically impossible to reach a shared vision of the past, the present, and the future. As such, it was critical for the government and the FARC to enjoy the support of robust technical teams, working to produce transactional and practical solutions for the disagreements that arose each step of the way. When a deeper impasse was reached, at times the parties could look to the guarantor countries for help, particularly Norway. It was thanks to the Norwegians, for example, that a serious standoff was overcome during agenda item 3 on the problem of drugs. Their intervention helped the FARC to acknowledge that they should extricate any link to drug trafficking that may have arisen in the course of their rebellion.

But it is important to emphasise that, despite the vital Norwegian and Cuban roles as guarantors – and the helpful accompanying roles of Venezuela and Chile – the Havana negotiations were not mediated. These were direct talks between the government and the FARC, from start to end. For the government, this was especially important since an international mediator might have abridged the advantages associated with their superior legal status and military position. Yet, these advantages proved insufficient to accelerate the process, serving to remind the government time and again that the FARC was not seated in Havana to work out the terms of its surrender.

23. Those in the FARC delegation who negotiated the transitional justice model were a rather urban and educated elite whose members, once demobilised, could reasonably aspire to elected office. Yet, those same people were the best candidates for criminal prosecution as the most accountable parties within the organisational hierarchy. This dual condition of the FARC negotiators explains in large part the enormous difficulty for the parties to reach an agreement regarding punishment. The FARC leaders constantly repeated the phrase that 'nobody negotiates peace in order to go to prison'. It should be no surprise, then, that while it took on average six months to reach agreements on points such as rural reform, political participation, or illicit crops, the discussions on agenda item 5 (victims) required a year and a half, not counting the extra time needed to negotiate final adjustments at later stages.

24. The time factor seemed to have a different meaning for the government and the FARC. Although it should have been important for the guerrillas to conclude the negotiations before a change of government in Colombia or in the United States, FARC delegates seemed to believe that they had all the time in the world. Their view of time may partly have reflected the slower pace of country life, despite the fact that the leadership had become more urban after the death of Manuel Marulanda (aka Tirofijo) and other leaders of peasant background. The government, on the contrary, laboured under the impatient pressures of the electorate, frequently leading it to urge a quicker pace inside the talks. In a context of rapid erosion of its democratic legitimacy – given its lack of peace talk results and the constant slings and arrows of former president Uribe – the Santos administration ended up having less endurance than the FARC in the push to decide which justice mechanism would finally be adopted.

25. President Santos used to say that drafting an agreement was like creating a work of art. The artist should show it to the public only once finished, so that it could be seen in all its splendour. In practice, however, things worked differently. Despite the rule of confidentiality, the FARC delegation would read communiqués and make statements to the media every day, while the government delegation remained silent. Because the government was silent and the FARC was speaking, the opposition in Colombia eagerly interpreted the silence as a signal of submissiveness to FARC demands. The effect of this was, at times, devastating for the government and for the legitimacy of the process.

B. VICTIMS AND THE POLITICS OF TRANSITIONAL JUSTICE

This chapter, which builds on the last, explores the concept of 'victim' and briefly attempts to reconstruct the story of how it came to occupy the centre of modern humanitarianism. It also explains the role of the victim as a major source of legitimacy for transitional justice institutions. The chapter explains how the Colombian armed conflict involved a predominantly horizontal victimisation model, with broad grey zones, and reconstructs elements of the discussions pertaining to victims in Havana.

Victimisation is a performative act that elevates the victimiser and diminishes the victim. The concept of victim denotes a power relation – the exaltation of the former and the humiliation of the latter. It affirms and reinforces the victimiser's capacity for action, and proportionally negates and weakens the victim's. Yet, it is frequently the case that, before being victimised, the victim has previously been dehumanised and rendered invisible by his or her adversary.

When victims don't die, they become survivors who remain entangled in a long chain of interactions, each of which further transforms their identity. It is against this slow and labyrinthine backdrop that we can see the reversal of roles that sometimes makes a victimiser of the victim, and vice versa – particularly in times of war. In such contexts, we see identities form within 'grey zones', whose archetype is that of the avenger.

A basic understanding of the victimiser as agent and the victim as patient – and an appreciation of the grave debasement of the latter's relative status – are key to understanding how human rights and transitional justice practices seek to re-balance these relationships. They involve acknowledging the victims, repairing the harm they suffered, and trying to guarantee that they recover their social standing and capacity for agency as preconditions for peace, reconciliation, and the guarantee of non-repetition. As such, it should come as no surprise that in order to lend greater legitimacy to a peace negotiation and to the transitional justice model chosen for a peace deal, the parties may allow the victims to participate, as free agents, in the design and implementation of the justice mechanisms agreed.

The idea of justice as re-balancing the exalted/humiliated relationship between victimiser and victim engages two enormous controversies. First, is it necessary, in order to elevate and acknowledge the victims and to give them back their dignity, that their victimisers be humiliated? Second, must they be made to beg for forgiveness and repent on their knees as a condition of their own redemption? This is the type of 'wounded relative status' retribution that Martha Nussbaum attributes to the inquisitorial figure of 'transactional forgiveness' in the Catholic tradition, embodied in the sacrament of confession.[3]

Applied to Colombia, it may be that the FARC's abysmal public rating and the final agreement's defeat in the plebiscite were largely due to the fact that ordinary people expected (and continue to expect) the FARC to show remorse and ask for forgiveness for the crimes committed, while the FARC cling to their identity as revolutionary combatants who refuse to kneel down, and merely acknowledge having made 'mistakes'.

Perhaps the best evidence of the FARC's resistance to relinquishing their self-image as good people who did some bad things by mistake was their decision to maintain the acronym FARC for the political party they founded after giving up their arms (albeit changing the complete name from Revolutionary Armed Forces of Colombia to the Common Alternative Revolutionary Force). Transactional forgiveness demands that, to demonstrate that they won't return to their old ways, they should first pass through the purifying ritual of humiliating themselves and renouncing their old identity in order to adopt a new one. By contrast, the privileged treatment of political crime, following a centuries-old constitutional tradition, demands that they lay down their arms but allows them to preserve their identity as ostensibly honourable leftist fighters, now under the wing of a democracy that had become more pluralist and agonal. The problem is that the idea of restoring equality without humiliation has depreciated under the new humanitarian conscience, which is highly retributive. In Colombia, it has also suffered the devastating blows of a right-wing rhetoric that posits a 'Castro-Chavista' threat from Venezuela.

As such, critics of the peace process would argue that if the guerrilla leadership doesn't go to jail and doesn't renounce its old revolutionary ideals, it won't pay any moral and psychological cost, and will preserve, intact, the willingness to take up arms at any moment. However, such arguments disregard the fact that the socialisation of individuals in the practices and routines of violence coalesce into an identity and that abandoning it already entails all kinds of changes and heavy costs. Those who relinquish their weapons leave behind an entire way of life.

This is where transitional justice enters in. As a form of justice crystallised in criminal trials, truth commissions, and reparation mechanisms, transitional justice entails the designation of an impartial third party, anchored in objective criteria, that determines not only who is a victimiser and who is a victim, but also the treatment that each shall receive. Although in principle the

---

[3] See generally Martha Nussbaum, *Anger and Forgiveness: Resentment, Generosity, Justice* (New York: Oxford University Press, 2016).

former is the legislator's job (as the lawmaker) and the latter is the judge's (as the law interpreter), it is well known that in extraordinary times, such as transitions, these functional borders often blur. For better or worse, the flexible mechanisms of transitional justice are often more open to allowing self-defined and self-organised victims be the ones who write the script and determine the terms of their appearance in the public sphere.

Insofar as it denotes justice for the victims, transitional justice is doubly anchored in the past and the future. It stands at the crossroad between the imperative of vindicating yesterday's victims and that of preventing tomorrow's victims. This is especially so in contexts of negotiation. Giving absolute priority to the right of yesterday's victims to see the victimiser receive retributive punishment proportional to the harm caused – assuming such right exists – can make negotiated peace impossible and raise the risk of continued, and even increased, production of future victims. Conversely, the commitment to preventing the victims of tomorrow can mean disregarding some of the demands and the rights of yesterday's victims.

The concept of victim is itself highly controversial, and the political consequences of defining victims in one way or another are enormous. For example, if the category of victims includes the poverty-stricken and socially excluded (who are subjects of so-called structural injustices), this expands not only the number of victims, but also the responsible parties that must provide reparations. This can lead to erasing the boundaries between involuntary, material constraints and intentional, voluntary violence. It could also stretch the concept of war beyond the limits of armed conflicts per se, extending it to all types of nonviolent social and economic conflicts, equating 'class warfare' with armed warfare.

Yet, an overly narrow concept of victim is just as costly. It isolates armed confrontations from their historical causes and from the social contexts in which they originate and unfold, to the point of making them incomprehensible, at least as political phenomena. This was a constant issue raised by the FARC, which formed its identity in the context of the Cold War struggle between communism and capitalism. As such, the FARC's discourse predictably focused on the victims of economic exploitation and political exclusion (preceding and superseding the war itself), whereas the government focused on the victims produced by the armed confrontation.

The category of 'victim' was subject to particularly bitter debate in Havana when seeking to distinguish between victims of crimes committed by the FARC (and guerrillas in general) and victims of state crime. The FARC insisted that the largest universe of war victims was those committed at the hands of the state (which for them meant crimes committed by state agents as well as paramilitaries). By contrast, the Colombian Retired Officers Association (ACORE), as well as the *Centro Democrático* party and the right in general, argued that the highest share of victims was attributable to the FARC. They also argued that this cohort was intentionally underreported by human rights organisations.

In the sections that follow, we will continue to see how an abstract conceptualisation of victims can give rise to an almost arbitrarily large number of debates: victims may be defined as innocent or defenceless, direct or indirect, products of structural violence or of the use of arms, and so on. The criteria for an empirical definition are no less debatable: victims may be individual or collective, and may depend on the victimiser's identity, the nature of the victimising event, the extent of the harm suffered, or a series of identity markers (e.g., ethnic, regional, ideological, gender, age, etc.).

On the Emergence of the Victim in Today's Humanitarian Conscience

It is now a well-known story how victims moved from an invisible periphery – in the philosophies of history, in the style of Hegel; in the national histories of modern states, such as those of Ranke and Michelet; and in the patriotic stories told to school-age children – toward the centre of collective memory. It should suffice to recall how Walter Benjamin's famous 'Angel of History' symbolises rebellion against the philosophy of history as a forward-gazing story in the form of progress, turning the pages of the past and making invisible the victims as a means and a necessary cost of the full realisation of national statehood in the central Western countries.[4]

This rebellion against the philosophy of history and against the great stories that embody it had its fulcrum in the crisis of the modern project, whose triumphant march led to the Second World War, and especially to the Holocaust. The Angel of History gazes not forward but backward, and its terrified eyes register the ruins that the idea of progress has left behind among vanquished peoples; the infamous flowers trampled by great conquerors who, like Napoleon, embodied the 'absolute spirit' in its path to glory. The old national histories, at the service of the collective memory and identity of modern national states, embody the story of the victors. Only the heroes and the martyrs are visible – the latter being the great exception to the victims' invisibility. These are the stories of armies and triumphant nation-states as great monopolisers of human agency. However, in the new collective

---

[4] Walter Benjamin, *Theses on the Philosophy of History* (1940; Frankfurt: Suhrkamp Verlag, 1955).

memories of post-Auschwitz postmodernity, the victims have reclaimed agency through their resiliency and through the fight for the recognition of their rights and dignity.

The intellectual and academic history of the birth of the 'victim-witness' isn't restricted to the reflections of philosophers like Walter Benjamin, Hannah Arendt, Theodor Adorno, Jürgen Habermas, and Paul Ricoeur. Sociologists of the Holocaust like Zygmunt Bauman and moral historians and literary critics like Tzvetan Todorov also played a significant role. The documentary *Shoah*, by the French filmmaker Claude Lanzmann, is just as important. Lanzmann famously declared that if there were photographic evidence of what happened in the death camps, he would destroy it so that only the testimony of the survivors could give an account of a reality whose horror transcends by far its factuality, a horror which would be incomprehensible were it not for the harrowing stories told by the survivors. There are also vital books by writers like Giorgio Agamben, whose well-known thesis is that what lies at the core of Auschwitz's intelligibility isn't the factual truth of the gas chambers but the figure of the *Muselmann*: the victim par excellence, the living dead, resigned to impending death.[5]

The central role in this intellectual history of the victim's emergence as history's protagonist also derives from the stories told by Primo Levi, Elie Wiesel, and countless other Jewish Holocaust survivors who made it their life's work to preserve the memory of those who died before they could be liberated. Projects dedicated to recording, classifying, and archiving the oral testimonies of Holocaust survivors like the one conducted by Yale University after 1982, and books such as Lawrence Langer's *Holocaust Testimonies: The Ruins of Memory*, analyse and categorise these daunting exercises in traumatised memory. They are indispensable for anyone who wishes to trace the steps in the rise of the figure of the victim to its current centrality in Western humanitarian conscience. Having said that, we must also acknowledge the debates by German, French, Italian, American, Israeli, and other intellectuals and historians about the relationship between history and memory, exemplified by Enzo Traverso's magnificent essays on the subject. Works such as *The Era of the Witness* by Annette Wieviorka also occupy a prominent position.

But the history of the emergence of the victim as witness saw its great beginning in the Nuremberg trials against twenty-four Nazi leaders after their defeat in the Second World War. In these trials, US Chief Prosecutor Jackson,

---

[5] Giorgio Agamben, *Remnants of Auschwitz: The Witness and the Archive*, trans. Daniel Heller-Roazen (New York: Zone Books, 1999).

in charge of indictments for the crime of aggression, preferred to prove unbelievable facts through ostensibly believable means, and thus favoured documentary evidence over victim testimony. Indeed, the footage of the horrific mountains of corpses and of prisoners in striped uniforms taken upon the liberation of the concentration and extermination camps and offered as evidence during the proceedings, has become the iconic visual representation of the Holocaust. Yet the famous footage contains voice-over narration that portrays them as prisoners of war and political prisoners, rather than as victims of the Jewish genocide.

The Nazi leaders who survived the war were given various sentences, including death by hanging, in a highly selective form of victors' justice that was nevertheless relatively observant of due process. Yet fifteen years had to pass before the holding of the 1961 trial of Adolf Eichmann, an office bureaucrat who, in Hannah Arendt's judgement, embodied the 'banality of evil'. The trial was one of the defining events through which the Holocaust and its victims stepped out of the representational periphery of criminal law and came to occupy the centre of the judicial scene. Eichmann, who had lived in protective hiding in Argentina for years, was abducted by the Israeli secret service and taken before the District Court Judge in Jerusalem, the capital of the young state of Israel. But whereas in the Nuremberg trials crimes against humanity took a back seat to the crime of aggression and to war crimes, in the Eichmann trial the prosecution focused on unveiling the role played by this SS officer, in charge of organising the transport of victims to the concentration and extermination camps. The Holocaust was here understood especially as a crime against the Jewish people.

The prosecutor, Gideon Hausner, gave the victim-witnesses priority by putting them on the podium. Before asking them to offer testimony to prove the charges against the defendant, he allowed them to provide expressive testimony, at times redundant and even irrelevant from an evidentiary standpoint, but cathartic for an audience made up largely of victim-survivors of the Nazi extermination campaign. Ada Lichtmann's testimony, made in Yiddish and broadcast on radio and television, brought the language of the dead into the courthouse, collapsing the past and present and transforming the conditions of the trial. Whereas the victims' testimony at Nuremberg was complementary to documentary evidence, in Jerusalem documentary evidence was complementary to the victims' testimony. In the Nuremberg courtroom, the impact of the images and tales of horror was mainly seen through the eyes of the accused. In the Jerusalem courtroom, it was through the eyes of the witnesses themselves, for the benefit of a local audience made up almost exclusively of victim-survivors.

The French also had a role in rendering the Holocaust visible. This is often linked with the dismantling of the Gaullist myth of a libertarian, republican France that resisted en masse the occupation by Nazi Germany, and with the equally tortuous efforts to re-signify the Vichy regime. Over the course of three decades, between the 1950s and the 1970s, the Vichy regime went from being seen as forced to adapt and collaborate with the enemy (with the central role in exterminating Jews played by German officials in the Nazi machinery, like Klaus Barbie, and only a few French collaborators betraying their homeland) to being seen as a regime of voluntary collaboration with genocidaires. The judicial history that spans from the Barbie trial in Lyon, to the trials of Vichy officials like Busquet, Touvier, and Papon, attests to this dramatic shift in the collective memory in which the martyrs of the resistance were progressively replaced by the Jewish victims.

All told, these varied countries, courts, and writers progressively turned the Holocaust into the central event in the moral history of the twentieth century. They also placed the Jewish victim – and later, victims in general – as protagonists and as the source of legitimacy for the tableaus of accountability for past atrocities in later transitions from dictatorship to democracy and from war to peace. How the centrality of the genocide also took root in the United States (including through the creation of the Holocaust Museum in Washington, D.C.) is yet another interesting chapter in this history of the rise of Holocaust awareness and, with it, the centrality of victims.

More recent chapters in the contemporary history of the victim's place at the heart of the new humanitarian conscience are less well known. They are not located so much in the intellectual and cultural history of the universalisation of the Holocaust and its victims, but in the rights discourse of the new national and transnational human rights and victims' movements. It is they who have been the more recent protagonists in situating a plural, abstract, and universal victim at the centre of contemporary human rights and transitional justice discourse and institutions.

One important chapter in this begins with the victims' and human rights movements in Southern Cone countries like Argentina and Chile, and those that became visible later or in parallel in many other parts of the world, not least South Africa. This new human rights and victims' movement has managed to influence international and domestic human rights, criminal law and humanitarian law institutions to such an extent that contemporary investigative commissions, national and international courts, and reparations mechanisms would be incomprehensible without their powerful footprint.

Thanks to the pressure applied by the human rights and victims' movement, the victim is not just the central category in the humanitarian conscience of the West (and of much of the rest of the world), but also of international standards for truth, justice, reparation, and guarantees of non-repetition that are part of the structure and practice of human rights and transitional justice bodies active today. Indeed, criminal law has done an about-face from the days of Marquis Cesare Beccaria – when it concerned itself almost exclusively with the rights of the convict, through the liberal and enlightened struggles against the judicial arbitrariness of monarchical absolutism – to being primarily concerned with the rights of victims. Evidence of this shift is everywhere – from the figure of the victim as the private accuser in ordinary criminal law to the multiplication of opportunities for victims and their representatives to intervene during transitional justice proceedings and the redefinition of sentences in reparative and restorative terms.

Truth commissions exemplify this centrality most of all. They were conceived first and foremost for the benefit of the victims, as a venue of both voice and evidence. They were meant to produce cathartic rituals as well as reports of the truth, in each case strongly anchored in individual memory and incorporated into social memory (albeit providing less direct relief to victims than reparations). Ultimately, they were expected to offer a venue in which the classical view of war and violence as a legitimate means to achieve political ends is replaced with a view of violence as a calamity that mutilates body and soul.

In this regard, it is worth recalling that at the root of the modern tradition, military and political elites could treat civilian populations as mere support networks, resources, and armies – basically, as the means to attain political ends. Consequently, they could be seen as such by enemy armies, and thus destroyed without mercy, their humanity rendered invisible. New perspectives –anchored in anthropologies, ontologies, and ethics of fragility – make the wounded bodies of the victims visible, demanding respect and reparation for them. In this sense, it should be deeply worrisome how – much like the old guerrilla ideology that treated civilian populations as 'the water that hides the fish' – contemporary terrorism tends to see civilians in its own jurisdiction as a human shield, and those under the enemy's as the enemy itself, loosely construed and expanded.

From a more philosophical perspective, the emergence of the victim at the centre of contemporary ethics might also be explained as the realisation of the ultimate ideal of Judeo-Christian ethics, which is anchored in original sin as the great symbol of human fragility and which is conceived for the benefit of the most vulnerable. 'The last shall be the first . . .'; not in heaven but here and now, as it should be in times of the hegemony of the human rights of victims. In terms of social ontology and the ethics of vulnerability, otherness, and recognition – as proclaimed by Emmanuel Levinas, Judith Butler, and Axel

Honneth – the fact that the victim is the other who embodies the deepest suffering and the worst humiliation triggers the necessity that it is victims, with their radical questioning, who raise the highest sense of responsibility in all who come across them.

The worrisome irony is that, by virtue of the recognition and empowerment of her capacity for agency, the victim becomes all-powerful, such that everyone wishes to occupy her role. The victim's enshrinement as 'innocent' by definition – not for her good behaviour but for having been at the wrong place and time – can lead the powerful to wage envious and merciless battles to be identified with the victim and the defence of her interests, and to abuse the privileges and rights that accompany this condition. Insofar as innocence becomes one of the concept's essential properties, victims – and especially their representatives – are immunised ex ante against any serious indictment for what they have done or will do. The status temporarily hands the powerful the magic wand that provides legitimacy to any peace and transitional justice arrangement.

Yet, if we wish to do justice to what takes place in any complex war – looking beyond the behavioural dynamics of warriors, and of those who mendaciously self-represent as victims or their proxies – it is problematic to include innocence as one of the essential properties of victimhood. For one thing, doing so makes it impossible to render complex political victims visible, or to understand the grey zone in which the roles of victim and victimiser collapse. In addition, if victims are innocent by definition, this turns war into an exclusively criminal phenomenon, thus hiding or eliminating its political component. Such a vision of war can be devastating to any effort to negotiate peace and transitional justice in places where, like Colombia, a political war unfolded against the backdrop of the Cold War.

Defencelessness, as such, is obviously the objective condition of many victims – and as such, it is and can be harnessed for good. However, because it triggers compassion, defencelessness can also be abused by actors seeking, for example, to garner support for their political project in a transitional electoral battle. In the wrong hands, victimhood is a powerful semantic weapon.

On War as a Dialectic between Victim and Victimiser

The Trojan War, in which the armies of a broad coalition of Greek tribes laid siege to and destroyed a prosperous city-state, is broadly regarded as a war of annihilation. Gathered around the just cause of avenging the kidnapping of Helen, which violated the laws of hospitality, the Greeks devastated Ilium.

Hannah Arendt notes that Homer, in a retrospective act of poetic justice, sang the glories of the victors and the vanquished equally, driven perhaps by the ancient Greeks' love of truth, or a deep awareness of how enemies in battle are equal in their frailty. In the process, he invented the impartial account of historical events.

But for a modern state with sovereign rule of law, in a context of internal war it is typical for the government and its agents to be protected by political-epistemic privileges that allow them to portray themselves successfully as victims, as victim representatives, and as the dispensers of justice, and to portray the rebels as criminals and victimisers. Likewise, from the standpoint of domestic law, it is normal to predicate the conditions of victim and victimiser asymmetrically in favour of the state and against its armed adversaries. Hegemonic moral and legal discourses that distribute the legitimate use of violence between the state and its armed opponents have a marked pro-state bias, particularly in liberal-democratic societies. Modern-day Colombia, despite the many faults and defects of its political system, is no exception.

In the past, by contrast, it was normal for warring parties to conceive their enmity in terms of a symmetrical, non-discriminatory game of mirrors. This happened in the framework of early modernity's law of nations (within European public law), which regulated relations between equally sovereign states in Western Europe between the sixteenth century and the early twentieth. It also happened, exceptionally, and almost miraculously, in mid-nineteenth-century Colombia, with an utterly weak central state and the quasi-internationalisation of the domestic political space. This circumstance created a preference for negotiated solutions and for broad and generous amnesties for the vanquished, rather than criminal trials.

During both world wars, the enemies gave each other mutually discriminatory treatment. Together with the enormous technological powers amassed by industrial societies and their states, this proved devastating for combatants, and especially for civilians. But during the second half of the twentieth century and the early twenty-first, a new humanitarian consciousness emerged, anchored in the experience of total warfare and the Holocaust of the European Jewish people, changing the balance between justice and peace. In the past, the value of peace had taken prevalence, and judicial impunity was the price to pay for it. Subsequently, the need for justice became increasingly dominant, especially criminal justice, if peace was to be sustainable. Since criminal justice operates on the basis of distinguishing between victimisers and victims, the old, symmetric, and horizontal dialectic of enemies who were equal in their sovereign dignity – typical in the interstate wars of old – increasingly turned towards the asymmetrical, vertical dialectic of victimisers and victims.

In past wars, portraying oneself as a victim provided significant benefits to the parties in conflict. It let one fight the enemy with hatred, yet simultaneously claim innocence; and it allowed armies to call upon the support of resentful populations that had been victimised by the enemy camp. However, guided by the shared expectation of an inevitable post bellum trial for the atrocities perpetrated by the parties, nowadays parties tend to self-represent as victims and to represent the adversary as victimiser, both during war and during peace negotiations. How much of this political-moral-legal game of inverted mirrors is sincere, and how much is fraudulent, is nevertheless difficult to tell. Both parties construct just causes and keep tabs on those crimes that allow them to self-represent as victims and/or as their representatives, and to portray the enemy as victimiser.

Through this victim/victimiser dialectic, all wars are ultimately wars for legitimacy. In the absence of a powerful and impartial third party capable of deciding who are the victims and who are the victimisers, and assuming that legitimacy belongs to those who claim to have this capacity and have others believe them, the party who most successfully self-represents as victim before its own audience – but especially before the public at large – can enjoy impunity and punish its enemy once the war is over.

An asymmetrical allocation of responsibilities is potent and multidimensional in its implications. It determines the distribution of punishment and reparations, as well as how the future narratives of historical memory and truth portray the respective heroes and villains. It may also define, at least in part, the future leadership of the broader society. As such, the interests at stake are quite immense. Yet, it is wrong to think that this is exclusively a strategic game of interests. For instance, the fact that many of the warriors started out as direct or indirect victims, before becoming victimisers, means that their self-representation as victims, and even the self-representation of the collective to which they belong, can often be anchored in facts. Indeed, the same may be true of the opposing side as well. As Paul Ricoeur says, identities are always aspirational, making them highly vulnerable to the temptation of abusing memory for their own benefit.[6]

---

[6] Paul Ricoeur observes that abuses of memory occur, not in the physiological realm of traumatised and repressed memory, but in its practical use; and that they often occur when memory is placed at the service of identity or justice. Following Clifford Geertz, Ricoeur points out that the aspirational nature of identity makes it vulnerable to abuse by memory, insofar as identity is profoundly tied to ideology. Regarding justice, Ricoeur says that such abuses are always (1) with the other, (2) where the other is, par excellence, the victim, and (3) expressed in

During the negotiation of transitional justice in Havana, the most perfect game of inverted mirrors took place between the FARC on one hand, and the more radical sectors of the military, the *Centro Democrático*, and the overall political right on the other. The right represented the state as a legitimate democracy attacked by FARC narcoterrorists, and thus exclusively as a victim, whereas the FARC represented the state as an oligarchic dictatorship disguised as a democracy, and thus as the great victimiser. Set apart from both, the government, as the representative of the state in the negotiation, was unable or unwilling to attribute to the FARC a monopoly over the condition of victimiser. As the partially failed guarantor of people's rights, the government organised around rights-based constitutionalism. It recognised itself as accountable (and even as part victimiser) and not only as victim.

The FARC's identity narrative, by contrast, was largely constructed upon victimisation milestones. Its foundational story begins with an act of 'aggression' by the army on the town of Marquetalia: a remote village in Tolima, forsaken by God and men, inhabited by peaceful farmers displaced by violence in the 1950s, whose only sin was being communist and following collectivised farming practices. This garnered the accusation of being an 'independent republic', whose mere existence threatened national sovereignty. The FARC's foundational myth says that, after the army's attack on Marquetalia, the peasant self-defence force mobilised and transformed into a mobile guerrilla.

As of the 1980s, the FARC's victim narrative was reinforced by the transformative event known as the 'genocide' of the Patriotic Union (UP): a political party, founded during the failed peace negotiations with the Belisario Betancur government, whose members were killed in devastating numbers by an alliance of paramilitaries, drug traffickers, and state agents. It should come as no surprise that, during the Havana negotiations, this was brought up countless times and ultimately included in the mandate of the truth commission. For them, this was a matter requiring recognition.

On Political Legitimation as the Dramatisation of the Victims' Authority

Victimisation is said to be a performative act where the victimiser exalts himself and degrades the victim. Transitional justice rituals seek to reorder things, inter alia, by exalting the humiliated victims.

> terms of 'settling a debt'. Therefore, any use of memory that doesn't respect these criteria – for instance, by putting memory in the service of oneself rather than another – can result in an abuse of memory vis-à-vis justice. See Paul Ricoeur, *Memory, History, Forgetting*, trans. Kathleen Blamey and David Pellauer (Chicago: University of Chicago Press, 2004), chap. 2.

By contrast, legitimation is an exercise involving the dramatisation of authority. Provided that those who represent the role of authority meet certain conditions, the ritual interaction that crystallises in the public believing an authority is legitimate is set in motion from the top down, and the primary evidence of its completion is a sort of mimetic contagion by the public, taking the form of acclaim.

Viewed this way, one can see how victims have emerged as a form of authority – often perceived as sacred – occupying a key position as source of legitimacy within the new humanitarian consciousness and within the modern rituals of transitional justice, such as criminal trials and truth commissions. In this environment, fierce competition unfolds between all actors involved – including victims themselves – for the role of victims, or their representatives. There is also competition to offer the various categories of victim a privileged position in the room. This makes it attractive for those who aren't victims to hold the same status, cost free.

What, then, is the nature of the authority attributed to victims? First, victims have the authority of being witnesses to their own direct or indirect victimisation, possessing privileged knowledge of the factual truth of what happened. This is communicated to others, such as the prosecution, the jury, the judge, the commission, or the public at large, depending on the ritual where the victims are called to declare. Given their condition of privileged witness, victims are also recognised as an expert authority. Victims know, better than anyone, the harm they have suffered and the effects it creates, and as a consequence, what they consider necessary for their own rehabilitation and reparation. This is why victims must be consulted, be it in their own voice or that of their representative, so that they may determine the type of measures required to restore their dignity and redeem their suffering.

Victims and their real or alleged representatives are also experts par excellence when determining the nature and magnitude of the punishment the victimiser deserves, and even the state policies needed for future peace and reconciliation. It could almost be said that the victim has the authority of both the government and the informed citizen. Moreover, criminal defenders sometimes complain that the 'sanctified' victim occasionally operates as a super-prosecutor, and that official judges don't dare to contradict their accusations. Having said that, their authority also depends on factors such as the degree of structure attributed to the ritual itself.

In any case, whereas the role of victim is one that many would like to play, nobody wishes to play the role of victimiser, unless it's that of the repentant sinner. This explains why the condition of victimhood is often self-attributed, while that of victimiser has to be attributed – through accusation – by another.

Peace negotiations – at least insofar as they are the continuation of war by other means – operate as a game of self-attribution of the condition of victimhood, and, by implication, of attribution of the condition of victimiser to the enemy. With the Socratic axiom that 'it is better to suffer harm than to inflict it' operative in the moral mind of the public, the dramatisation of authority – accompanied by argumentative or rhetorical discourse, when a party affirms being the 'Only True Victim' – is a way of legitimising oneself and de-legitimising the other, who, explicitly or implicitly, becomes the 'One True Victimiser'.

To successfully dramatise her authority, the victim doesn't always need to shout it from the rooftops. When the condition of victimhood is broadly known and recognised, it can be more beneficial to refrain from discussing it. A political leader can, for example, demand harsh punishment against the victimisers using retributive or prevention-based arguments, without arousing suspicion that he does it out of a thirst for revenge. This increases his capacity for mimetic seduction on the public stage.

The example of former President Álvaro Uribe in Colombia serves to illustrate this point well. The story of the murder of his father during a kidnapping attempt by the FARC is broadly known. However, Uribe, as the leader of the opposition *Centro Democrático* party and main antagonist of the Havana talks, has rarely referred to himself as a victim. Instead, he has used a prevention discourse, decrying the bad example set by treating guerrilla leaders with leniency because it sends the message that 'crime pays'. Only when confronted by national leaders from the political left who, like himself, are victims of the war (e.g., Senator Iván Cepeda, whose father is presumed to have been murdered by right-wing paramilitaries) does Uribe brandish the authority imparted onto him by his own personal tragedy.

Assuming that the state represents the highest authority in the political and legal arenas, as is the case in most countries, government officials who defend the state are much more likely to gain recognition from their dramatisations than those who confront it. In general, it is understood that the use of violence by the state is legitimate, but not so the use against it. And this authority has even more force if or when government officials also speak on behalf of the victims.

The opposition, which plays an important role of authority in modern constitutional democracies, can, under certain conditions, successfully challenge the government's legitimacy by wrestling away the victim's authority. But this is much more difficult in societies that, like Colombia, have emerged divided from war. Here, determining who is a victim and who is a victimiser is highly disputed, and any rituals of justice, truth, and reparation are inevitably called into question by one or more sides.

Powerful political-epistemic privileges in favour of the modern state also serve to reinforce its image as the victim, when confronted by a non-state armed group. For example, the label of terrorism is attributed almost exclusively to those who confront the state but rarely to states themselves, much less those that are structured as liberal, constitutional democracies. As a response to the experience of totalitarian dictatorships, Auschwitz, and Kolyma; as ratification of the anti-state sympathies of much of eighteenth-century continental European liberalism; and as a retaining wall against monarchical absolutism, the post–World War II legal scaffolding for human rights was conceived as a set of checks on state power to limit its capacity to abuse individuals and minorities, having been delegated the monopoly over violence within its borders. In other words, it has been possible to correct the pro-state bias of sovereignty by producing an anti-state bias within human rights discourse. The problem is that this bias creates serious epistemic dangers in regards to justice, especially insofar as the discourse can be so easily manipulated by violent enemies of the state.

All of this can help us understand what took place in and around Havana. Since human rights and victims' NGOs are grounded in the epistemic-legal logic of state distrust, and haven't fully evolved towards the more impartial logic of international humanitarian law (IHL), they give prevalence to the grievances of victims of state crimes. In Colombia, this results in such groups tending to be perceived as allies of the FARC by other sectors of society, and often by the state itself. Certain sectors on the political left that are separate from but ideologically akin to the guerrillas likewise prefer to frame their work within the discourse of human rights, at the cost of being stigmatised. Only rarely, and almost reluctantly, do they interpret events through the lens of IHL, or work to articulate and present the grievances of the victims of FARC crimes.

The classical human rights discourse representing the state as the great victimiser is nevertheless counterbalanced today by IHL's treatment of the militarily weaker side in an asymmetrical war. As noted earlier, in 'legal' but asymmetrical wars, which are reliant on air and technological superiority, the stronger party is often aided by expert IHL advisers who select legitimate and proportional targets as they prepare their attacks, and who keep detailed accounting of war crimes perpetrated by the enemy, whose strength lies precisely in its willingness to behave savagely and outside of IHL. In such wars, IHL acts de facto as authorisation for the stronger party and as prohibition for the weaker. In that respect, IHL offers an impartial yardstick for all parties in conflict, but also functions as an instrument and a battlefield in the construction of the weaker (and anti-state) party as the great victimiser. Without the counterweight provided by human rights, IHL – even when applied in good faith in contexts of asymmetrical warfare – tends to mask state liabilities because it is inherently less able to capture them, particularly when they occur outside the battlefield.

On the Place of Victims in the Havana Negotiations

Wars degrade into victimisation enterprises between those in battle and, all too often, against civilians in general. It should thus come as no surprise that – against the backdrop of a humanitarian crisis of immense proportions in Colombia, and where the majority of public opinion has viewed the FARC as the main victimiser and rejected concessions on delicate matters like the terms of imprisonment, participation in politics, and the connection between drug trafficking and political crime – the Santos government and the FARC agreed to put victims at the centre of the accords.

During transitions from war to peace, the old mind-set of war and the emerging mind-set of peace coexist, and the parties self-represent ambiguously as enemies, adversaries, victims, and victimisers. In their drive to garner public support, enemies negotiating the end of an armed conflict often adopt strategies in proportion to their level of willingness to transform identity. From this perspective, the parties often sway between two extremes. The first involves both sides dramatising the claim that they have supreme authority, derived from being the only true victims and/or their representatives, in the hope that the credibility of this dramatisation secures the support of their constituency (or the population in general) and takes support away from the adversary. The second involves acting unilaterally or in association with the adversary to invite the victims to come forward as agents of supreme authority in the hope that, in their generosity and plurality, they support any agreed commitments by the parties.

The parties at the Havana talks, but especially the FARC, employed both of these legitimation strategies: minimising moral risk by discursively and performatively asserting their victimhood – and, by implication, attributing the condition of victimiser to the *other*, and inviting the war's civilian victims to participate, thus permitting the moral and practical risk of being labelled as the victimisers. The parties sought further legitimation of the process as a whole, through the creation of a mechanism whereby the public could submit ideas and proposals to the negotiating table.

Of course, the first strategy can be seen as legitimising only if it is practised in a setting that is somehow open to the public, for example, through public communiques that convey what the parties say behind closed doors (a device frequently used by the FARC). In a closed negotiation without witnesses, representing oneself as victim and the enemy as victimiser can only fulfil the expressive function of seeking the moral high ground, and the instrumental function of making one's proposals and grievances sound coherent and justified to the other negotiating party. Without witnesses or audience, there is no gain in broader legitimacy.

The first strategy is also anchored in the understanding of negotiation as the continuation of war by other means, and implies a conservative view of oneself and a low perception of moral risk.

The second strategy, by contrast, is anchored in an open understanding of one's own capacity to change, and thus associated with the moral risk assumed by the invitation to victims to participate. In their free expression, the victims may raise accusations beyond the expectations of the party that invited them and may even shake the latter's moral certainty, forcing it to wonder what it did wrong and whether it is more victimiser than victim. As such, the second strategy generates greater legitimacy than the former, being more respectful of the free agency that characterises individuals and groups in liberal-democratic societies.

While the first strategy relies on controlled communiques to seduce the masses, assumed to be ignorant and passive, the second is based on recognition of victims' autonomy. From a normative standpoint, the first strategy stems from the self-affirmation of one's moral identity, the second from the willingness to have that identity challenged. The former isn't open to moral learning; the latter is.

As such, those who take the risk of being accused by victims of being a victimiser can naturally be assaulted by fears, as we will see further on when we reconstruct the victims' visits to Havana. There, both sides feared that the victims, upon seeing them, would succumb to repressed anger and insult them. Some of the delegates also feared that some victims might make outrageous declarations to the media which, instead of supporting the process, would destroy the legitimacy of the negotiations. Preoccupied with their own fears, these delegates failed to notice that some of the victims were also scared of having to come face to face with their tormentors. Indeed, rather than 'letting them have it' – as some victims reportedly intended to do – the opposite happened in a number of cases. Perhaps this was partly due to the historical responsibility of the occasion: the visiting victims may have wanted to avoid jeopardising the negotiation as a whole, by spoiling the ceremony to which they had been invited.

Of course, both strategies (controlled press statements and uncontrolled victim testimonies) can prove politically successful. The success of the first depends largely on the adequate selection of the audience for the theatre of authority (which must be friendly and captive), the quality of the acting, and the limited information the victims and the public have about who is responsible for the harm inflicted during the conflict. The success of the second, by contrast, depends on a more nuanced audience selection (which must include spectators who are new, indecisive, or even hostile to the hosts) and the quality of the choreography; but it also depends on the capacity of participating victims' and human rights organisations to support and articulate their accusations and demands and to communicate the truth convincingly to other social sectors.

Still, the question remains, what constitutes an adequate response in the eyes of the public? In a Catholic – and, more generally, Christian – society like Colombia, the public expects that those enemies accused of being victimisers by their victims respond with remorse and ask for forgiveness. This is in fact what public opinion polls showed, especially vis-à-vis the FARC. Yet, there was a deep mismatch between the overwhelming social expectation – reinforced by the political right – that FARC leaders should humiliate themselves to show that they have undergone an identity and attitude shift, and the rebels' self-representation as proud revolutionary warriors who shouldn't have to kneel before anyone to ask for forgiveness. Thus, the FARC's legitimation strategy required less controlled approaches through which the public could judge on its own.

As to the Colombian military, the public was more benevolent. Only the perspective of victims of state crime, as well as the impartial gaze of those who regard it from afar (such as the international community), tended to question the political-epistemic bias in favour of the state and its agents. The *Centro Democrático*, the more doctrinal sectors of the Conservative party, and the political right in general, skilfully tuned in to this bias in favour of the liberal democratic state and against the FARC and guerrillas in general. As such, rather than helping the cause of public support, the Santos government's acknowledgement of its double condition of victim and victimiser earned it the unfair accusation of 'selling out' and committing 'treason'. This played a decisive role in the lower-than-expected legitimacy of the negotiated agreement, including its transitional justice provisions.

In practice, the victims portrayed themselves in different ways, including (1) as abstract, and thus universal, victims; and (2) as specific victims of one of the parties in conflict. The first portrait is based on the notion that it matters neither who the victimiser was nor the reasons for the victimisation. This allows the victim to portray himself, or to be portrayed by others (including the parties), as an equidistant 'third party' and as a shared reference that can inspire the victimisers to recognise themselves as such. The second, in contrast, involves the victim pointing an accusatory finger at his specific victimiser and thus lends weight to his counterpart at the negotiating table. In this respect, the victim who self-represents (or is represented as victim of) a specific party becomes, perhaps unintentionally, a functional ally of his victimiser's adversary and thus a participant in the political game of enmity more than in the cause of reconciliation.

On Victimisation Models and Grey Zones

To fully understand the disputes that took place in Havana between the Santos government and the FARC around the issue of victims, we must make the analytical distinction between vertical and horizontal victimisation models, in spite of the fact that these often intermingle. Vertical victimisation occurs typically in repressive dictatorships uncontested by violence. In such circumstances, the state-victimiser has a monopoly over barbarity, whereas the victimised social groups have a monopoly over defencelessness. The defining trait of vertical victimisation is the clear separation of the roles of victim and victimiser. By contrast, horizontal victimisation occurs typically in wars, in which the conflicting parties, supported by segments of the population, cross-victimise the reference populations of their enemies. Here, there is little clarity in terms of jus ad bellum and jus in bello about who are the good guys and who are not. Instead, there is an abundance of 'grey zone' agents: individuals or groups in which, to different degrees and in different ways, the roles of victimiser and victim collapse.

Claiming that all wars are simply cross-victimisation scenarios between great masses, where the entire population is divided neatly between warring sides, can be a gross exaggeration. This disregards large segments of the population, often the majority, who have nothing to do with the armed actors, and who have been unjustly victimised. Claiming that wars are always and essentially 'wars against the people', as many human rights advocates prefer – and suggesting that they consist of dual vertical victimisation models in which the war machines, with no social or political support, 'ally themselves' to kill and harm civilians who are almost by definition innocent – is equally exaggerated. Turning a blind eye to the fact that wars aren't only waged against, but also with the population, denies the agency many victims exert, and conceals the nuances.

In order to observe those in the grey zone through the most elementary factual lens, it suffices to recount the events where those who inflicted and suffered unjust pain were involved individually or collectively. Bringing these trajectories into a coherent narrative and understanding the tense subjectivity of those in the grey zone are matters that belong to the realm of interpretation. The child, forcibly recruited by an armed group, who becomes a habitual killer, belongs in the grey zone. So does the landowner who, after an armed group kidnaps his child, becomes the voluntary and habitual financer of his victimiser's enemy. Even the guerrilla fighter who is detained, tortured, and murdered outside of combat can be a rightful inhabitant of this ghostly grey zone that morality and law often wish to ignore.

Grey zone figures exist in both vertical and horizontal victimisation models, but tend to be more abundant and varied in the latter. The clear separation of victim and victimiser in vertical models (whose defining example is the concentration camp, and more broadly, dictatorial states) often excludes a very large variety of grey zones. The open and unstable nature of interactions between enemy camps in horizontal victimisation models, by contrast, favours the proliferation and more varied configuration of grey zones. Of course, the size of the grey zones also changes as a function of the size and nature of the support offered by the population to the various war machines. But it is worth noting that the less ideologically mobilised the reference population subjected to domination by a military apparatus, the sharper the contrast will be between the victim and victimiser camps.

Within horizontal victimisation models, the debate over grey zones is largely focused on the 'avenger': the victim-victimiser par excellence, who in the past, was the explanatory axis for war, especially in tribal societies. In the Oresteia (457 C.E.), Aeschylus already understood that tribal wars in ancient Greece were collective hatred traps, dominated by an archaism (embodied by the Erinyes) that compelled parties to avenge the harm inflicted on members of their own kind. The Oresteia has an inter-generational scene in which Agamemnon and Orestes switch roles, from hunters to prey, and from victimisers to victims. Agamemnon and Orestes are thus portrayed, throughout this long history, as grey zone figures. Only the establishment of justice and clemency imparted by an independent and impartial party, embodied by the courts at the Polis, provided the great civilising leap needed to escape this trap.

In nineteenth-century Colombia, and up to the middle of the twentieth century, civil wars were likewise interpreted as 'chains of revenge' based on 'inherited hatreds'. The National Front power-sharing arrangement, which put an end to 'La Violencia' of the 1950s, arose with the goal of overcoming the heavy burden of the legacy of hatred between liberals and conservatives.

However, subsequent moral and legal developments (such as the exclusion of revenge as a source of justification in liberal criminal law based on the civilising illusion of greater self-control by modern individuals over their drives) as well as theoretical and methodological developments (such as those related to understanding wars and armies through the individualist paradigm of 'rational choice') contributed to rendering invisible the importance of anger and vengeful hatred among the deep motivations that drive warriors and their social backers, particularly in contexts of highly fragmented, prolonged, and degraded wars like the Colombian one.

On Pure Victims

The principle of distinguishing between combatants and non-combatants in modern IHL grants the position of victim to civilians and unarmed combatants, the wounded, and the ill, in virtue of their defencelessness rather than their innocence. In the logic of IHL, one can be a victim without being innocent.

Yet, explicitly and implicitly, innocence is often seen as a core trait of the definition of victim. Supposing that, in a liberal culture, an individual can be guilty only for what she does and never simply for what she is or what she has, it is clear that European Jews were taken to the extermination camps not for what they did but for what they 'were'. In this sense, the Jews exterminated by the Nazis can only ever be understood as innocent victims. And, since the Holocaust has had such a disproportionate impact on modern notions of victimhood, the very concept of victim has, over time, surreptitiously incorporated the quality of innocence.

The victims of Stalinism, who were victimised for what they 'had' and not for what they did, were likewise innocent victims; indeed, the two great forms of totalitarianism of the twentieth century resemble each other in their production of innocent victims. The 'bomb', with its death that falls from the sky and makes victims of those who happened to be in the wrong place at the wrong time; the victims of the Guernica bombing; the indiscriminate 'terrorism' of suicidal jihadists; all of these have contributed to this conceptual development of victims as fundamentally innocent.

The idea of the guilty victim, and with it that of grey zones, was coined by Primo Levi in his famous text *The Drowned and the Saved*.[7] In it, he referred especially to the Sonderkomandos and the Kapos, central figures in the Nazi

---

7   Primo Levi, *The Drowned and the Saved*, 1st Vintage ed. (New York: Vintage, 1989).

death factories, as the epitome of this notion. However, the concept of guilty victim is bothersome to those who, like the Spanish philosopher Reyes Mate, have made innocence part of the definition of victim. The idea of the guilty victim encumbers the purification of roles required to sanctify the victim and demonise the victimiser, as criminal law would prefer, ruled as it is by the binary rationale of imparting sentences. The purification of roles for victimiser and victim facilitates the attribution of judicial and non-judicial blame to groups as well as individuals, but often at a very high political price: stimulating polarisation.

What grey zones reveal are the complex moral identities of those who interact in contexts of dictatorship or war, calling attention to the frequency, degrees, and ways in which the roles of victim and victimiser dissolve into a single person or group. Those who reject this idea claim that it simply legitimises victimisers by making the victims accomplices in their own demise. In light it is easier to understand, for example, the Jewish community's adverse reaction to Hannah Arendt's efforts to put on the table the issue of Hungary's Judenraete in her book, *Eichmann in Jerusalem*. The nascent Israeli government of the day and its support base throughout the diaspora, operating in a hostile political environment, found it intolerable for Arendt, on the occasion of Eichmann's trial, to shine light on the uncomfortable phenomenon of Jewish collaboration. Arendt may have lacked tact, and even factual information when she passed judgement on the matter, but the issue was real; and in any case her intention was neither to bash leaders of the Jewish community in Eastern Europe, nor to excuse the victimisers. Yet, Arendt's ideas, and concepts like Erica Bouris's 'complex political victim', have generally had little welcome in moral and legal debates.[8]

Having said this, if we aim for an honest understanding of wars like the one that may finally be ending in Colombia, what happened in black and white must be represented in black and white. Those who were victimised for their class status or simply for being in the wrong place at the wrong time, when the war and terror machines from either side caught them by surprise at their workplace or home and destroyed their lives, have the right to be represented and recognised as innocent victims. In Colombia, as in many other places, these spotless victims are certainly the norm. However, we must also make room for grey zones and the portrayal of complex political victims. Doing so can be important because such figures are the great witnesses of the

---

[8] Erica Bouris, *Complex Political Victims* (Bloomfield, Conn.: Kumarian Press, 2007).

shared humanity between victims and victimisers. Without them, war cannot be represented, at least from the perspective of the victim, as a political phenomenon, but merely as a criminal one. Indeed, it is ultimately a representational and moral error to bestow the quality of innocence upon all victims based on the fact that the majority possess it, thinking that this will benefit them all.

This is yet another reason why judicial mechanisms must be complemented by non-judicial truth-seeking mechanisms, such as truth commissions and similar bodies of inquiry. The work of the Historical Memory Group, a non-judicial body created in 2005 under the Justice and Peace Law that was adopted by Álvaro Uribe's government as part of its settlement with the AUC paramilitary group, demonstrates that, while criminal trials tend to render those in the grey zone invisible, special truth-seeking bodies may do otherwise – especially when they are not set up simply as an 'auxiliary to justice'.

Without such non-judicial bodies, the likely outcome is a double purification of the roles of victimiser and victim, respectively. To wit, during the initial stage of the Justice and Peace Law's serious crimes prosecutions, the prosecutors often demanded that paramilitary commanders, in making their confessions (called 'free versions' under the law), limit themselves to the facts and refrain from presenting their deeds as heroic. Out of respect for the victims, they had to avoid attempts at portraying themselves as legitimate counter-insurgents or as victims of the guerrillas (which they often were). In parallel, attorneys for the victims in the parallel civil redress scheme were known to make the private recommendation that their clients disavow any guilt that may have played a role in their own victimisation and thus avoid the risk of self-incrimination. Fortunately, the Historical Memory Group (and its successor, the Historical Memory Centre), rather than fashioning a narrative of humiliation of the victimiser and exaltation of the victim, occasionally offered a different discourse that gave visibility to grey zones and produced a levelling effect on public understanding.

Yet, the tendency to construct black-and-white narratives that consciously or unconsciously disregard the existence of those in the grey zone is not exclusive to law. In interdisciplinary areas such as transitional justice, many social scientists and humanitarian activists practice it also, tending to conflate the 'victim's memory' with the 'victimising event'. This creates a short circuit between historical memory and victim testimony, and between historical memory and judicial truth, spuriously following the footsteps of the investigative paradigm of liberal criminal law in its most traditional version, which prosecutes individuals for their individual acts. When the victim's story loses its condition of being a life story in which episodes follow each other in a long trajectory, and when the subject may only occupy the role of victimiser or victim (thus reducing the story to the temporal and spatial terms demanded by the reconstruction of the 'victimising event'), many grey zone figures are made invisible. The more horrendous the story of the circumstances and the mode of victimisation, the more untouchable and sacred the victim's image becomes.

In a segmented, short-term narrative, aimed exclusively at proving the victimising event, it is evident that few grey zones can survive. Those that do are the grey zones that stem from the temporal proximity of the situations where the same person or group occupies the roles of victimiser and victim (e.g., a guerrilla fighter who, having been caught killing a soldier from behind, is immediately tortured and disappeared, or the minor who, having been forcibly recruited a few days before her eighteenth birthday, is criminally prosecuted for a homicide she commits in combat the day after her birthday). The problem is that many figures in the grey zone are visible only from their long stories, full of vicissitudes, like those told by many who participated in the fourth delegation of victims at the Havana talks, whose stories were as inconceivable as they were long and complex.

Whereas in Chile the empirical grounds for the near-exclusive responsibility of the dictatorial state and its officials were decisive in making transitional justice there a story told fundamentally in black and white, in Colombia it could never be thus. Due to the partially horizontal character of the victimisation dynamics that occurred in Colombia – and the existence of all manner of grey zone figures composed of land owners, merchants, peasants, truckers, recruited minors, etc. in whom coercion and willingness blend – the roles of victim and victimiser are more fused. This makes it very difficult for the parties to be willing to recognise their responsibility as victimisers unless their condition as victims is simultaneously recognised. After all, recognition of the victimiser as a victim runs the moral risk of justifying what otherwise would be considered unjustifiable. However, the opposite stance also carries risks. Giving visibility to victims' moral and legal responsibilities could lead judges to stop treating them as victims and prosecute them as victimisers. This is reason enough for them to want to keep grey zones out of sight.

Only those who have been (1) indicted, politically or criminally, for perpetrating serious crimes and (2) compelled to recognise their condition as victimisers, have a powerful incentive to portray themselves, truthfully or not, as victims, and thus as inhabitants of the grey zone. They rarely have incentives to show sympathy or support for one of the parties in conflict, since this weakens the justice of their cause and the force of their demands, and thus risks forfeiting their treatment as victims. Nevertheless, there will be some victims, always few in number, who feel that part of their dignity consists in being able to exercise their political agency and acknowledge (with or without regret) that their ideological convictions were, at least in part, the cause of their victimisation. As for judges, the ancient debate about the causes for justification and acquittal, and the contemporary concern with extenuating circumstances and mitigating factors, offer them sufficient reason to illuminate grey zones. Yet, given the binary character of the distinction between guilt and innocence, which lies at the heart of law as a machine for allocating responsibility, justice has internal epistemic constraints in accounting for grey zones, especially in matters of sentencing.

Yet, despite our conviction about the importance of making grey zones visible, in practice they tend to remain in the shadows. Colombia suffered a degrading decades-long armed confrontation – thoroughly infused by the economics of illicit drugs – between the state and its paramilitary allies on one side and multiple guerrilla groups on the other, reaching its peak during the so-called 'war of massacres' at the turn of the millennium. But in spite of the war's grey zones, victims were seen, above all, as victims of state crimes or as victims of the guerrillas: a sort of branding left on their skin by the political identity of their victimiser, independent of their own guilt or innocence. It hasn't been the victims' endogenous political identity derived from their ideological sympathies or voluntary actions to benefit one camp or another, but rather the exogenous political identity imposed by their victimiser through the very act of violence committed against them, that has defined the struggle for victim recognition in Colombia, including in the Havana negotiations.

As though faced with a dictatorship, the FARC would claim that the state had a monopoly over barbarity, and they – the guerrillas – had a monopoly over innocence and quasi-defenceless. In a game of inverted mirrors, the *Centro Democrático* claimed that, short of a true war, what the country faced was a situation in which a stable, functional, and legitimate democracy was under siege by terrorist groups with no popular support. The government, representing the liberal democratic state, started from a horizontal victimisation model, which made it morally and politically impossible to adopt the role of victim in a sharp victim/victimiser dialectic.

In this light, it is unclear whether it will be possible for the Special Jurisdiction for Peace (JEP) or the Truth, Coexistence, and Non-Repetition Commission (CEV) to reconstruct the conflict's black-and-white victimisation dynamics, as well as study the ghostly figures of the grey zone. As with the 2005 Justice and Peace Law, disregarding victims' political guilt protects them from legal or physical retribution, but it also deprives society of the chance to understand the complexity of what happened in all its dimensions. Without such understanding, it isn't possible to construct a collective memory that is able adequately to contribute to reconciliation and the guarantee of non-repetition. That is because figures in the grey zone simultaneously inhabit the camp of victimisers and victims, and as such, are proof that good and evil aren't fully static. This is why making them visible helps to depolarise. It is the means for helping those sectors that are trapped in the ideological illusion that Colombia suffered a vertical victimisation process to discover the sharply horizontal character of the victimisation that took place, and react accordingly.

On the Difference between Negotiating Transitions from Dictatorship and from War

Victory in war and victory against authoritarian regimes both produce models of unidirectional justice. They distribute blame in distorted, asymmetrical fashion, for the benefit of the victor and to the detriment of the vanquished. Negotiated transitions out or war or dictatorship are entirely different. They demand (especially in the case of negotiated ends to conflict) reciprocal compromises in which, if there is to be justice, it will be issued at the hands of an independent and impartial third party, allocating responsibilities among all parties involved in serious transgressions.

In spite of efforts made by the winning powers and their judges to make justice that respected liberal principles of the rule of law – rather than the political and administrative justice that the Soviets practised at home and wished to replicate in the Allied military tribunal – the Nuremberg trials were in fact an exercise in victors' justice. Neither in Nuremberg nor in Tokyo were serious Allied war crimes tried. Allied bombings of northern German cities and what occurred in Hiroshima and Nagasaki are, at least for the vanquished, monuments to the impunity of victors.

In both the war's cause (jus ad bellum) and conduct (jus in bello), the Nuremberg trials attributed all guilt to the vanquished. The priority conferred to the charge of aggression played a prominent role in the exercise. The just cause of defensive war meant that the victorious powers could ratify the political-epistemic privilege of remaining untried for their own war crimes. As a consequence, the horizontal victimisation endemic to 'total war' was judicially portrayed as vertical victimisation.

Nuremberg created three problematic corollaries in and for the international human rights framework, and eventually, transitional justice: (1) an excessive separation between the victim and victimiser camps, which has expanded into humanitarian law; (2) the idea that the state is, par excellence, 'the' great victimiser, expressed in the anti-state bias built into human rights law; and (3) an increased punitive logic in IHL, disavowing the old liberal conviction which held that criminal justice is better at maintaining peace than at bringing it about.

The Nuremberg heritage fits like a glove vis-à-vis the transitions from dictatorship to democracy in the Southern Cone during the 1980s. The vertical representation of victimisation phenomena, typical of human rights institutions post-Nuremberg, constituted the perfect legal-political yardstick to judge the victimisation dynamics of Argentina, Uruguay, and Chile, all markedly vertical by different degrees. But the biggest defect of the Southern Cone cases lies in their de-contextualised generalisation. Human rights and transitional justice doctrine and jurisprudence tend, even now, to represent transitions from war, in which reconciliation dynamics usually prevail over criminal justice ones, as if they were transitions from dictatorship, in which criminal justice dynamics should prevail. Although the effect of this is starting to be corrected, it is not an easy task because the principles and pathways that structure the hegemonic discourse on transitional justice, despite their youth, have become legally dogmatised and sanctified.

In dictatorships, it is often clear from the outset, or soon after, who are the bad guys and who are the good. When transitions arise, such clarity tends to awaken retributive sentiments that manifest as strong social demands for punishment. However, where the facts are more ambiguous regarding who are victimisers and who are victims, as is often the case in transitions from war, this epistemic confusion tends to favour the tragic view and a preference for the mind-set of coexistence and reconciliation over punishment. The exception, of course, is when society is dominated by a false clarity that resists debunking – a reality which, sadly, occurs all too often.

In Argentina, the human rights movement that rose to power after the dictatorship has remained dominant. Until the victory of the centre-right president Macri, the Argentinian state was represented by successive centre-left governments, as the crystallisation of the full victory of the ideals of transitional justice over dictatorship. The anti-militaristic memory of resistance became the official memory of the Argentinian state. The Mothers of the Plaza de Mayo moved their headquarters to the notorious Navy Mechanical School that had been used as a torture centre during the dictatorship. Trials abounded against members of the military of every rank responsible for the repression.

For these reasons, the Argentinian case has been heralded by many, both at home and abroad, as a model to be imitated. Argentinians turned their experience with transitional justice into an export. For decades, its activists and judges have occupied strategic posts in many regional and global bodies related to the fight against impunity, and have travelled the world preaching their particular gospel on how to handle justice during transitions. The Inter-American human rights system has appeared to function, at least until recently, to the beat of their dictates.

But in the El Mozote sentence,[9] the Inter-American Court of Human Rights began to send signals that it is willing to recognise that transitions from dictatorship and from war should receive different treatment. Likewise, Pablo de Greiff, the former UN Special Rapporteur on the promotion of truth, justice, reparation, and guarantees of non-recurrence, called attention to the difference between transitions from cases where the state is a coherent unit with a functioning justice system, and those in which it is not.[10] He doesn't explicitly mention the difference between dictatorship and civil war as starting points for transition, but one can read between the lines that such difference is there.

Civil wars are generally a mixture of vertical and horizontal victimisation dynamics, putting justice goals in tension with peacemaking ones. Just like dictatorial bureaucracies, the armed bureaucracies of war tend to operate like repressors of their reference populations, and not just of the enemy's. Similarly, reconciliation dynamics aimed at building stable and lasting peace can work in either direction. Curiously, horizontal reconciliation among enemies, especially when it involves reciprocal pardon, appears to have a greater chance to come about than vertical reconciliation between victims and victimisers.

In the vertical victimisation contexts of the Southern Cone, the word 'reconciliation' was used ad nauseam by the dictatorships' ideologues and henchmen to advance, if not impose, their impunity. When added to the militancy of those who rightly rejected the nefarious role of much of the Catholic Church during the dictatorship, the term became discredited. And yet, there is no obvious alternative in ordinary language that – with equal cultural resonance and semantic force – is able to define the ultimate horizon toward which transitional justice policies must aim. The term 'reconciliation' can mean anything from a willingness to coexist politically to respect for the

---

[9] The Massacre of El Mozote and Nearby Places v. El Salvador (Merits, Reparations, and Costs), Series C, No. 252, 25 October 2012.
[10] Pablo de Greiff, 'Informe del Relator Especial sobre la promoción de la verdad, la justicia, la reparación y las garantías de no repetición' (Asamblea General, Consejo de Derechos Humanos, 9 August 2012, 21° período de sesiones), 5–6.

rules of the democratic game or even forgiveness for wrongdoing (although we must steer away from anything approaching the vile notion that victims must forgive their victimisers). As such, reconciliation is an idea that has sufficient bandwidth to bring together priests, shamans, politicians, psychiatrists, social workers, and everyday citizens in the task of restoring the social fabric, and, with it, the quest for strong guarantees of non-repetition. Nevertheless, in the Havana talks, the parties opted for the safer term of 'coexistence' in lieu of reconciliation when it came to negotiations on the subject of a truth commission mandate.

Granted, there is nothing pre-set about privileging justice over reconciliation at the end of a dictatorship. For example, in Spain the political settlement after Franco's death determined from the outset that the transition from a dictatorship of over forty years would be treated as a negotiated transition from civil war. Its model of transitional justice, based on a sweeping amnesty and broad political reconciliation, is now criticised. In part, this is because Spain is increasingly polarised around whether it must unveil, prosecute, and repair the crimes perpetrated by the Francoist fighters during the civil war and by the long dictatorship in which they consolidated their victory.

In Colombia, the transitional justice solution fell somewhere between Argentina and Spain, as it included significant justice measures, but within a horizontal victimisation model. It reflected a balance between the mindset of reconciliation and that of retributive justice, albeit one more favourable to the former. Indeed, the nature of the transitional justice system agreed in Havana and the concomitant political integration of the guerrillas are clear indications that this was the case. However, it remains to be seen whether, despite the formal end of the war with the FARC, the political right manages to convince the country that, due to the injustice of the FARC's attack on the state, Colombia's victimisation model needs to be completely asymmetric.

Debates such as these bear upon the format of any negotiation out of war or dictatorship. Here, we recall that the pacts negotiated in transitions from dictatorship to democracy – such as that of Chile – tend to be informal, hidden, and shameful. This can be explained by the fact that they are built over the backdrop of vertical victimisation models, where it is generally clear that dictatorship embodies evil and the emerging democracy embodies good. Such pacts can be understood only as pacts of impunity, involving concessions that the good guys offer the bad guys to keep them from derailing the transition. As such, it should come as no surprise that many human rights advocates are quick to assert that these pacts are undeserving of respect, and that although they must be tolerated for a while to avoid jeopardising the transition, in the medium term it is permissible to hunt down the bad guys and bring them to justice.

By contrast, the pacts negotiated in transitions from civil war to peace tend to be formal, public, and honourable for those who sign them. In such contexts, transitions often occur over the backdrop of predominantly horizontal victimisation models, in which the responsibility for crimes is distributed among all the parties in conflict, with an abundance of grey zone figures such as avengers that collapse the roles of victim and victimiser. This makes it prima facie very difficult to determine who are the good guys and who are the bad. It also explains, along with the independent benefits of war's termination, why peace deals are given a higher moral value and premised on the respect of the *pacta sunt servanda* (agreements must be kept) principle. This makes it all the more obvious how out of keeping the efforts of certain human rights defenders are when, in search of judicial prey, they set their targets on those who signed peace deals. Their error can be explained only by a kind of hypnotisation by the Nuremberg heritage and experiences like the Southern Cone transitions, causing them to treat transitions from civil war as if they were transitions from dictatorship.

Of course, the generally solemn, public, and honourable nature of peace agreements is no guarantee of compliance. Developments in Colombia after the 'No' victory in the 2016 plebiscite to ratify the Havana peace deal make it clear that the legal force of the *pacta sunt servanda* principle depends on the robustness of the political ground on which the deal stands. The Havana negotiations took place with the support of four countries (Cuba and Norway, plus Venezuela and Chile), in addition to the intermittent presence of various international actors, such as special envoys from the United States and the European Union. The first version of the agreement was formally deposited in Geneva before the ICRC, and then submitted to the United Nations in the form of a unilateral declaration expressing the willingness of the Colombian state to meet its commitments. The UN Security Council adopted a unanimous resolution of support for the agreement. Yet, all of this was in vain. The public rejected the deal, leading to its partial renegotiation and subsequent legal codification, without a new plebiscite.

While many implementation bills were adopted up to November 2017 under a special 'fast-track' procedure, others were buried before they could even be submitted or debated. Of twenty-seven bills that, by official accounts, should have been ratified by that time in order to implement the agreement adequately, only eight were passed. But on a positive note, in the summer of 2017, the UN certified the successful demobilisation of more than thirteen thousand FARC men and women and the destruction of sixty-nine tonnes of weapons and ammunition that had been in their possession.[11] This, after all, was the minimum goal of the entire process of negotiating an end to such a bloody, decades-long war that produced such a great number of atrocities and victims.

[11] 'Declaración conjunta del Representante Especial del Secretario General de la ONU para Colombia, Jean Arnault y del Enviado Especial de la Unión Europea para la Paz en Colombia, Eamon Gilmore, sobre el segundo aniversario de la firma del Acuerdo de Paz' (24 November 2018), https://colombia.unmissions.org/declaración-conjunta-del-representante-especial-del-secretario-general-de-la-onu-para-colombia-jean.

2

The Experience

A. VICTIMS VERSUS VICTIMISERS

In June 2014, before the negotiations in Havana on Point 5 ('Victims') of the 2012 General Agreement began in earnest – and thus before Mark Freeman and Iván Orozco formally began their work as independent advisers to the government's negotiation team – important conversations and decisions regarding victims had already occurred.

For example, during the secret exploratory phase of 2012 that led to the General Agreement (in which the agenda and procedural rules for the talks were outlined), it is said that the FARC representatives opposed the mention of transitional justice and the inclusion of all of its constitutive elements. Discussing truth and reparation was fair game, but discussing justice wasn't. The government, meanwhile, wished for the negotiations to be guided by a mix of local and international standards, which encompassed the need for justice. This diversity of concerns eventually led to Point 5's compromise language about how fixing the harm caused to victims would be 'at the centre' of the negotiation process between the government and the FARC.

Putting the victims at the centre was a counterintuitive act. That is because it suggested that the parties were negotiating not for their own benefit but for that of a third party. It also hid from view the very different ways in which each side understood who was a victim, who was a victimiser, and who was neither. All along, while reading the word 'victims', the FARC could think that the term referred mostly to victims of state crimes. The government, for its part, could think that it referred to all victims, as befits a government that understands that the state must assume the ultimate responsibility towards all victims of the conflict. However, because human action often occurs in the midst of such divergent understandings, it wasn't difficult to live with both assertions;

and overall, the choice to put the victims at the centre enabled more than impeded the negotiation process.

This did not, however, preclude some ugly moments. For example, at the official opening of the negotiations in Oslo on 18 October 2012, FARC leader Jesús Santrich infamously sang the refrain 'Perhaps, perhaps, perhaps' (from a well-known Cuban song by the same name) in responding to a videotaped question about whether the FARC would be willing to acknowledge responsibility for 'their' victims. Naturally, this was received very poorly by Colombian public opinion, leading to a harsh questioning of the FARC's bona fides and an early weakening of the legitimacy of the process. Another sign of divergent sensitivities and views around the identity of the victims for whose benefit the parties were negotiating occurred in relation to the requirement to achieve the 'structural transformation of the countryside' (under Point 1 of the 2012 General Agreement). In one view, the victims were persons who suffered structural injustices like land usurpation and political exclusion, dating back to the 1930s, and even back to colonial times. In the other, they were victims produced by the parties during a national armed conflict that began with the birth of the FARC as an armed group in the early 1960s. However, aware of the abyss that separated their worldviews, which could make their discussions long and sterile, both parties managed over time to put their ideological differences on the back burner and find solutions to concrete issues and problems.

By June 2014, with the risk of President Santos being defeated in his re-election bid – an eventuality that would have ended the peace talks in their tracks – the negotiating parties managed to reach agreement on the adoption of ten principles on victims. These created an initial vocabulary and minimally shared terrain for the full negotiation of Point 5, which would last until December 2015 – representing three times the duration of the previous agenda items. Why it took so long is recounted below.

The Road to Victim Participation in Havana

The failed 1999–2002 Caguán negotiations between Andrés Pastrana's government and the FARC took place within an enormous 'demilitarised zone' located in the heart of Colombia. A large area in the eastern plains of the country, with very poor state presence and infrastructure, it was nevertheless relatively easy to reach from the capital in Bogotá. This proximity facilitated access by scores of visitors who flew in from the capital or arrived by land to participate in all sorts of events and discussions that were taking place there, based on a negotiation agenda that encompassed every conceivable topic.

It was thought that opening the negotiations to the world would give them greater legitimacy. In practice, it resulted in discussions that were scattered and plagued by daily interruptions caused by the pilgrimage of politicians, experts, and onlookers who came to be photographed with the guerrilla commanders while they dined and talked together.

The Havana process drew a number of lessons from the errors of Caguán, one of which was to hold any new talks outside Colombia. The relative isolation of the island of Cuba helped to ensure that political and military developments on the mainland wouldn't interfere with the discussions. The goal was to facilitate privacy, prevent excessive exposure to leaks, and maintain better control over third-party visits in order to ensure a more fluid and uninterrupted negotiation routine. In the beginning of the 'public phase' of the talks in the fall of 2012, there were only two mechanisms for third-party participation: the so-called '2 for 2' (in which the parties could jointly invite specialised experts to give confidential, technical presentations in the negotiating room) and a separate, special mechanism for civil society groups to submit proposals electronically. Both mechanisms were initially conceived as a resource to enrich the negotiating table with policy ideas, and thus new and better elements for reaching agreements. A third mechanism, added later and applied to agenda items 1 (rural reform), 2 (political participation), and 4 (illicit drugs), involved mega-conferences held in Colombia on the corresponding themes. The organisation of these was placed exclusively in the hands of the United Nations and the National University, while the Havana process stayed to one side, maintaining contact with the forum organisers through a liaison committee.

Only when the government and the FARC began to prepare for agenda item 5 (victims) did the notion of third-party participation take a sharp turn. Under pressure from victims' organisations, the parties realised that the victims were no ordinary third party, and that their participation should be understood not only in information-gathering terms, but also as an interactive process to face up to the awful consequences of the armed conflict and, indirectly, increase the legitimacy of the negotiation itself and of any resulting agreements. The United Nations and the National University continued to act as organisers, but were joined by the Catholic Church (Episcopal Conference). Rather than acting autonomously, it was decided that the three would coordinate closely with the government and FARC delegations in Havana, so that the latter would retain some control over the process by, for example, setting the general selection criteria for the diversity of victims who, eventually, would travel to Havana to meet the parties.

The Civil Society Participation Mechanisms in Practice

Starting in December 2012, the official website of the Havana talks (www.mesadeconversaciones.com.co) allowed anyone to fill out a form and electronically submit proposals to the negotiating parties. In addition, the national mail service offered to deliver hard-copy proposals, free of charge. Paper forms were also distributed, allowing citizens to present ideas at local government offices nationwide. But the FARC distrusted all this. They said that such mechanisms, and especially the electronic one, were vulnerable to tampering. As such, they preferred to have submissions written on paper and sent by courier directly to Havana. Ultimately, it was agreed that each of the parties would receive the proposals and could use them in whatever manner it saw fit.

The FARC contracted the publisher José Martí in Cuba. Three employees would digitise the proposals that arrived in Havana and add them to those uploaded directly on the official website, so that they could all be processed together. However, the procedure was quite slow and the use that the FARC could make of the information was rather limited. Handwritten proposals that would constitute the future memory of this participatory experience were stored in humid places and deteriorated rapidly. The government's OACP (Office of the High Commissioner for Peace) ended up bringing to Havana an expert in archival conservation to assess the situation. The paper documents were eventually returned to Colombia and stored at the National Archives.

The OACP contracted the Ideas for Peace Foundation (FIP, by its acronym in Spanish) to process the submissions it received. FIP was to set up a database intended to support the government at the negotiations, make it possible to track the degree to which civil society proposals materialised in some form in the final agreement, and preserve the historical memory of civic participation and victims' involvement. FIP had a dedicated team of up to twenty people working exclusively for the government's negotiating team to organise the proposals that arrived in Havana. However, its role was not to interpret the proposals received, but merely to submit descriptive reports. The analysis and assessment of the relevance of each proposal were entrusted to the OACP and the government negotiating team in Havana.

The government and the FARC agreed that in order to consider that a proposal had been read, its electronic record had to have two check marks, showing that the file had been opened by both parties. Only then could a reply be issued to the original sender. Without both check marks, there would be no reply, and thus the author of the proposal wouldn't know whether her proposal had been taken into account. This led to arguments between members of the

OACP team and members of the FARC. The former told the latter that many proposals lacked the double check mark, showing that they hadn't been read by the FARC, meaning that a reply couldn't be issued: something the government considered reproachable.

As for the mega-conferences (called forums), when the time came, the UN, the National University, and the Episcopal Conference organised four of them on victims. They were all held in Colombia (in Barrancabermeja, Villavicencio, Medellín, and Cali); and they were held in parallel with the sequence of negotiations in Havana, on the one hand, and with forums organised by Peace Committees at the Senate and the House of Representatives, on the other.

Although there were many heated public discussions as to whether the forums were dominated by cases of state-crime victims as opposed to FARC-crime victims, it should be said that the Havana delegations were concerned with guaranteeing that all types of victims were represented. They agreed with the organisers to seek broad, plural, and balanced representation (following criteria such as the nature of the victimising event; regional, ethnic, and gender balance; the identity of the victimiser; etc.). Moreover, cognisant that in practice it would be impossible to avoid imbalances between the categories of victims (due to discrepancies between those invited and those who would actually attend), the government decided to have four forums for victims, rather than three, as had been the case for other agenda items. The impartiality exhibited by the organisers and the fact that the victims' forums encouraged the creation and involvement of organisations of FARC-crime victims are made evident by the fact that in the Cali forum, victims of such crimes – and of guerrillas in general – demanded and were granted a table that operated independently.

Ultimately, however, it was impossible for the delegations in Havana to prevent the most experienced and engaged victims' organisations from dominating the forums. It was inevitable, for instance, for those organisations whose representatives brought precise proposals in carefully written documents to fare better than smaller and less experienced organisations that were less cognisant of what was at stake. A precise, written proposal drafted by an organisation with direct or indirect presence in many locations could be submitted multiple times, and in more useful and intelligible terms, than a vague, oral proposal made spontaneously. This reality, rather than any favouritism, explains why proposals by women's organisations and by human rights and state-crimes' organisations like Movice and Marcha Patriótica were more abundant, better differentiated, and more impactful than those made by the more recently established organisations representing FARC-crime victims.

Those in charge of the complex operation of processing proposals for the OACP quickly suspected that this dynamic was at play. They could observe the comparatively greater experience, organisational capacity, and ideological unity and clarity of human rights and victims' organisations devoted to recording, reporting, and filing judicial claims for state crimes. Such organisations had broader networks across the country, enabling them to multiply and clone their more strategic proposals, so they appeared as mass appeals from a myriad of victims. The organisations belonging to victims of FARC crimes, by contrast, were less structured, had less ideological unity and clarity of purpose, and had less national presence through networks, so their influence on the negotiation was not as deep. Yet, there was little the Santos government and the Havana negotiators could do to counteract this asymmetry.

During the four-year FIP project, 168 reports were submitted to the Havana process, of which 108 were statistical, 47 analytical, and 14 comparative exercises. The first reports produced by FIP for the OACP were lengthy documents, rather dry and difficult to interpret, and full of descriptive statistics. Over time, as the government learned to express its concrete needs as a function of what was discussed in Havana, and as FIP learned to adapt to its requests, the reports became more refined. The last FIP reports were comparative statistical charts, revealing a step toward more refined data management to facilitate interpretation.

At the end of the contract between FIP and the government, and to verify the hypothesis of disproportionate participation by human rights and state-crime victims' organisations over those of FARC ones, Professor Orozco requested that the FIP try to determine the number and percentage of each among the total civil society participants under Point 5, and the number of contributions (based on a customised FIP calculation formula) made by each. Of a total of 4101 organisations that participated in the regional forums and that sent proposals on all the agenda items of the negotiation, 3178 participated in topics related to Point 5.[1] Of this number, 97.1 percent were organisations self-identified as 'victims' organisations' or 'peace organisations' without additional qualifiers, and with the latter far more numerous than the former.

---

[1] The 'Memoir Document: Civil Society Participation in the Havana Peace Dialogues' states that 'of the 4101 participating organisations, the highest percentage was from those that represent the victims of the conflict with 21.8%. The second group consisted of peasant organisations with 10.8%. Women's organisations had a significant share with 10.6%, followed by internally displaced persons' organisations with 8.85%. Those with smaller numbers included those representing illicit drug consumers with 0.68%, miners with 0.53%, and the Armed Forces and law enforcement with 0.24%'.

It was assumed that all of these organisations focused on defending the rights of victims of both state crimes and guerrilla crimes, or that they concealed their bias for the benefit of one or the other behind abstract labels like 'victims', 'war', or 'peace', making it impossible to recognise them at first glance without having studied their membership and objectives from their websites and their proposals. 'Displaced persons' organisations', including those in exile and refugees, represented a small percentage of the total, and it was assumed that they also didn't offer clues as to whether they were victims of state or guerrilla crimes. Forced displacement, after all, is a crime that all parties have perpetrated to similar degrees in Colombia, and in today's public perception it isn't associated exclusively or predominantly with either party. Aside from that, it's also worth noting that not one organisation on the long list had a term like 'victims of the paramilitaries' in its name. This gave the impression that victims of the paramilitaries tend to fold into the category of victims of state crimes.

Overall, the more militant organisations that could be easily identified with the polarities of the war in the context of the peace talks were few in number compared to the diverse aggregate of civil society organisations who offered their proposals freely to the Havana process. Such organisations participated with unanticipated vitality in the forums and the written proposal mechanism, and did so overwhelmingly guided by a genuine concern for the drama of all victims and the desire to achieve peace without victors or vanquished, leaving behind the divisions of wartime. Yet, the fact that the number of human rights and state-crime victims' groups who made proposals on Point 5 was slightly larger than those of FARC crimes is, as previously noted, indicative of the high level of organisation of the former compared to the latter.

The analytic chart produced by FIP was quite enlightening, since it ranked civil society organisations by the number of contributions made on Point 5. In isolation, none of the 849 best-ranked organisations made significantly more contributions than any other. The chart makes it clear that the highest percentage of contributions, 6.41 percent, emanated from individuals rather than organisations. Next came the category of 'undetermined', with 5.75 percent. In third place was the Alianza Iniciativa de Mujeres Colombianas por la Paz, with 1.73 percent. In this sense, interviewed FIP staff said they were under the impression that women were better organised than all other participants and that they had conducted a sort of 'sting operation' to clone their proposals, making them arrive from multiple sites and organisations throughout the country.

What remains hard to assess, however, is the actual degree of reliance that the FARC and government delegations placed on all the contributions. FIP officials in charge of constructing the database simply said that when the partial agreements under Point 5 were made public (e.g., on the truth commission mandate), they were under the impression that the submissions had been read by the parties at the table and that these were 'reflected' in the agreements.

Victimhood within the State Apparatus

Beyond the third-party input mechanisms of the Havana process, various public offices also played a major role in the transitional justice choices made, including the Victims Unit (*Unidad para la Reparación Administrativa de las Víctimas*) and the Historical Memory Centre (*Centro de Memoria Histórica*). The human rights movement in Colombia has a long history, dating at least to the 1980s; and it is reasonable to suppose that the human rights activists educated in the doctrine of the state's greater responsibility, given their better training and experience, were the best candidates to staff the government's human rights offices and to advance transitional justice ideals.

To put some of the budding bureaucracy of transitional justice in perspective, we could evaluate the work conducted by the Historical Memory Centre, which has its remote origins in the Historical Memory Group created during the Uribe government pursuant to the 2005 Justice and Peace Law, which focused on the paramilitaries. The initial group was composed of a few academics, including Álvaro Camacho, María Teresa Uribe, María Victoria Uribe, Pilar Riaño, María Enma Wills, Fernán González, and Iván Orozco, among others. It was directed by Gonzalo Sánchez, chaired by Eduardo Pizarro, and attached to the National Reparation and Reconciliation Commission (CNRR – *Comisión Nacional de Reparación y Reconciliación*). Although lacking representatives from the country's political right, it was an ideologically pluralistic group, recruited from public and private universities rather than the realm of humanitarian activism. Its International Advisory Council was composed of renowned members of academia and humanitarian activism, who could hardly be said to have shared an ideological bias.

Something similar could be said of the parallel administrative and research assistance team. The first report by the Historical Memory Group examined the Trujillo massacre, and it dealt harshly with the state by delving deeply into the responsibilities of members of the Palacé Batallion in Buga – though it also bore witness to the enormous responsibility of the ELN guerrillas in the same events. The group went on to investigate all kinds of phenomena and crimes involving the state, such as mass executions, land usurpation, and displacement involving state agents. It likewise sought every opportunity to gather information allowing it to investigate and report on mass crimes, such as kidnapping, committed mainly by the guerrillas. To do so, it requested full access to state institutions, the military, and civil society organisations like *País Libre* (Free Country). The goal was to preserve investigative balance, considered necessary to ensure the body's legitimacy.

During the Santos administration, as part of the strategy leading to the Havana negotiations, the Historical Memory Group transformed into the Historical Memory Centre, becoming a sort of ministry of memory. Its payroll grew exponentially, especially as the state's finances weren't yet in crisis. But in the merit-based competition for recruitment of staff and in the outsourcing of contractors, people educated in the human rights creed ended up in a plurality of positions, as they were seemingly better suited and more experienced than other candidates. This might have been a factor, over time, in the exponential production of Centre reports in which the narrative began to take on a representational bias that produced an over-visibility of state crimes and a comparative invisibility of FARC crimes. A Centre official said that this bias was evident, for instance, in the fact that the report on forced displacement published under the title *Una Nación Desplazada* (A Displaced Nation) opened with a long tirade that construed displacement as a state crime, and ended with a set of statistics that, contrary to its discourse, proved that most displacement was caused by the guerrillas rather than the state.[2]

The final report of the Centre, titled *Basta Ya* (Enough is Enough), was a major effort to fit a very plural universe of information sources into a single story. Sources included the inputs of human rights NGOs, but also the Prosecutor General, the National Ombudsman (Inspector General), and others. However, the document was strongly rejected by some sectors of the military, who complained of bias and information asymmetries. If these existed, however, they primarily arose from the reticence of the military to share information with the Centre, rather than the Centre's intention to write a narrative that benefited the political left and its perceived allies in war.

In June 2013, ten months into the Havana talks, the *Basta Ya* report was presented to President Santos by the director of the Centre in a public ceremony, and the President apologised on behalf of the Colombian state for its identified responsibility in the war. In the months that followed, there was an important exchange of letters between the Defence Ministry and the Historical Memory Centre's director. In a December 2013 letter, the Ministry blamed the Centre for having disrespected the principles of presumption of innocence and due process enshrined in the Constitution, by making

---

[2] Centro Nacional de Memoria Histórica, Una nación desplazada: informe nacional del desplazamiento forzado en Colombia (Bogotá: CNMH-UARIV, 2015).

judgements and attributing responsibility to members of the military, supported exclusively by highly biased (human rights) sources and in the absence of a court sentence. The letter further complained that the Centre's report failed in its duty to dignify the members of the military who had fallen in combat, as victims of the guerrillas' actions. Mostly, however, the letter expressed the military's indignation toward the Centre for purportedly equating the state's forces with those of the guerrillas, without taking into consideration the fact that the former acted out of a constitutional mandate, whereas the latter acted outside the law.[3]

In its reply to the Ministry, the Historical Memory Centre argued that it was false to claim that it had only used human rights and victims' NGOs as sources, emphasising that it had also used official sources including the testimonies of various high-level public officials and the voluntary confessions of paramilitaries made under the Justice and Peace Law. The Centre then explained the difference between producing judicial truth and historical truth: while the first is constructed by following judicial evidentiary standards, leading to a binding verdict, the latter uses the methods and benchmarks of social science with the intention of contributing to a debate that never fully concludes. The Centre's reply also clarified that although it documented the responsibility of members of the Armed Forces in serious crimes such as massacres and forced disappearances, it never claimed that this was a systematic policy of the institution. As for the inclusion of military victims, the Centre recognised that this constituted an information gap and expressed its willingness to fill it by working jointly with the War College.

What resulted was a long effort of confidence building to bring together the 'militant memory' of the Armed Forces and the 'historical memory' of the civilian officials and social scientists involved with the Centre (which was also perhaps militant, but in a humanitarian sense). However, the beginning phase of this process was quite difficult. The military's first reaction was to set up its own office devoted to building an institutional historical memory. With strategic, more than humanitarian goals, the Armed Forces dedicated themselves to investigating and reporting the crimes of the FARC and the ELN. This was a kind of game of mirrors with the guerrillas, one that the latter took up in the production of equally simplistic memories, disregarding the complexity of the context and the facts of war. Yet, there were moments of

---

[3] See generally Maria Emma Wills, principal rapporteur, 'Conversaciones inéditas entre la fuerza pública y el centro nacional de memoria histórica: Aprendizajes de una experiencia (2012–2017)' (Bogotá: CNMH, 2018), www.centrodememoriahistorica.gov.co/noticias/noticias-cmh/download/620_0926fcda11ab42807e5d2daaed21fc0b.

consensus between the military and the guerrillas: for example, when seeking to open room for a more complex narrative than either of the party's memories, the military attributed the highest responsibility for the war and its excesses to the country's civilian governments and to civilians in general.[4]

We can thus see how and why the field of memory was initially understood as a battlefield between antagonistic accounts. In Colombia, memory often acted as a space for unarmed confrontation that prolonged the war by other means. The political left's militant memory relied on the anti-state mind-set of human rights, whereas that of the Armed Forces conveyed its mirror opposite. Yet, the fact that the Historical Memory Centre was not directly involved in the armed confrontation helps explain why, over time, it was more capable of transcending this polarising inertia – as reflected, among others, in its work with the victims of anti-personnel mines. This resulted in the report *Guerra Invisible* (Invisible War), which accounts for the ravages caused by this perverse weapon of war, whose use increased massively in Colombia as the guerrillas' response to the state's aerial superiority. This and other reports (on kidnappings, the recruitment of minors, and more) show that the crimes of the FARC, and not only those of the state, were indeed part of the Centre's investigative scope and activities.

Nevertheless, it's not unreasonable to think that the anti-state bias of traditional human rights discourse could have influenced the weight given to state crimes in the aggregate of the Centre's reports, attributing more numerous and more serious responsibilities to the state than to its armed enemies. Yet, the hegemony of the 'democratic security' policy that penetrated and embedded itself in Colombian society under the charismatic leadership of President Uribe, arguably did a lot to counteract the organisational capacity of human rights' and state-crime victims' NGOs in the battle of victim narratives. Likewise, despite being less organised, the victims of FARC crimes eventually found shelter and a powerful sounding board in the military and its retiree organisations, such as ACORE, as well as in business groups attacked by the guerrillas, like FEDEGAN.

But after the triumph of the 'No' vote in the October 2016 peace plebiscite, and after the demobilisation of the FARC, it seems that the victims of state crimes lost their capacity to be heard as fully, whereas the victims of FARC crimes gained capacity to influence legislative and policy decisions. In parallel, historical memory has been given a more preponderant role in the administrative redesign of the Armed Forces to adapt them to the reality of

---

[4] Ibid.

no longer having the FARC as their enemy. After the end of the armed conflict with the FARC, it would seem that the military is preparing to enter into a nonviolent confrontation for memory with the Historical Memory Centre.[5] Yet, the newer and bigger battleground of judicial and historical memory – not just for the military, but also for human rights and victims' organisations – are the post-conflict tribunal, truth commission, and missing persons' unit, created as part of the implementation of the peace deal.

Victims in Havana

As noted earlier, the Havana negotiations were structured around the procedural condition that they should unfold in isolation. That is why third parties initially participated only through the '2 by 2' mechanisms, the national forums, and the system of written submissions. However, shortly before the formal talks began on Point 5, the parties agreed to one important exception to the rule of isolation: five delegations of victims would be selected – again by the UN, the Episcopal Conference, and the National University – and allowed to visit Havana to meet directly with the negotiating parties. While it is said that this idea formally emerged as a variant of the 2 by 2, based on the idea that there were no better experts relevant to the issues than the victims themselves, it likewise resulted from the High Commissioner for Peace's emphasis on the need to increase attention to victims in the process.

It is also true that the victims' visits were intended to breathe an air of legitimacy into the negotiations, which were being harshly questioned in Colombia at the time. If the victims, in their diversity, told the country that they were in favour of peace and reconciliation – symbolised in the very act of accepting to travel to Cuba to meet their victimisers – this would undoubtedly provide much needed oxygen to the peace talks. The negotiating parties (but especially the government) also believed that the exercise could help improve the internal dynamics of the talks, to the extent that it could encourage the victims to challenge their victimisers so strongly that it would force them to acknowledge their responsibility, thus eliminating the moral and emotional resistance that was impeding agreements on the issue.

---

[5] See, e.g., *Conflicto en Contexto* by José Obdulio Espejo Muñoz, published on 20 November 2017 in *El Espectador*, in which the author, after celebrating the partnership between the military and Javeriana University in producing works that put the war in context, disqualifies the work of the Historical Memory Centre as a kind of 'denial' in reverse, which, according to him, blames the state for everything.

However, confronting the victims meant, for both parties, exposing themselves to enormous risk. It was an experiment with uncertain results that could undermine, rather than increase, the legitimacy of the negotiations; and could even end the talks as such. If the victims collapsed emotionally in the presence of their victimisers or didn't appear willing to forgive and reconcile, the scandal, if leaked to the media, would deliver a deadly blow to the process. Consequently, the makeup of the victims' delegations had to be carefully managed, and the meeting between the negotiating parties and the victims' delegations had to take place under conditions of total isolation and confidentiality. The media should only witness what the negotiating parties and the visit organisers permitted – which, in the end, consisted of the staging of an opening ceremony that lasted until the victims crossed the threshold of the meeting venue.

The authors, Freeman and Orozco, arrived for the first time in Havana in August 2014, just as the first victims' visit was being planned. The atmosphere was already tense and the issue all-consuming. At an early meeting, the parties were anxiously awaiting the provisional list of participants comprising the first delegation of victims who would visit Havana. When the list was sent to the parties, the government team met at the residence of the Colombian ambassador, Gustavo Bell, to discuss the matter. It was said that the FARC delegation was dissatisfied with the first list of victims selected by the organisers, perceiving it as highly biased against them. It was also said that among the organisers there were strong differences of opinion on the criteria for assembling the list and the persons that should be included.

The relations between the visit organisers and the negotiating parties were far from easy. It was said that the organisers had been emphatic in demanding that the first visit, scheduled for 16 August 2014, not be postponed for any reason, because that would send the dangerous message that there were serious problems in Havana. Meanwhile, Colombia's High Commissioner for Peace, Sergio Jaramillo, read and reviewed again and again the names and biographies of the twelve selected victims and of the three substitutes, seeking to make sure that they had made a flawless and balanced choice.

Balancing the number of victims from each side wasn't easy because the number of victims classified as victims of state crimes depended on the classification of many victims of paramilitary crimes. Also, among the victims were some who, though they had been victimised by the FARC, were known to have deep resentment against the state for failing in its duty to protect them, and it was not known to whom they were finally going to direct their main reproaches. The head of the government delegation, Humberto De La Calle, examined the list at one point and said there were serious cases against all sides and that the whole picture was representative of the complexity of the horror. But he and others remained concerned because the mere fact that certain victims were included and their names published would lead to toxic speculation in Colombia. Most concerning of all was the case of the sister of Erika Bautista, an M-19 guerrilla fighter, disappeared during the counterassault on the Palace of Justice in 1985. Although it was the only old case in a list of comparably more recent victims, the tragedy of the Palace of Justice was an open national wound and source of bitter controversy. Yet another victim whose presence arose concern was one of the 'mothers of Soacha', whose mentally disabled son had been among the 'false positives' (murders of civilians by state agents that were falsely presented as rebel crimes in order to inflate war figures).

Beyond the list of names, the government delegation also worried about how it should respond if the FARC were to behave badly with the victims, a worry that played out unexpectedly on the days prior to the 16 August 2014 visit by the first delegation of victims. For one, the FARC wanted the negotiating parties to manage the protocol and the visits themselves, and were against having psychosocial counselling for the victims' delegation. However, the government insisted successfully on the need for third-party organisation of the visit, and said that without psychosocial counselling there would be no visit. In the end, it was apparently agreed that Cuban psychologists would provide the necessary support to the victims.

Two days before the victims arrived in Havana, an informal grouping from each negotiating team came to inspect the site where the official hearing with the victims would take place. The conference hall was large and rectangular, and could be divided by sliding walls into smaller spaces depending on the needs of the event. The hall had broad windows on one side, overlooking a landscape with large trees, and on the other a set of doors leading to the bathrooms. It was located in a corner of El Laguito, a short walking distance from the houses where the government and FARC delegations lived. During the visit, the Cuban guides proudly explained that the site was visited frequently by President Castro and, for security reasons, nobody had photographic records.

Yet, what was foreseen as a merely informal, operational visit to the conference hall site, turned into a broader discussion about some issues that would have to be agreed by the parties. It began when Marcos Calarcá of the FARC said that his delegation wanted to send representatives to the airport to receive the victims and that he understood that greeting them was in itself a gesture of reconciliation. The government delegation was taken by surprise with this proposal. It wanted the first encounter with the victims to occur at the ceremony itself, proposing that everything should begin with the two delegations standing, as a sign of respect, as the victims entered the ceremony's premises. But Calarcá was aggrieved; he complained that the government was trying to deter his side from engaging the victims, treating the FARC as though they were 'monsters' who had to be kept at a distance from the visitors. In the end, the controversy was resolved by having members of both sides go to the airport to greet the victims.

For their part, the Cubans meticulously explained various planning measures in the course of the site visit. For example, they informed the FARC and the government that they could guarantee there would be no journalists inside the nearby hotel where the victims stayed, but that they could not prevent journalists from hovering at a certain distance, noting that completely driving them away could come at a high political cost. Then, in the middle of the inspection of the venue, the head of security for the Cuban delegation asked, 'And what do I do if a victim suddenly comes across his victimiser?' He was the only one in that tense morning who used the word 'victimiser', and the word landed with a thud. Fortunately, Calarcá wasn't in the room.

Members of the government delegation, meanwhile, addressed concerns about medical care. They expressed the view that it was unlikely that the victims would collapse emotionally or physically, since those selected for the first visit were used to the spotlight, having just participated in the regional and national victims' forums that preceded the negotiations on Point 5. It was also emphasised and agreed that the visit should take place in a ritual atmosphere of great solemnity. Later, at a government team meeting at Ambassador Bell's house, the point was reinforced. There was a kind of tacit consensus in the team that they should address the victims by saying things such as 'we are here not to speak but to listen', 'the government and the state have accepted their responsibilities and that is why President Santos has asked for forgiveness on several occasions', and 'your story and the pain you have endured are the reason why we must stop this war'.

When the victims arrived at the airport in Havana, the joint reception committee from the government and the FARC was there to greet them. The government delegation's María Paulina Riveros mentioned that, while they were waiting for the visitors, Calarcá had said to her that he was nervous. Thus, despite the fact that he had been offended because the representatives of the government treated the victims as if they were made of porcelain, implying that the FARC was a monster whose mere sight might break them, the truth is that he was scared (and rightly so) because the experience of a direct encounter with the victims was a leap into the morally unknown and emotionally unpredictable. In that respect, the victims' visit was comparatively less nerve-wracking for the government delegation. After all, with the exception of General Mora and partly of General Naranjo, the members of its delegation hadn't been directly involved in the war. By contrast, the FARC delegation was made up of much of the guerrillas' military command.

According to Riveros, no unpleasant incidents occurred at the airport. She reported that Constanza Turbay, whose family members had been murdered by the FARC, embraced Calarcá.

The Visit and the Ceremony

As planned, on the morning of Saturday 16 August 2014, in an atmosphere charged with anticipation, the victims entered the hearing venue in a procession. The room was very elegant and soberly arranged with bouquets of flowers. The negotiating parties, who waited much like guests for a surprise party, stood simultaneously when they saw the twelve victims appear, and welcomed them with a round of applause.

Following the instructions of their companions and according to a strict protocol, the victims sat one by one in the seats that were assigned to them on a long table occupying one of the sides of the room. Another, equally long table had been occupied in advance by the representatives of the institutions managing the event. Monsignor Castro officiated as moderator and was accompanied by Alejo Vargas of the National University, Fabricio Hochshild of the UN, and representatives from the guarantor and accompanying countries. The remaining sides of the ceremonial rectangle were occupied by the negotiating parties: first the heads of the delegations, then the rest of the plenipotentiaries and behind, in a second row, the advisers and the rest of the delegations. By design, the government and the FARC delegations were separated, facing each other, while the victims' delegation sat on one side and the moderators and witnesses on the other, closing the ritual space and serving as a 'bridge'.

In a gesture suggested spontaneously by Monsignor Castro, there was an opening minute of silence after which all the attendees held hands. Thereafter, the first to speak was Hochshild; his speech, very short, was one of gratitude for all, but especially for the victims and for their commitment. Vargas, who spoke second, said that 'the victims have set for us a great example'. Afterwards, Humberto De La Calle, head of the government delegation, and Iván Márquez, head of the FARC delegation, made their own opening remarks. When the victims were given the floor, it followed a precise sequence that alternated victims of state and paramilitary crimes, and victims of guerrilla crimes. One by one, all the victims spoke. Their interventions, undoubtedly well prepared in advance, mixed textual reading and spoken remarks, personal testimony and the representation of the various categories of violations: forced disappearances, displacements, massacres, extrajudicial executions, kidnappings, sexual violence, and more. It was a three-hour deluge of almost uninterrupted tales of pain and blood – which fell like a dark and acid rain, barely tempered by the diagnoses and recommendations to which it gave rise.

In the very incomplete personal notes taken by Professor Orozco, one could read about the following elements from De La Calle's opening speech: '... We believe that this meeting must serve as a turning point ... The conflict has been devastating, but that won't keep us from stopping it ... We must guarantee non-recurrence ... We think of the victims of yesterday and of tomorrow ... We are not here to negotiate away the rights of the victims ... We want to listen to your stories and your proposals ... This is not a formal hearing; we want something more human ... We reiterate our willingness to assume the responsibilities that correspond to us'.

In relation to Márquez's opening speech, Orozco's personal notes begin with a comment on how the head of the FARC recognised the victims present, one by one, by their own names. It was a personal and respectful greeting, like a host who opens the door when his guests arrive. His ensuing phrases retained the same spirit: 'We feel the pulse of your pain ... Thank you for being present ... Thank you for being protagonists of reconciliation'. Yet, the guerrilla commander's speech at moments became a formalistic discourse ('we salute you as subjects of rights') or veered into the ideological construction of the FARC as a representative of the victims of state crimes, and of themselves as victims. Orozco's unofficial notes include messages such as the following: 'We greet you as part of a society subject to intolerable segregation and that calls for justice as a basis for reconciliation ... We have not come to exchange impunities ... The war was imposed on us by exclusion ... After the Caguán talks came the "Authoritarian Spell", an expression coined by the Colombian Commission of Jurists in a report about the government of Álvaro Uribe ... We regret that the press wants to blame us, and we praise President Santos for recognising that everyone should assume their own responsibilities ... We have exercised the right of rebellion ... We are recognised as subjects of a command structure, regulated by the law of armed conflicts ... There must be a political act of contrition that proclaims "never again" ... We want humanisation with a partial agreement, we want a bilateral ceasefire and we want the truth ... You [the victims] are a beacon to guide us all, and we recognise you without caveats ... True reparation is peace with justice, democracy and sovereignty. Peace will prevail in Colombia'.

The first of the victims to speak was José Antequera, son of the murdered leftist leader of the same name. Monsignor Castro gave him the floor after saying that we were witnessing a 'dialogue of hearts' and after describing the victims as 'survivors'. Professor Orozco's incomplete notes suggest that Antequera's was a very articulate speech, perhaps the most ideologically consistent and with the greatest strategic projection of all those heard in that long day of tales of horror interspersed with accusations, recommendations, and urgent calls for peace. Orozco's unofficial notes record Antequera saying, 'I want my story to serve peace and not war ... This is not a battle of legitimacy; the military and the insurgents are not victims ... The victims have a responsibility in reconciliation ... I represent the victims of state crimes ... State crimes started the war ... We ask that the state accept that the genocide of the Patriotic Union was the beginning of the degradation of the war ... It was not a matter of a few rotten apples'. Antequera proceeded to present a book on the Patriotic Union stating, among other things, that the Historical Memory Centre's *Basta Ya* report was not sufficiently comprehensive and that is why a truth commission was needed. In his closing remarks, echoing his introduction, Antequera spoke directly to the FARC, saying, 'We want the lives of Antequera and others to be an argument for peace and not war ... To recognise me is to recognise the existence of state crimes'.

Afterwards, Monsignor Castro gave the floor to Ángela María Giraldo, sister of politician Francisco Javier Giraldo, who was kidnapped and murdered by the FARC. The tone of her speech was very different from Antequera's. It was more reticent and showed more hesitation in assigning responsibilities. Although it was clear to her that direct responsibility for the crime fell on the guerrillas, her resentment against the government that had ordered the rescue of her kidnapped brother, and thus precipitated his murder, was evident. Giraldo's first words, according to Professor Orozco's unofficial notes, were, 'I did not want to come here. I know who killed the deputies. But I made the decision to forgive. The question of the victimiser became secondary ... To classify the victims according to their victimiser is to continue the war. The pain is the same for all victims. My task is to raise awareness that a victim is a victim ... Forgiveness is an act of love with oneself and with others ... My brother wrote from his captivity: "I have to forgive". I can't fail to live up to that legacy'. Addressing the FARC directly, she asked them to tell where the anti-personnel mines were located, stating that she agreed with their participation in politics, but only if they asked for forgiveness for their crimes; failing which, all would have been in vain.

After the interventions of the other ten victims concluded, the heads of the negotiating teams offered thanks and attempted to summarise some of the diagnoses and recommendations made. They said that they would utilise them as a 'guide' for the future negotiations on Point 5, which was just beginning. The guarantor countries then invited everyone to an impressive lunch inside the protocol hall. At the many tables arranged for the purpose, members of both delegations, victims of all backgrounds, organisers, hosts, and guarantor countries sat and dined together. It was an important occasion for the exchange of impressions and for building relationships.

In retrospect, the hearings as a whole constituted a unique space in which the victims of the Colombian war were able to speak one by one with their own voices, express their pain, and scold the parties at the negotiating table for unforgivable crimes. Humberto De La Calle, a sensitive and empathetic man, able to enjoy the moral comfort of knowing that he could not be personally accused of being anyone's victimiser, limited himself to stating his willingness to listen and to assume a measure of responsibility on behalf of the state. By contrast, Iván Márquez, a very ideological guerrilla commander directly involved in the war, offered long, complex, and morally tortured interventions, struggling between recognition and denial, between listening and issuing accusatory tirades. Much more than De La Calle, he made use of expressions that interspersed the humble willingness to listen and acknowledge, with the ideological construction of the FARC as victims, recalling historical grievances that ostensibly justify their own actions during the armed confrontation.

As for the victims, it must be said that they were, in all cases, committed to seeking a political solution to the conflict and achieving a negotiated peace. This was the premise behind their desire to participate and probably also part of the selection criteria. Indeed, the victims selected to speak at future visits expressed the same underlying commitment. For example, General Mendieta had been kidnapped by the FARC and held in the jungle, under miserable conditions, for more than a decade. In his testimony, he refrained from openly speaking against the Havana talks despite his strong proximity to ACORE (the Association of Retired Members of the Armed Forces), the *Centro Democrático* party and, in general, the leading political opponents of the peace process. Likewise, the sister of Garzón, the great comedian murdered by hired assassins in Bogota, did not challenge the legitimacy of the process or the visits themselves, despite making harsh statements against General Mora, who was part of the government delegation in Havana. On the contrary, these and other victims often used the moral authority vested upon them to demand from the parties that under no circumstance should they abandon the talks without a final agreement. The victims who were outright enemies of the peace process simply didn't attend or were not invited.

In conjunction, the victims of state and paramilitary crimes on the one hand, and the victims of FARC and ELN crimes on the other, always represented an accusatory finger by their very presence and stories of pain. Nonetheless, the differences between them were clear. As noted, these derived, at least in part, from the more organised and ideological character of the former compared to the latter, who remained more emotional, more scattered, and less homogenous in their denunciations and proposals. Nevertheless, as several members of the government delegation observed, some of the victims of FARC crimes preferred to reproach the state for minor sins and treat it as the universal depositary of the responsibilities derived from the armed conflict, rather than directing their blame at the FARC. This may have been influenced by the victims' fear of directly confronting their rebel victimisers and their understanding of the state as the ultimate legal guarantor of the rights of all.

The Government Delegation's Assessment of the First Visit

On the day after the first victims' hearing, a meeting took place at the residence of Ambassador Bell to evaluate the experience and to correct errors for the remaining four visits and hearings. One team member mentioned that there had been a lot of concern by the UN when one of the victims had made unexpected statements to the media. It was said by another that Antequera had set a high bar with the quality of his testimony, while someone else noted that the victims had met the night before the encounter and had expressed their desire to spend more time together. It was also noted that the Church had brought a psychologist to accompany the victims during the flight.

In terms of the content of the testimonies, one team member said that she had liked very much that a few of the victims had said 'I do not forgive', because it showed that there was 'a long way to go' and it debunked the simplistic idea of 'reconciliation express'. Another one of those present said that it was harmful for the organisers to treat the victims as 'heroes' because to lionise them was to provoke a sector of public opinion that despised such notions. There were also some strongly held opinions about the tendency by some victims to use the idea of Colombia as a 'criminal state' as the starting point of everything.

Above all, however, there were reflections on the difference between the inward and outward impact of such a closed experience. Facing inward, there was criticism of the FARC's self-interested claim that the state should bear ultimate responsibility for the 'errors' committed by all sides. More positively, it was observed that 'nobody had ever told the FARC what they were told today' and that in any case the victims' visits were not determinative of any attributions of individual criminal responsibility. As for the outward impact of the first visit, it was said that the correct message had been sent and that 'the victims had destroyed the argument of their invisibility'. It was also noted that 'we have to look at the selection carefully' for the planned future visits, and that 'we can delegate the task, but we must supervise it'. As far as possible, it was said, we should aim for visits to take place on the penultimate day of the eleven-day negotiation cycles and never on the first, in order to start each cycle with a clear focus on the primary task of negotiation.

The Remainder of the Visits

In total, sixty victims went to Havana over the course of five separate visits. Each encounter followed broadly similar patterns; however, the issue of the selection of each small sample of victims – conducted by the Church, the UN, and the National University – remained highly controversial, both in Havana and in Bogota. For example, on the fourth visit, which took place on 2 November 2014, the internal battle over the balanced representation of victims of state versus FARC crimes spilled over to the meeting itself. After the government's Humberto De La Calle greeted the victims as 'citizens with rights' and told them that they were the 'moral anchor' of the process and would be heard 'with devotion and without arguing', the FARC's Iván Márquez lashed out against the imbalanced representation of victims. Professor Orozco's unofficial notes include the following utterances: 'The state did not grant permission for the imprisoned rebel [Alonso] to come. There is an empty chair that stands as a monument to exclusion. The living conditions for political prisoners are deplorable'. In addition, Márquez denounced several of the crimes attributed to the state that were taking place at that time in Colombia against trade unionists, political activists, and human rights defenders. He also called on the state 'to stop refusing to acknowledge the crime of the Patriotic Union'.

The condition of political prisoners was an especially important issue for the FARC. Symbolically, its denunciation was a way for the commanders who were negotiating in Havana to affirm the victimhood of their side and send their troops a message of solidarity; practically, the denunciation was meant to try levelling the moral playing field with the state. Reporting the mistreatment of prisoners of war in state prisons was a *tu quoque* (you also) argument to try to shake off the unbearable weight of the denunciations that fell like an endless avalanche on the FARC itself, for the prisoners of war and kidnapped civilian hostages they held under their power for many years. This was one of the main reasons for the guerrillas' low moral and political reputation with the public.

But the most striking difference in this fourth hearing in Havana was undoubtedly that the sample included people who, over a long and winding history, had sequentially occupied the roles of victim and victimiser, and in relation to all manner of armed actors. If other samples had shown the horrors of war, this one also showed its absurdity and pointlessness. The accounts of several of those who spoke were an accusation against everyone at once, and against the war itself. Their unusual biographies made them unwitting figures of the 'grey zone'.

Politically speaking, the selection of the victim participants for each visit was the only aspect of the ritual that took place under the close surveillance of the media and political parties. It was always subject to morose scrutiny and was the object of many ill-intentioned challenges by those who opposed the negotiation. Measuring imbalances in the representation of victims became a morbid game for some. As such, the three organisers sought to make sure that the samples always reflected a balance of regional origins, categories of crimes, organisations, and forms of criminal victimisation. Their intention was to offer an aggregate picture of the horror, symbolising its complexity, but also the temporal and geographical extension of the humanitarian dramas caused by the war. Yet, the public reception of this message depended on many factors beyond their control. The country was entrenched in its polarities. In this respect, it is possible that the effect of the victims' encounters was more positive facing inward than outward.

Did the victims, with their powerful stories and accusations, manage to take the negotiating parties out of their ideological comfort zones? With regard to the guerrilla elites, who saw themselves as social and political fighters and as military enemies, but not as victimisers, perhaps we should say that the experience demonstrated the obvious: that fracturing and transforming one's identity is a very difficult personal and group process, full of ups and downs, and with very uncertain outcomes. Professor Orozco recalls that, during a break at one of the victim hearings, he came across two members of the FARC delegation with their backs to him at the urinals, talking about the ceremony that was taking place and remarking on 'the terrible stories we are hearing'. Orozco recalls that he left the bathroom convinced that the visits were in fact fulfilling the function of softening the hearts of the warriors and leading them to recognise themselves, at least in part, as victimisers, by acknowledging their victims.

The next day, however, the same people who had seemed so moved by the stories they heard were once again donning the moral and emotional armour of the victim and the revolutionary fighter. In that sense, it was both naive and awkward that some of the plenipotentiaries on the government team devoted themselves for such a long time to the task of classifying the individual members of their FARC counterparts according to their current place in the stages of mourning the loss of their identity. It was thought, above all, that once that 'mourning work' was done, which was thought to follow an implausibly linear sequence, the members of the guerrilla elite would be willing to present themselves as persons bearing heavy responsibility for war crimes, and prepared to go to jail. It was just a matter of patience, and therefore, it was necessary that the negotiation of Point 5 take the time needed.

However, the reality is that warriors who allow themselves to be challenged by victims incur high emotional and moral costs. To grasp their size, it suffices to observe how, in the kind of Judeo-Christian moral culture hegemonic in the West – mediated by the secularising discourses of modernity – acknowledging responsibility usually requires an exercise in 'humiliation'. As shown in the Catholic practice of confession, those who acknowledge their sin must also repent under the eyes of God or their confessor, and, in so doing, denigrate themselves. Only after the sinner self-flagellates, crawls, and denies his own identity has he accumulated the required merits to be forgiven. That is why Martha Nussbaum interprets the sacrament of confession, in Nietzschean code, as not merely an exercise of 'transactional forgiveness' but also, and above all, as a modality for satisfying the expectation of 'retribution'.[6] As such, it should come as no surprise that in today's Colombia, it is mostly the ordinary people living in big cities (who have been less directly affected by the war) and not the direct victims of political violence (who live mostly in the countryside), who want the FARC to rot in prisons. It is they who demand that the FARC at least show their repentance through humiliation.

Although it was common for members of both delegations, and the participants in general, to tell each other that after listening to the victims they had been transformed, it is difficult to gauge the depth of that feeling or the sincerity of the statements. Even if we assume that the stories told by the victims touched the hearts of those who heard them, it is important to bear in mind that affirming in front of others that listening to the victims 'transformed us' merely proves our quality as moral subjects; it is hard to resist the temptation to make such affirmations. To the extent that almost everyone utters the statement, it creates the impression that the visits were a

---

[6] Martha Nussbaum, *Anger and Forgiveness: Resentment, Generosity, Justice* (New York: Oxford University Press, 2016), 72–74.

turning point in the dynamics of the negotiation. However, this may turn out to be an exaggeration.

The First Transitional Justice Strategy Meeting at Ambassador Bell's House

During the same eleven-day cycle when the first victims' visit occurred, an important internal meeting of the government team took place at Ambassador Bell's house. This meeting had a different register: more abstract, general, and strategic. The question by which High Commissioner Jaramillo opened the discussion was 'how should we frame the discussion on Point 5'? He started from the fact that the ten principles on victims, already agreed between the negotiating parties in June 2014, should be the guiding criteria for the discussions that were to take place during the months to come. But among the big questions that was raised at the time by several of the attendees was, 'what definition of victims should guide the position of the government delegation in the discussions at the negotiating table'?

Someone recalled that the FARC spoke of victims of 'the economic system' and that it should be established from the outset that there would be no 'victims' of the economic model. It was remarked by another that the issue of economic rights had already been addressed in Points 1 (rural reform) and 2 (political participation) and that it was now time to address the issue of the rights of victims to truth, justice, reparation, and the guarantee of non-recurrence. It was likewise identified as necessary for the delegation to find a way for the FARC to recognise its responsibilities in the armed conflict, noting that a conditionality system should be devised to justify the benefits that would have to be granted to the armed actors on all sides of the conflict.

Another member of the delegation asked, 'are we interested in a culture of victimisation, or rather a culture of overcoming the condition of victim'?, and 'what does it mean for the victims to be at the centre of the agreement'? He said that he did not like the term 'survivors' because he thought it implied a 'mystical' construction. He said that the expression 'citizens' seemed better when referring to the victims, and he worried that the FARC might be attracted to saying that they themselves were 'victim-survivors'. Another member focused on a broader issue: war itself. He believed we should frame the discussion on victims by saying that we were not in Havana to make peace but to end the conflict. Colombian society, he said, was caught in the middle of a confrontation between the state and the FARC, giving rise to victimisation at the hands of each. He also said that we should not forget that it was the Armed Forces that prevented the FARC from taking power in Colombia, arguing that the common standard of IHL was the right one to apply under any accountability formula, notwithstanding the risk of equating actions by the illegal guerrillas with those of a democratically controlled military that had defended the state.

Since talking about victims involves talking about who victimised them, the discussion also turned to the importance of consulting directly with the military and police forces in Bogota about their definition of victims. De La Calle said that it was necessary to 'weave together' a differentiated treatment for the guerrillas and the military, and agreed on the importance of active consultations in Bogota, understanding that the Ministry of Defence had its own ideas and initiatives. This debate on the need to find a solution that could satisfy all parties led, eventually, to the creation of a technical commission in Bogota to discuss truth, justice, and reparation with the Ministry of Defence, the National Police, the different security forces, and other state agencies. While the Santos government reiterated in speeches that negotiating reforms of the state's military was a 'red line' that wouldn't be touched in the negotiation, De La Calle and Jaramillo consistently explained the importance of finding a way to include them in the solution of Point 5; failing which, there would simply be no negotiation.

Yet, the ambiguity over the issue of ensuring access to legal benefits for the Armed Forces under the final agreement, without equating them with the FARC, was never fully resolved. During the days after the renegotiated 2016 agreement was announced, the military dramatically distanced itself from the symmetrical spirit of what was negotiated in Havana, favouring a differential treatment for themselves far superior to that of the FARC. Out of the blue, they appeared in Congress, with a surprise series of provisions that held them less responsible than the FARC, and that were justified in virtue of the military's special status.

The Historical Commission on the Causes of the Conflict and Its Victims

States like Colombia have followed sixteenth- and seventeenth-century patterns of development similar to those of midsized European nation-states. Georges Duby suggests that in these states, it is in history that we discover the ideological differences that separate political parties in future times of peace and war.[7] In Havana, this intuition was confirmed when the ideological differences that formed a chasm between the government and the FARC

---

[7] Georges Duby, 'Ideologies in Social History', in *Constructing the Past: Essays in Historical Methodology*, ed. Jacques Le Goff and Pierre Nora (Cambridge: Cambridge University Press, 1985), 151–165.

materialised as a debate about the past, with its implications for the present and the future.

During the first victims' visit to Havana, in August 2014, it was announced that the government and the FARC had reached an agreement on the creation of an ad hoc Historical Commission to examine the causes of the conflict. During the months before the formal opening of negotiations on Point 5, the FARC had been pressuring the government to allow such a commission to be created, holding it up as a precondition to officially enter the discussion on Point 5. They argued that in Colombia, the opposition represented by the *Centro Democrático* party (and the political right in general) considered them to be mere criminals and attributed to them all the responsibility for the war and for the crimes perpetrated. They said that the media, serving as an instrument of the forces in power, had been broadly manipulated to construct the image of guerrillas as nothing but drug traffickers and war criminals in the eyes of Colombian society. To the FARC, peace would be possible only if this extreme perception was replaced by one where their cause represented a response to structural and historical injustices, with the recognition that their armed struggle was the continuation of a protracted social conflict rooted in a history of peasant dispossession and exclusion of the political left.

Ultimately, the government delegation found a creative middle ground involving the selection of twelve academic experts for the Commission, of which six would be chosen by each side. The government calculated that even if the FARC appointed commissioners akin to them ideologically, the government could neutralise the effect by its own appointments. It could select individuals of noted academic excellence, with a critical and independent, but pluralist view of the origins of the armed conflict. The final result would therefore be a narrative showing the 'complexity' of the debate on the historical causes of the conflict and of the conflict itself. Also, anticipating the impossibility of agreeing on a single report that would make a common appraisal from the twelve essays, an agreement was reached in which there would be two spokespersons: Víctor Manuel Moncayo would summarise and present the writings of the academics and intellectuals chosen by the FARC, and Eduardo Pizarro would do the same for those chosen by the government. The FARC accepted the formula, making it possible to advance in what really mattered to the government: the negotiation of the different mechanisms of transitional justice that would constitute the binding text of Point 5. Nevertheless, within and across delegations, it took several weeks to negotiate a whole series of practical decisions regarding the functioning of the Historical Commission, including the terms of its mandate, the names of the members, the relationship with the larger negotiation process, the deadlines for the delivery of draft reports, and so on.

Naturally, the names of those selected, once made public, provoked the biggest controversy and debate. For example, at one point the government complained that ANCOL, the news agency linked to the FARC, had made statements that Gustavo Duncan, one of the members selected by the government, was not qualified to serve. The government delegation complained to the FARC that this was unacceptable, pointing out that the exercise would be 'doomed to failure' if such actions persisted. Members of the FARC delegation responded that ANCOL was not a FARC subsidiary and that they had no control over it. They also said that the government blaming them for what ANCOL said, was analogous to the FARC blaming the government for what *El Tiempo* newspaper said. This short and bitter discussion was indicative of the climate surrounding the selection of commissioners; their names were caught in a crossfire of demeaning statements, some from the right and others from the left.

The Historical Commission was formally inaugurated on 21 August 2014 in a small ceremony that took place on the ground floor of Hotel El Palco, very close to the room where the negotiating parties routinely met. The night before the event, there was a small meeting between some members of the government team and its six appointed commissioners. The latter were told that they had full intellectual autonomy but should consider that if their writings 'went too far' and established too broad a historical time frame in their definition of the armed conflict's origins, they would do serious damage to the negotiations that were meant to put an end to the war that had begun with the formal emergence of the FARC as an armed group in the early 1960s. Another member of the government team told the commissioners that they had an enormous responsibility and should have the courage to tell 'the real truth' of what had happened. Yet another noted that the government's hope was that their writings would give an account of the 'complexity' of the armed conflict, thus laying a constructive foundation for the negotiations on Point 5.

Then came the commissioners' answers. One member expressed concern for their collective safety. Another drew attention to his fear that the Commission would be divided into two antagonistic 'factions' that would give rise to two blocks of incompatible narratives, 'making the Commission a continuation of the war'. Reflecting on this, the government team responded that the most important thing was to avoid having the Commission's work, important though it was, dictate the investigations or findings of the future truth commission that the government intended to negotiate with the FARC. The aggregate of all the essays in the Historical Commission's final report should produce diverse perspectives of the truth, rather than a single causal account of 'the truth with a capital T'.

Professor Orozco took unofficial notes on the speeches by the heads of the government and FARC delegations at the Commission's inauguration ceremony. De La Calle, in his inaugural address, began by saying that the points he was about to make on behalf of the government were not at all binding for the Commission. He recalled that an agreement had been reached on the creation of a 'pluralistic' body of experts. He noted that while the FARC wanted the commissioners to build a long-term historical vision of the causes of the conflict, the government instead preferred that the essays concentrate on studying the more immediate factors that had facilitated the emergence and spread of the armed conflict. He likewise said that while the government understood that there were structural conditions that had contributed to violence, this violence was also the expression of 'human decisions' not predestined to become a full-fledged armed conflict. While pointing out that the inclusion of the two spokespersons was 'a tribute to realism', he explained that the government was not seeking 'an official truth' and that the Historical Commission was 'neither a watered-down truth commission nor a court'.

Sergio Jaramillo struck a similar tone. Orozco's unofficial notes record him as stating, among other things, that 'the Commission is not a mere academic exercise but rather one conducted in the midst of a negotiation'; 'adding complexity is in itself a great contribution towards peace'; 'the conflict that the text refers to is the military conflict that arose with the FARC, and this is the one we want to end – the rest is simply context'; 'no fresh investigation is requested, just a forty-page essay'; 'the issue of truth is going to be central but cannot predetermine the course of the negotiations or the work of the future truth commission'.

Then came Iván Márquez and the FARC delegation. According to Orozco's loose notes, he said things such as 'history is an organic process, and the past is inseparable from the present'; 'there is a political opposition in Colombia stubbornly seeking the continuation of the war and fixated on demanding surrender, seeking to construe history as a story of victors'; 'it is not true that we waged a war against society or that we are a victimising machine'; 'there is ample evidence of the structural causes that gave rise to the armed uprising, which include the ideology of anti-communism and the national security doctrine'; 'we must ask why the forces of the political left were mostly exterminated, and why there was an alliance formed with paramilitaries to fight an internal enemy'; 'there is asymmetry in the confrontation, but we are going to assume our responsibilities'; 'we want the facts to be elucidated and that is why we understand that this work and that of the truth commission are part of a broader whole'.

As other members of the delegations took the floor, they tried, in their own way, to instruct the commissioners to do their job well. The government representatives at the table spoke, in general terms, of subsidiary truths, of decision-making and individual responsibilities, and of ruptures and discontinuities in the history of the guerrillas. They spoke of medium- and short-term conditions for the initiation and spread of an armed confrontation that began in the 1960s, and of the importance of building a joint story that would account for this complexity. The FARC representatives, by contrast, spoke of a truth written in capital letters that was being hidden by the regime, and of manipulation of public opinion with respect to this truth. They talked of structural continuities that made the FARC the expression of long-lasting social and political problems, and of the remote causes of a violent social conflict of which the FARC were, in their account, merely an expression.

Another key dividing line between the negotiating teams concerned the question of whether the final report of the Historical Commission would be binding on the parties or on the future truth commission. The government was adamantly opposed to the idea. It insisted that historical truth should serve only to illuminate the contextual factors about the armed conflict. In contrast, the FARC insisted that the report be binding. Ultimately, the government position won out.

The Commission's essays were supposed to be structured following a common thematic index. They would deal with the historical causes of the conflict, as demanded by the FARC, but also with the story of its spread, as demanded by the government. In terms of academic excellence, however, the final results were very uneven and were presented a couple of months late. Apparently the six commissioners appointed by the government were very independent-minded and could hardly even meet and discuss among themselves. The six commissioners appointed by the FARC, by contrast, were said to share epistemological and ideological postulates that allowed them to work together, distributing tasks to produce, if not a single story, at least a set of congruent ones. However, Víctor Moncayo and Eduardo Pizarro, the two chosen spokespersons for each 'side', were unable to communicate with each other to attempt shared reflections and appraisals.

In the government's interpretation, the final report of the Historical Commission assisted in showing the complexity of the armed conflict, related to both its causes and its course, whereas the FARC interpreted it as having helped to highlight that the armed conflict had deep historical roots, while purportedly showing the greater misconduct of 'the regime and its imperialist supporters'. The strong coherence between explanatory accounts that emanated from the FARC's six appointed commissioners, combined with some elements of social and political criticism contributed by the government's commissioners, was seen by the FARC as sufficient to prove that the truth they proclaimed had been confirmed. Meanwhile, the government team found itself awkwardly having to argue, in a more liberal and less dogmatic way, that the essays, in their plurality and diversity, had demonstrated the complexity of things.

In retrospect, the experiment of the Historical Commission can be described as the expression of a radical disagreement. A deep epistemological, theoretical, and ideological schism underlay the negotiating parties' visions of history and war. This predetermined how the commissioners' essays would be interpreted by each side, precluding the possibility of achieving a minimally shared narrative. The handpicked choice of commissioners was itself the reflection of a dispute that had been evident since the negotiated text of Point 1 (rural reform) in early 2013.

With the support of its commissioners' essays, the FARC hoped to be able to build a favourable narrative of jus ad bellum, that is, a proof of just cause for the recourse to violence. It was to be oriented toward material and political causes (such as land dispossession and political exclusion) that had underpinned their exercise of the right of rebellion, and toward the claim that this had been a defensive war against an aggressor state that fought dirty. The FARC seemed to imagine that any resulting judgements of responsibility against them became unnecessary, or at least more lenient, than they would otherwise have been in terms of jus in bello. In other words, the identification of the FARC as examples and representatives of the victims of historical grievances was a central element of their dignity as combatants and rebel-revolutionaries.

By contrast, relying on the writings of the other six commissioners, the government hoped to be able to build a narrative of jus in bello, focused on the crimes perpetrated by both parties inside the armed conflict, with IHL as the essential legal framework. It wanted to maintain the separation of jus ad bellum and jus in bello, following the tradition of European public law prior to the Nuremberg trials. As far as the government was concerned, matters associated with the material causes of the war had already been sufficiently addressed under Points 1 (rural reform) and 2 (political participation) of the negotiation agenda. As such, by the time the discussions on Point 5 arrived, the government's interest was in focusing on the development of transitional justice mechanisms which would serve to pass judgement, under the standards of IHL, on the degraded armed conflict that had taken place, without contaminating the process with considerations of jus ad bellum.

Yet, it would be a mistake to conclude that the mechanism of the Historical Commission was a failure merely because an epistemological, theoretical, ideological, and philosophical-legal dialogue between the negotiating parties proved impossible. To the contrary, by separating out and containing the discussion of the war's root causes under a separate process, the creation of the Commission made it possible for the bogged-down negotiations on Point 5 to move forward. This was fundamental to the very survival of the negotiation. The Commission process also demonstrated, in all its dimensions, the kind of underlying disagreements that Colombia will have to face as part of any post-conflict future. Indeed, it would have been naive and even unfair to expect that, in the midst of the armed conflict, or indeed in the early post-conflict phase, the explanatory accounts offered by the commissioners could have given rise to a shared foundational truth and conciliatory memory.

Further Evolutions in the Dialectic of Victim and Victimiser

In between visits to Havana by the various groups of victims, there was time for the government and FARC delegations to mingle and develop work routines in the relative seclusion of Cuba and El Laguito. The discussions on substantive issues took place in the plenary sessions, but particularly in the drafting committee. There, how one vision regarding sensitive matters unfolded and finally prevailed over another ended up depending on the ability and efficiency in writing sentences and adding or changing periods or commas here and there. While the plenary sessions were led by the heads of the delegations, Humberto De La Calle and Iván Márquez, the drafting committee was headed by Sergio Jaramillo and Jesús Santrich, both of them formidable, astute, and attentive grammarians. A central role was also played in those dizzying, rhetorical, and grammatical tasks by those who managed the written text, that is, Elena Ambrosi, Santrich himself, and Lucas Carvajal, as assistant to the latter. Any lapse in attention or concentration could have dire consequences that would be difficult to rectify later.

In general, the party that best managed to represent itself predominantly as a victim and/or representative for victims (and conversely to represent its negotiating counterpart predominantly as victimiser) was the one able to set the starting positions and delineate the playing field. Thereafter, the parties tried to kick the ball of discussion into the net of a single text and a shared narrative. Throughout, the vertical dialectic of victimiser and victim outweighed the horizontal dialectic of enemies within a common conflict.

The First Big FARC Proposal: 'Towards a New Colombia without Victims'

Within the government team it was customary to point out that the excessively bombastic, ideological, and rhetorical texts of the FARC rarely formed part of the written agreements. More austere texts written by the government, consistent with the canonical language of human rights, were usually the cornerstone around which the narrative of the agreement under construction was finally woven (after the guerrillas had folded). It is therefore striking that the FARC supplied the discussions of Point 5 with a well-organised debut by means of an elaborate proposal that they progressively made public under the title 'Towards a New Colombia without Victims', first published in *Liberación* on 11 September 2014. It was around that same time that the FARC presented their initial vision of Point 5 inside the Havana talks, never ceasing to refer back to their proposal as the great synthesis of their diagnosis and demands.

Based on the FARC's vision for realising the ten principles on victims that had been agreed by the parties in June 2014 (hereafter the 'Decalogue'), their proposal was meant to steer and control the negotiations that were to come. Their document reiterated that the parties had not come to Havana to 'exchange impunity', yet very little was said about criminal justice. Instead, the emphasis was placed on truth, reparations, and guarantees of non-recurrence. The document did, however, state that if there was going to be justice it would have to be applied to everyone, including state agents and third parties, who in one way or another were responsible for crimes perpetrated in the course of the armed confrontation.

There was not much talk of criminal justice by the FARC because their objective was, above all, to assign a new meaning to the term 'justice' in the context of the transition. In their communiqués and public statements, the FARC purported to be seeking to leave behind an 'archaic' vision of justice, based on retribution and revenge, to open the way to a modern, reparative, and restorative vision of justice – more in line, in their view, with the needs and rights of victims. The distance between the government and the FARC on this issue was enormous, because the government had a very different expectation and was more attentive to the demands of both Colombian society and the international community. Nevertheless, both the government and the FARC defended alternative visions of justice and impunity that could, at least partially, transcend mere retribution.

To get an idea of the FARC's initial position and the degree of ideological distance from the government view at the time, it is useful briefly to reconstruct the guerrillas' extensive inaugural document, following the order of its sections. To begin, the document lays out their moral, political, and identity cards. In a self-congratulatory manner, the text emphasises the historic and admirable choice reflected in the negotiating parties' 2012 General Agreement to give centrality to the issue of victims. But immediately thereafter, almost as if the first sentence had never been written – and after endorsing the UN's definition of victims – the text goes on to characterise the FARC as victims and as representatives of the universal victim which, in their view, is a party that has been the object of state crimes. A footnote argues that their diagnosis is supported by the *Noche y Niebla* database, created by the Colombian group CINEP; by reports from the Office of the UN High Commissioner for Human Rights; and by the proposals made at the national victims' forums. The document then goes on to say (excluding the footnotes),

> The FARC-EP adopt the clear definition of victims established by the United Nations as our own, while simultaneously showing our criteria and point of view on the origin of the armed conflict, its causes and its course, on the internal armed conflict that existed before our constitution as a guerrilla organisation, the character of our organisation arising from the victimisation of the peasant population and the poor, as well as our recognition of the reality of victimisation in Colombia manifested by the most rigorous studies and reliable statistics, elaborated by independent academic organisations and international institutions, even if we may partially disagree with them ... We recognise in the victims of the armed conflict the active political subject on which the New Colombia must be built, which we hope to enlighten after the arrival of peace with social justice, in a process in which they [the victims] should play a leading role.

The FARC document goes on to lead the charge against Law 1448 of 2011, promulgated by the Santos government and better known as the Victims and Land Restitution Law, which regulates the reparations scheme administered by the government. The guerrillas had previously asserted the existence of a social and armed conflict whose origins can be traced back to the 1930s, in which the FARC are merely another manifestation, in their capacity as direct victims and representatives of equally victimised social and political sectors. As such, the document argues that Law 1448's selection of 1 January 1985 as the starting date for the determination of the universe of victims that must be repaired is arbitrary. The document advocates that comprehensive reparation should be extended to all the victims, going back decades, including the victims who fought against dispossession and in favour of land restitution under the terms of Law 200 of 1936.

Based on this proposed redefinition of the universe of victims to be repaired, the document then makes a series of recommendations. A particularly striking one – centred on IHL's distinctions between combatants, non-combatants, and the civilian population – is the call to determine who the victims and victimisers were during each period of the long confrontation. But against expectations, the FARC did not argue for the need to elevate the national reparation policy to the level of a distributive-developmental policy within the framework of the state. It would thus seem that they understood that stretching the definition of victimhood and the universe of recognisable victims too much would be unmanageable.

The next section of the document offers a diagnosis and recommendations relevant to Principle 2 of the Decalogue, which concerns 'recognition of responsibility'. This section of the FARC document is the most ideological, defensive, and radical one of all in terms of the deployment of the identity dialectic in its representations of victimiser and victim. It begins by recognising the imperative of 'establishing who the real perpetrators are in this war that was imposed on us'. It then proceeds to denounce the reluctance of the Santos government, as the representative of the Colombian state, to accept responsibility for violations attributed to it by various international and domestic bodies.

Having singled out the state as an unrepentant victimiser, the FARC go on to say that they are willing to recognise their own responsibilities – but only under very limited conditions. Their self-representation as victims in the document, and their very limited willingness to be judged, are so radical that they deserve a longer excerpt (again excluding footnotes).

> The FARC-EP have insisted that ... just as we demand the acknowledgment of responsibilities by the multiple responsible actors, with all the measures and actions that derive from them, we express our willingness to take on ours, always observing the political-military character of our organisation, our purposes and programmatic definitions, our military plans for the seizure of power, our internal norms and relations with the civilian population and, of course, the laws of war and the norms of International Humanitarian Law ...
>
> When some of our military actions during the conflict have produced non-combatant victims, it has never been due to the perpetration of intentional attacks against the civilian population, but instead due to unpredictable situations in some cases and unjustifiable mistakes in others, invariably caused by military operations in a position of tremendous military disadvantage in relation to our adversaries. Because of this, we the FARC-EP do not recognise ourselves as a 'victimising agent', but as persecuted, and in that condition, we have exercised our right to rebellion, recognised in the US Declaration of Independence of 1776, the French Declaration of the Rights of Man and of the Citizen of 1793, and the Universal Declaration of Human

Rights of 1948. A peasant and people's army cannot have the same requirements as the gigantic standing army of a state, even though we have always strived to include in our regulations provisions of strict respect for human rights and IHL and to comply with them.

In the first paragraph, in addition to suggesting that 'what's good for the goose is good for the gander', they spell out the very restrictive criteria under which they are willing to be judged for 'residual' responsibility. The criteria are conveniently derived from the FARC's own strategic plans, statutes, and internal legal procedures. Any mention of criminal justice thus shines by its absence. As for the second paragraph, the FARC appeal to criteria of jus ad bellum to specify that they have acted in the exercise of the 'right to rebellion' proclaimed, inter alia, in the seminal declarations of the US and French revolutions. As such, only 'errors' can be attributed to them, because they recognise themselves not as 'victimising agents' but rather as victims of the asymmetric war of a state against which they justly rose up in arms. Thus, in the recommendations that follow the above excerpts, the FARC demand that the determination of the 'victimising agents' be made based on information from human rights NGOs and entities such as the United Nations, and not based on national governmental sources like the Prosecutor General's office and the judicial police.

The subsequent section of the FARC document looks at the theme of 'satisfaction of the rights of victims', which is Principle 3 of the Decalogue. Here the FARC demand the removal of all existing factual and legal obstacles preventing the full satisfaction of victims' rights. They call upon the state to make funds available and put in place programmes of all kinds to advance this huge undertaking. They go on to remind the government that the people are asking the parties to agree on a bilateral ceasefire, so that the war machine that is still producing victims can stop.

Section 4 of the FARC document, on 'victim participation', discusses rights infringed as a result of serious violations of human rights and humanitarian law. Convinced that they created far fewer victims than the state, the FARC declare their willingness to make victims an additional party in the talks and have them play a formal role in all the eventual transitional justice mechanisms. The document then builds on this in Section 5, characterising truth as a human right of the victims and of society and arguing that this truth applies specifically to criminal practices perpetrated by the state and its paramilitary allies. It then makes a list of state crimes committed since 1936 that must be elucidated, including expatriations and forced disappearances. A demand is also made for elucidation of the responsibility of non-state actors in the war (i.e., private financiers of violence) while denouncing the victimisation of opposition political parties and movements, peasant organisations, trade unions, and so forth. More generally, the section speaks of the importance of establishing an 'extrajudicial' truth, built with broad participation from society, which allows 'the normalisation of coexistence and reconciliation of the different sectors of Colombian society'.

Section 6 of the text deals with reparations and begins by saying that 'the greatest reparation is truth and justice' and that it should be sought not only for direct victims but also for social sectors victimised by premeditated policies and serious omissions of state protection. It redefines justice as comprehensive reparation and restorative justice as redistributive justice, and it declares insufficient, almost insignificant, the reparation work carried out by the Colombian state since 2011. In this regard, the FARC effectively characterise the state as a great siphon through which all the active and passive filth of a complex and degraded war runs. Because of this, they ask for everything under the sun on behalf of the victims, and still regard it as little.

The remaining four sections of the text deal with 'guarantees of protection and safety for the victims' (Principle 7 of the Decalogue), 'guarantees of non-recurrence' (Principle 8), 'reconciliation' (Principle 9), and the 'rights-based approach' (Principle 10). The first urgently restates the need for a bilateral ceasefire or at least a progressive de-escalation of hostilities to stop paramilitarism and the production of victims: a theme that resonates strongly in post-conflict Colombia, in which large numbers of social leaders, including many human rights defenders and victims reclaiming dispossessed lands, are being murdered in the territories abandoned by the FARC.

The FARC's approach to Principle 8 on the guarantee of non-recurrence was especially hard to reconcile with the government's. Their offer to disarm and enter civilian life constitutes a powerful guarantee of non-recurrence that has no equivalence in the actions of the state and its Armed Forces because they do not demobilise. As such, the FARC urged that fundamental changes be made to the doctrine and organisation of the military, while also demanding, with even greater insistence, the dismantling and accountability of the paramilitaries. Yet, as noted earlier, the Santos government refused to negotiate any reform of the Armed Forces with the FARC; it was simply not on the agenda. As such, whenever the FARC interpreted the guarantee of non-recurrence in a way that implied military reform or retooling, the government was forced to remind them that the termination of the conflict, the entire agreement, and its execution were, in combination, the greatest form such guarantee could take.

In Section 9, on the principle of reconciliation, the FARC spoke of the importance of forgiveness as a necessary condition to achieve social objectives and suggested, in a somewhat odious manner, that the mere recognition of responsibility should serve to mitigate the victim's pain. As if this wasn't enough, Section 10 began by repeating long, bold-type, and sacramental formulas of human rights, explaining – to the outrage of the enemies of the process, who saw in it an insult to the Constitution and an assault on popular sovereignty – that the FARC were committed to the task of designing, together with the government, a new jurisprudence consistent with the satisfaction of victims' rights.

As much as the FARC's ten-point proposal may have offended, it also contained some ideas that were constructive and reasonable, and that found their way into the final agreement. Yet, it was never clear the degree to which the document represented the expression of a calculated, tactical position; a genuine statement of convictions and vision; or an amalgam of both. Likewise, it was hard to assess the veracity of the FARC's claim that its document encompassed many ideas included in the proposals collected through the third-party participation mechanisms of the Havana process.

Initial Obstacles in the Discussions on Point 5

Especially on the question of truth and justice, the negotiations in Havana were booby-trapped from the start. On one side, the military preferred schemes of justice over those of truth. They felt that decisions by judges were the only ones that granted legal security. On this point, there was a surprising coincidence between the military's primary lawyers, like Manuel J. Cepeda, and prominent national human rights defenders, such as Gustavo Gallón. On the other side, the guerrillas preferred truth commissions and rejected what they saw as the retributive, depoliticised, and humiliating justice of the 2012 Legal Framework for Peace (see Annex 2). They wanted a formula similar to that of South Africa – with amnesty for political offences and connected crimes, and truth-telling spaces rather than courtroom justice. However, many soldiers hated and feared truth commissions, based on the view that they mimic the anti-state language of human rights used by NGOs.

The early FARC communiqués on Point 5 – which the rebel group's leaders read out before a throng of reporters in a morning walkway ritual held daily in front of the hotel where the talks were taking place – explained that they had not been defeated and thus sat as equals at the negotiating table. Because the government's Legal Framework for Peace, in their view, had been unilaterally constructed and implied the submission of the FARC's leadership to the state's justice, they described it as unacceptable and inapplicable to them; it was 'legal underbrush' that had to be yanked out. By contrast, the government remained unwaveringly loyal to the Legal Framework, wagering on a judicial model dominated by IHL and in which the list of crimes directly connected to rebellion for purposes of amnesty was very small. In other words, the space it would countenance for the privileged judicial treatment of political offences was practically nonexistent. As such, there were hardly any obvious points of convergence between the two parties' core visions. It would be necessary to wait one long year for the insertion of an ad hoc legal committee that partially replaced both negotiating teams, to open a space for more accommodating formulas.

Public debate prior to the negotiations in Havana had revolved around the Legal Framework for Peace's model of justice and its promised prioritisation of those bearing greatest responsibility for the most serious and representative crimes. The debate, organised by important human rights groups like the Colombian Commission of Jurists, initially addressed whether such an extreme selection of those maximally responsible within the leadership was compatible with the satisfaction of victims' right to access justice, especially as prescribed in the Inter-American system. For them, the victims of perpetrators falling below the Framework's restrictive threshold would be denied their right to have a justice of their own.

The government replied that, among other things, a prosecutorial focus on persons bearing maximal responsibility would lead to a better judicial understanding of the criminal structures that had perpetrated crimes in a systematic or generalised manner, and thus a better determination of the true perpetrators. It would also prevent the system from collapsing when faced with the impossible task of having to judge hundreds of thousands of cases of serious crimes committed over the course of more than fifty years of war. The government noted that a collapse due to overload would be the greatest source of impunity and, rather than vindication, would produce evisceration of victims' right to justice. It argued that there had to be an explanatory process for the victims, to show them how a focus on the punishment of those maximally responsible was a better way to fulfil their right to justice, even if, on account of the selection criteria, most who directly inflicted harm would not be judged and punished.

When the design for what would later become the Special Jurisdiction for Peace (JEP) finally began to be discussed at the negotiating table, the most difficult debate, in Havana and back home in Colombia, concerned prison. The ad hoc legal committee, which drafted the principal elements of the JEP framework, had to work out a formula that involved a mix of reparative, restorative, restrictive, and non-custodial accountability for persons willing to disclose and accept responsibility for their crimes.

At this point, it is important to recall that the classical discourse of human rights has an anti-state leaning that highlights the crimes of the state, thus serving to legitimise and empower human rights organisations which fight for the visibility of the victims of such crimes. This is to be contrasted with the 'sovereign rule of law' discourse that privileges the actions of state, giving its agents the presumption of legality and a political-epistemological privilege against those who, like the guerrillas, are structurally outside the law.

It should not be surprising, therefore, that the Office of the Prosecutor General in Colombia, as the entity that investigates and prosecutes, has a pro-state and anti-subversion bias reflected in the statistical fact that it had many more open investigations and convictions against guerrillas than against state agents. Yet, this may also be explained by the fact that the Office is, compared to NGOs, better resourced and equipped to work on cases against the guerrillas. The issue, then and now, is how to square the different pictures of victimisation presented on the one hand by NGOs, which disproportionately highlight state crimes, and the state on the other. The risk is that these different biases and priorities could result in a disorienting picture for society about the war's great wrongdoers, in which the judicial truths produced by the JEP may tend to have greater anti-guerrilla focus than the non-judicial truths produced by the truth commission, where NGOs may feel more at home. This would put at risk the whole exercise of accountability embodied in the transitional justice system.

Discussions on Truth

The parties at the negotiating table were always attentive to what was happening in Colombia, to the extent that every morning the government's team received a printed summary of the news that had been published the day before in the national press pertaining to the negotiations. However, the negotiations themselves transpired in the more rarefied environment of Cuba, in the El Palco Hotel in Havana. Sitting face to face in plenary sessions and in drafting committees, the parties, but especially the FARC, would repeatedly don and remove the victim's costume when discussing the configuration of extrajudicial and judicial bodies. At the same time, both parties were configuring the doors through which the victims of state and FARC crimes alike would be able to access the different mechanisms once established. In this regard, the internal discussion within the government team and the external discussion with the FARC were first and foremost scenarios for determining a definition of the victims and perpetrators following sociological or criminal categories, as well as establishing the size and characteristics of the procedural doors through which the victims themselves could eventually access truth, justice, and reparation.

The FARC wanted the truth, which supposedly had been established by the Historical Commission as jus ad bellum and to their benefit, to be determinative of the narrative that the future truth commission should produce. They wanted to show irrefutably the asymmetry that, in their opinion, characterised the distribution of responsibilities between the state and the guerrillas, which in turn could shape the construction of the reparation and justice mechanisms.

Believing themselves to have achieved victory (through the Historical Commission) in their 'scientific' fight over the origins of the war, the FARC's next move was to seek the creation of a truth commission that would allow them to leverage this first 'triumph'. As such, they advocated a vision in which the issue of justice could, in fact if not in name, be resolved in a non-judicial setting. This aim persisted even though the FARC articulated it only through euphemisms in the statements read by the different members of their delegation every morning in the daily briefing with the media. They thought that if the work of a truth commission had to be complemented with a criminal justice mechanism, it should be residual; the idea was that the truth would favour their account of history, and thus the tribunal would end up judging those maximally responsible among their enemy's ranks rather than their own.

The government team had a very different vision. It was aware that it needed a comprehensive strategy that articulated the sequencing and relationship among truth, justice, and reparation. In August 2014, High Commissioner Jaramillo said that the strategy should be ready in one month at the latest, as his office had already spent years developing concept and strategy documents on different strands of transitional justice. But it was also determined that in the meantime, and for practical reasons, the government should begin by discussing the terms of a truth commission with the FARC. The thought was that it would be easier to begin with truth than with justice, not so much because the FARC were requesting it, but more so because the issue of justice and punishment was viewed as a kind of 'dynamite', capable of blowing up all of the negotiation effort. However, it quickly became apparent that reaching agreements in the area of truth would not be easy either.

Presentation by Mark Freeman on Truth Commissions

Early in the negotiation over the mandate of a future truth commission, High Commissioner Jaramillo officially introduced Mark Freeman to the table as an external advisor of the government, asking Freeman to present his expert view on the 'minimum requirements' a truth commission should satisfy to be considered as such from an international perspective.

Freeman began by presenting his prior experience, with a level of detail that in another context might have seem pedantic, but had, in this setting, important tactical value. The intention was to have the FARC appreciate him as a key independent authority on the topic and thus be listened to attentively. Freeman subsequently was asked to make similar presentations with key actors in Bogota, including the President, who was keen to know international standards on the matter.

Orozco's unofficial notes on Freeman's inaugural address to the FARC recount how he started by asking, as a didactic preamble, 'Where did truth commissions come from'? to which he answered, 'The first one was in Argentina'. He then explained, 'Before the advent of truth commissions, decisions on how to face the past were presented as a false binary between forgiving everyone or punishing everyone. Truth commissions offered a third way, no longer focused on the perpetrators, but more so on the victims'.

Next, Freeman observed that before thinking about a truth commission tailored to the needs of Colombia, one had to ask what a truth commission is, and in that sense, define its 'minimal identity'. He then enunciated and explained its basic features, drawing largely on the definition he developed in his 2006 book, *Truth Commissions and Procedural Fairness*, where he defined it as 'an ad hoc, autonomous, and victim-centred commission of inquiry set up in and authorized by a state for the primary purposes of (1) investigating and reporting on the principal causes and consequences of broad and relatively recent patterns of severe violence or repression that occurred in the state during determinate periods of abusive rule or conflict, and (2) making recommendations for their redress and future prevention'. Freeman emphasised the importance of tailoring a commission's mandate to the needs of the particular context, seeking above all to build something with legitimacy: an attribute that depends on a wide variety of elements, including operational independence, the choice of commissioners, and much more.

Having made the above observations and others along the same lines, Freeman asked himself, 'how could a commission be conceived for Colombia'?, to which he answered, 'It is important to think beyond the models of Latin America. It is true that the most widely-read commission report is that of Argentina, but South Africa popularised the use of public hearings, which helped to humanise the work and achieve a more transcendental impact going well beyond the final report. The key is to customise a design that fits the context, which in this case includes the fact of an armed conflict and the prism of a negotiation process'.

Freeman went on to ask himself further questions that he considered had special relevance to Colombia. He noted, for example, the importance of distinguishing between 'knowing' and 'acknowledging' the truth in a context like Colombia, in which considerable information was already available. Following the famous phrase of Michael Ignatieff, he explained that truth commissions can help 'reduce the number of lies that can be circulated unchallenged in public discourse' and that it was better for commissions to serve, in a minimalist way, to 'clarify' facts rather than seeking to establish 'the Truth' in capital letters.[8] He noted that after Chile, South Africa, and other commission experiences, the inclusion of the word 'reconciliation' had increased, and he went on to discuss the different complementary meanings of the expression. He said that it was a word with a bad reputation, but useful, since it could help incentivise commissioners to interpret their mandate in a more creative and dynamic fashion, rather than legalistically. Finally, he talked about the relationship between truth and justice. He raised the question, 'does truth have legal consequences'? and offered various reflections, including the observation that truth and justice could never be entirely separated since, among other things, national courts do not disappear simply because a truth commission is in operation. Freeman concluded his presentation by saying that a truth commission was a 'great opportunity' that could potentially serve as 'a lung' for the post-conflict period, provided that (1) other truth commission experiences and lessons are examined, and (2) a design is reached that reflects the positive and negative attributes of the Colombian context in particular.

After the presentation, High Commissioner Jaramillo briefly summarised it by saying that Freeman had merely set a 'baseline' and that now was the time to listen to the FARC. Thus followed a good number of questions, broadly anticipating the difficult discussions that would come later. Iván Márquez, head of the delegation, commented that the commission that was negotiated in Havana should not be exclusively run by lawyers because it would lead to 'depoliticising' the conflict. Jesús Santrich, another delegate, engaged with a critical question about the time frame of events a commission should cover, asking: 'Where should we identify the origins of an armed conflict'? He explained that, for some, the historical origins of the conflict in the former Yugoslavia were in the fourteenth century, while for others everything began

---

[8] M. Ignatieff, 'Articles of Faith', *Index on Censorship* 5 (1996): 113.

in the Second World War. He wondered, 'Are the 1930s the remote past'? Then came the turn of 'Rodrigo Granda', who was uneasy about the fact that truth commissions focus on establishing patterns and asked: 'Could it be possible to reveal who killed Gaitán'?, adding, 'And will the political genocide of the Patriotic Union be explained'? Freeman responded with an exposition about the difference between the broad historical context and the more contemporary focus of a commission's work, and about the possibility of incorporating a mix of specific events and broader patterns of violations into the eventual mandate.

Thereafter, Enrique Santiago, external legal advisor to the FARC, asked whether South Africa's commission complied with international standards, talked about the relationship between truth and justice, and inquired, 'What is an *official* commission'? As if they had agreed to ask and answer each other's questions, commander Catatumbo spoke next, saying that 'official' does not mean created by the state, since several commissions have been created through peace agreements (e.g., El Salvador and Guatemala); and that, more than being official, it was about being 'legitimate'. In the reflective tone of those who think that the keys to the present must be sought in the long stretch of history, Catatumbo continued, according to Orozco's unofficial notes, by making a variety of observations, such as, 'Colombia is a sui generis country'; 'We have to be very creative in structuring this truth commission'; 'Recognition of the armed conflict and a logic of reconciliation are required'; 'In Colombia there have been attempts to reconcile with our history, but none has managed to string everything together, offering a single connected story'; and 'The Colombian political class has never acknowledged its mistake in killing Gaitán'. Near the end, he said that there was a need to 'defeat the propensity to make truth nonbinding'.

With rhetorical formulas typical of someone who had been, at one time, a parliamentarian on behalf of the Patriotic Union during the peace negotiations of President Betancur, Iván Márquez recapitulated and expanded what was covered by his comrades. According to Orozco's unofficial notes, he said things like, 'There is a fog of lies that obscures the truth'; 'As the Gospel says, the truth shall set us free'; 'The Commission will show that the path of reconciliation involves inclusion'; and 'Violations of social and economic rights should be treated as generators of victims'. Then, to the surprise of many, he individually addressed General Mora of the government delegation. In a tone of solidarity with a fellow warrior, he told him that 'the greatest originators of victims are neither you [the army] nor us [the guerrillas]', asking aloud, 'Where is the author behind the author'? After a pause he returned to the mode of asking and answering his own questions, including about how to combine truth and justice in the agreement; to which his answer was, 'We have to produce new law rather than wrapping ourselves up in the international legal framework, or the weed of the Legal Framework for Peace'.

In the weeks that followed, it became increasingly evident that truth commissions were also a subject of great interest among many high military commanders and their closest technical advisors. Through discussions with them, the picture emerged of a non-accusatory truth commission composed exclusively of Colombians. Their hope was that the commission would take into account the fact that the 1991 Constitution represented a turning point in the history of the Armed Forces, reflecting a new relationship between civilian and military powers in the country, very different from the National Front period (1958–1974) when the military had followed counterinsurgent doctrines derived from the Cold War. In the discussions that took place both at the Presidential Palace and at the Ministry of Defence, the concept arose of a truth commission that would operate as a podium for debate, where representatives of the Armed Forces, among others, could tell the story of the institutional transformations that had taken place during the last decades, including in terms of their immersion in IHL norms and values.

The Internal Negotiation, Followed by More of the External

Internal discussions within the government team were at least as difficult as those with the FARC. For General Mora, who had a special responsibility in looking after the interests of the Armed Forces within the process, the burden of responsibility was especially acute. Throughout the negotiation on the truth commission, he expressed his deep concerns about various issues within the delegation, often disagreeing with the rest of the team, which was almost exclusively civilian, comprising individuals who could not be candidates for prosecution on the basis of command or superior responsibility.

During the long months in which the issue of the truth commission was under negotiation with the FARC, General Mora often conveyed to his team members the conviction among many in the Colombian military that such commissions tended to disparage the Armed Forces. As proof, he cited the examples in the Southern Cone. However, team members argued that Colombia was not like Argentina and Chile, countries that underwent transitions out of military dictatorships that had practiced state terror against rather defenceless opponents. This was not the case in Colombia, where there was a transition out of a long war in which the military had defended democracy. The Peruvian truth commission was also presented to him as a counter-example. There, the commission had begun its work convinced that the military had a greater responsibility than the guerrillas in the country's humanitarian tragedy, but in the end its investigations showed that the Shining Path, and not the military, bore the largest responsibility for the crimes perpetrated during the war.

General Mora's concerns also rose to the surface when the government team discussed the issue of whether Colombia's commission should operate in a centralised or regionalised manner. In a country with a huge accumulation of historical information on human rights violations and war crimes, and even a Historical Memory Centre that had produced enormous amounts of data about the horrors of war, High Commissioner Jaramillo considered the 'recognition' of the truth just as important, if not more, than simply finding it. For this reason, he thought that it would be beneficial if the commission could operate through decentralised offices, as this would allow it to carry out cathartic hearings with victims and local populations of all political persuasions in the areas most affected by the war, such as Urabá and the Nariño jungle on the Pacific coast. The rejection of this model by General Mora was blunt. He thought that such regional scenarios would come to be dominated by left-wing social and political organisations, many of them purportedly partial to the guerrillas, and that hearings held there would serve only to subject the military to public scorn. In the General's view, the truth that would be constructed at such hearings would be highly biased.

But the biggest internal battle about the truth commission revolved around the question of whether it should have the authority to make attributions of institutional responsibility in its final report. The High Commissioner and others on the team put forward the logic that courts are concerned with judicial findings of individual responsibility, whereas truth commissions, acting in a complementary manner, contribute through non-judicial findings of collective or institutional responsibility. But for General Mora, the risk of unfair tarnishing of the military's image was too high: it could cast a cloud of suspicion upon each of the members of the institution and facilitate their prosecution. So great was General Mora's concern with truth commissions and their focus on institutional responsibilities, that on one occasion he travelled to Bogota to meet with the President and offer his resignation. Finally, the disagreement was laid to rest by replacing the adjective 'institutional' with 'organisational'.

The tension around the issue nevertheless persisted. General Mora thought that truth commissions were, in general terms, platforms that tended to be dominated by human rights NGOs and victims' groups. Since state crimes have had a larger historical focus in Colombia than crimes committed by the guerrillas, he thought the final result would likely be most unfavourable to the state and the Armed Forces. His opposition to the creation of a truth commission might have been even stronger, were it not for transitory Article 66 of the Constitution (part of the Legal Framework for Peace), which required the establishment of such a commission. Ultimately, it was understood that the military, like the FARC, would have the opportunity (and corresponding expectation) of engaging with the truth commission, in a national process aimed at non-repetition and better conditions for peaceful coexistence.

Regarding discussions with the FARC at the negotiating table, these operated as a zero-sum battlefield at times. For example, if the government included kidnapping as one of the crimes that should be investigated by the truth commission, the FARC would seek to even things up by including forced disappearances. As such, to avoid this kind of tit-for-tat dynamic, the parties were at times forced to describe, in a very generic and non-specific way, the conducts that would have to be investigated.

According to advisor Orozco's unofficial notes, an early May 2015 discussion of the truth commission was particularly noteworthy, occurring in the context of a profound crisis derived from the military confrontation in Colombia and a sense of immobility in the conversations in Havana. Led by Santrich, the FARC insisted that the commission investigate 'crimes against humanity' and 'systematic' patterns of violations. General Mora quickly opposed this, as it seemed to him that the term 'systematic' was directed against state agents. Then, the FARC demanded that the commission investigate the responsibilities of governments, military forces, and the police. This naturally led the government team to demand that the responsibility of the 'insurgency' be investigated. And so it went for some time, with each delegation pointing out the cowardice of the other in its unwillingness to risk being listed as a potential subject of investigation in the commission's mandate. Finally, the FARC accepted that a generic formula be sought, such that the commission would investigate the responsibility of 'the state' and 'the insurgency', and that the specific contents of those expressions would be determined by the commission itself. (The FARC additionally proposed that the commission be authorised to investigate 'foreign governments', but this was rejected as unnecessary as well as counterproductive in the preservation of international support for the negotiations.)

The next day the discussion continued, as High Commissioner Jaramillo suggested that the truth commission be empowered to investigate the phenomenon of drug trafficking. Santrich responded that investigating drug trafficking would require a mechanism separate from the commission, since trafficking was merely part of the 'context'. The guerrilla leader then responded with intricate vengefulness by demanding that the commission investigate 'the existence of the paramilitary phenomenon, its causes, origins, forms of manifestation, as well as its organisers, beneficiaries, instigators, collaborators and impacts'. Two days later, there was an expectation that the FARC would deliver a response regarding a compromise proposal suggested by the government team. Instead, Santrich and his people seemed unwilling to budge from their position: paramilitarism in, drug trafficking out. Jaramillo explained that the term used should be 'criminal gangs' since paramilitarism, as such, had ceased to exist. He explained that investigating and combatting the ongoing actions of these surviving gangs – as part of Point 3 (conflict termination) of the 2012 General Agreement – was separate from the exercise of clarifying the paramilitary phenomenon in the terms that correspond to a truth commission. But Santrich, insistent that investigating paramilitarism was more important than investigating drug trafficking, said that if the government wanted a specific mention of the latter, it should be accompanied by other equally important elements of context such as 'corruption associated with the conflict', 'military contracting', 'the dispossession of lands', 'the violence of multinationals', 'the role of the media', and so on. The discussion of the commission's mandate thus became a war over the use of precisely targeted narratives as a tool for the construction of the other as victimiser.

Other examples of similar dynamics and divides abounded. For instance, the parties spent multiple cycles discussing issues such as whether or not the truth commission should, following the Salvadoran example, have the authority to 'name names'; whether it should have powers to access confidential intelligence files; and whether its recommendations would or would not be binding on the government and the state. On the first issue, the FARC – wanting a super-empowered truth commission to resolve every issue of law and justice – preferred giving it the power to name individual culprits; by contrast, the government – preferring a strict separation of truth and justice between the commission and the courts – preferred the opposite. On the second issue, an agreement was reached when the government, after consulting at length with the Ministry of Defence in Bogota, ensured that current laws on access to intelligence files (which prohibit national security arguments from trumping ongoing investigations on human rights violations) could regulate the matter. The third issue was settled with an intermediate formula that balances state responsibility to give an accounting of any non-implementation of the commission's eventual recommendations, and the irreplaceable role of the elected legislative and executive branches of government whose judgement cannot be substituted by an unelected commission.

Unfortunately, by the time the many debates about the truth commission mandate were resolved, the Havana talks as a whole were suffering a growing crisis of public legitimacy due, among other things, to the fact that they had lagged far longer than promised. The government team realised that the working methodology of the negotiation that had been used up to that time (involving a strict sequence of cycles and working and rest days) had reached its limits. The team also concluded that an in-depth negotiation of the issue of justice, postponed thus far, had to be brought forward in order to untangle the discussions on truth. As such, when a consensus on the basic design of the truth commission came within reach, the government's detailed proposal on justice (its so-called Plan A) was at long last presented at the plenary session. However, in some ways the timing could not have been worse, as it was preceded by three consecutive aerial bombings against the FARC with a significant number of casualties, including two members of its negotiating team. Unsurprisingly, the FARC interpreted the attacks as a way to pressure them to accept a surrender to justice.

The Discussions on Reparations

Despite various shifts in names and faces – for example, Foreign Minister María Ángela Holguín and businessman Gonzalo Restrepo were added to the government team – both delegations were downtrodden and dejected by the end of the negotiation of the truth commission mandate. The feeling was widespread that the negotiations would be interrupted or dissolved at any moment.

In the midst of this, the parties initiated discussion on the topic of reparations, recognised as the most directly helpful patch of transitional justice for the victims. The fact that truth and justice can be characterised as forms of reparation gave it even more appeal as a topic.

As a concept, reparation offers a kind of double-recognition opportunity, comprising recognition *of* the victim and recognition *by* the victimiser. Under this logic, the government sought to inject multiple and successive formulas of recognition across the accord's transitional justice system. This is the origin of the 'early acts of recognition of responsibility' (Section 5.1.3.1 of the final agreement) that the parties pledged to perform. These were meant to provide an initial shot in the arm for the transitional justice ritual, avoiding the symbolic vacuum that could result from nothing significant happening in the realm of reconciliation and victim acknowledgment between the accord's signature and eventual implementation. This broad concept of recognition was also the origin of the idea that the truth commission should be concerned not only with fact-finding, but also with the creation of platforms and dialogues for the reciprocal recognition between members of regional and local communities torn apart by the armed conflict, such that 'the journey was the destination'. The same thinking likewise contributed to the idea, which arose later, that the penalties to be imposed by the post-conflict tribunal should combine reparative as well as retributive dimensions.

In short, both the government and the FARC agreed to put the concept of reparation at the centre of their concerns, even as the concept itself, and the manner of distributing the obligations associated with it, remained undefined. For the government team, ending the conflict was also a great opportunity to add reparation contributions by the guerrillas into the existing reparations scheme of the state, producing a potentially synergistic effect. As such, the government was disturbed to discover the FARC's apparent desire to link the commitment to carry out activities of recognition and reparation of the victims with opportunities for political gain. The government thought that if these were not clearly separated, the reparative intention would not be recognisable and the average citizen would indignantly reject such transitional justice as a 'farce'.

Institutional Arrangements for Reparation

The fact that the Historical Memory Centre and the Victims Unit were already in place – one in charge of symbolic reparation, the other of making administrative reparation a reality for the victims of the armed conflict – led the government to define its initial negotiating position as one of building upon existing foundations. The Victims Unit served the government team as a constant source of relevant information on what the state was already doing in terms of reparation and as a source of additional proposals on what needed to be corrected and improved in a post-conflict scenario. The Historical Memory Centre, by contrast, was absent during the Havana negotiations on Point 5. But this did not mean that it had been excluded; for example, Gonzalo Sánchez, its director, participated in discussions that took place in Bogota in the Office of the High Commissioner for Peace, which shaped the government's position regarding the FARC's demand for the creation of the Historical Commission.

The government team was fully aware of its role as a representative of the state and of its position as guarantor of the safety and well-being of all the inhabitants of its territory. It thus understood that it had a subsidiary responsibility to make reparations that extended to victims of all sides of the armed conflict. Yet, within the framework of the negotiations, it also had the task of demanding that the FARC, being responsible for serious harm to the population, undertake to contribute to the reparation of its numerous victims with its ill-gotten assets and through community work. The government team in Havana pointed out that the Victims Unit, according to a study conducted by Harvard University, was responsible for managing one of the most ambitious reparation programmes since the Second World War, accounting for 1 percent of Colombia's GDP. As such, the government argued that the parties' sub-agreement on reparations should be limited to correcting and expanding the existing and successful reparation effort, addressing gaps that could be filled on account of the end of conflict.

The FARC, however, detested the model of administrative reparation embodied in the Victims and Land Restitution Law. Among the stated reasons for this animosity were the following: (1) that the legislation excluded the historical victims of land grabbing and political exclusion, and only included war violations committed since 1985; and (2) that the law recognised the military, even those killed in combat, as victims for purposes of reparation, whereas it completely excluded that the guerrillas and even their relatives could be recognised as victims.

The Evolution of Discussions on Reparation

With these abysmal disagreements on the basics, the negotiation of the sub-agreement on reparations proceeded in three phases. The first was a kind of honeymoon phase during which the government, capitalising on the existing scheme, made proposals or listened to requests by its counterpart, to improve the scheme in aspects jointly considered deficient. These included the reparation of a variety of social and political collectives affected during the armed conflict and which were not yet covered; the coordination of reparation activities with those derived from the territorial development plans ('Pdets') contemplated under Point 1 (rural reform) of the final agreement; the coordinated return of persons in exile; and psychological counselling for individuals and groups affected by the war.

A second and much more contentious phase started when, apparently echoing demands from social and victim organisations, the FARC advocated that the government overhaul the Victims and Land Restitution Law through a highly participatory process that would have placed the Victims Unit in limbo. High Commissioner Jaramillo tenaciously resisted this demand, while accepting that there could be participation by victims in the design of the implementation mechanisms. The discussion on the eligibility criteria for the policy of administrative reparations and on the very concept of victim were then reopened. This led to discussions on, among other things, the convenience of expanding the universe of victims of the conflict to well before 1985; the possibility that guerrilla members and their families could be recognised as victims, just like the military and their families; and possible arrangements for the management of the reparations funding.

The fact that, for budgetary reasons, only the victims of the war from 1985 onwards were eligible for reparations made it vulnerable to criticism by the FARC. But the government was willing to accept that, at least for purposes of symbolic reparations, the universe of recognised victims could be partly expanded. As for the issue of funding the reparations policy, the FARC demanded that it be guaranteed, on a constitutional level, by high fixed percentages of the national budget, which in practical terms implied that the policy of reparations cease to be a government policy and become a state one. The FARC also sought some kind of control over the distribution and administration of the reparation funds; but the government defended the preservation of exclusive state control, maintaining that it should continue to be run by the Victims Unit, as well as arguing for an updated design for the funding model.

The negotiation of the reparations issue ended with a highly contentious third phase in which the government demanded, in vain, that the FARC contribute to the material reparation of its victims with its own assets and financial resources. For the government, it was politically and ethically imperative to demand the FARC to articulate what they would contribute to the reparation of their victims, not only symbolically or through their labour, but using their wealth. However, the idea outraged the FARC delegation. Not only did they revisit the old tirade about being victims rather than victimisers; they also claimed that they had no assets and that everything they had raised had been invested in funding the armed struggle. Day after day, through endless sessions, they asserted their Franciscan poverty. The government then warned that the issue of reparations was governed both domestically and internationally by the principle that 'all parties responsible for damages are obligated to repair them', implying that if the FARC refused to contribute to the financial compensation of its victims, the state would be forced to find and seize its assets until the end of time. In response, the FARC's delegation was reduced to expressing amazement and outrage, offering to 'let them frisk us'. It took the 'No' result in the referendum for the FARC finally to agree to deliver an inventory of its assets, during the frantic renegotiations that led to the revised agreement in late 2016.

As a side note, it may be mentioned that the forms that must be completed to be listed in the National Registry of Victims include questions about who the victimiser was. During the negotiation, the Victims Unit was asked to give an estimate of the comparative proportions of victims of state crimes, guerrilla crimes, and so forth who were represented in the Registry. Contrary to what was expected, the statistics revealed that the highest percentage of victims had declared that they believed that their victimiser had been the FARC and not the state. The percentage of crimes attributed to the state by registered victims was barely 3 percent of the total; and not even after adding those who declared themselves to be victims of the paramilitaries did the aggregate percentage reach the magnitude of those who named the FARC as their presumed victimiser. Having said that, the statistics had the disadvantage that about 35 percent of the total registered victims had not given any information about who they believed their victimiser had been. Moreover, some of those who chose to identify an alleged victimiser may have thought it was inappropriate, or unwise, to point an accusing finger at the same state they were soliciting compensation from.

The Sequencing Debate

Across the negotiation of Point 5, there probably wasn't a more difficult and illuminating, but less conclusive, discussion than the one about the sequencing of the different transitional justice measures.

In earlier phases of transitional justice's development, a rather disjunctive international debate asked the narrow question of whether criminal courts were a better solution than truth commissions to the demands of victims and society facing a legacy of mass abuse. In more recent times, it is widely believed that justice, victims' rights, and even the reconciliation needs of societies in transition are better served if the mechanisms of justice, truth, and reparation work in an integrated manner, as this is thought to better ensure the satisfaction of victims' composite rights.

The previous experience of the Justice and Peace Law trials, which grew out of the pact between the Uribe government and the paramilitary United Self-Defence Forces of Colombia (AUC), had nevertheless shown that it was a mistake to collapse the search for truth, justice, and reparation into a single procedure. Having prosecutors and judges try simultaneously to reconstruct historical truth and judicial truth, while providing reparations to victims in the same criminal proceedings, had been a source of confusion, huge delays, and very erratic hearings for unsworn depositions. However, the FARC, as much interested as the government in consistency with the international community's perceived standards and preferences, acceded to its adversary's position of favouring a comprehensive transitional justice model that would operate through distinct and complementary mechanisms.

Yet, the discussion remained inconclusive as to whether these mechanisms should operate simultaneously or sequentially and, in the latter case, what the sequence should be – especially in terms of the placement of the *núcleo duro* (hard nut) of justice. After some initial hesitation, the government delegation advocated a formula entailing that the selection for trial of the persons bearing greatest responsibility for the most serious and representative crimes would occur before the truth commission commenced formal operations. Partly inspired by Article 66 of the Legal Framework for Peace, the idea was that immediately after the final agreement was signed and ratified, a special prosecutorial committee would be created and set in motion. This committee would be responsible for the production of a 'crime repository', drawing on credible existing reports that would be made available by prosecutors, the courts, human rights and victims' organisations, and so forth.

However, there was never agreement within the government team about whether the most serious and representative cases were only those that reflected systematic patterns and violations, or whether isolated criminal acts of extraordinary gravity, like a sudden or unplanned massacre, could also qualify. The internal discussion on this issue partly reflected disagreements within the team regarding the degree of internationalisation that should be present in Colombia's transitional justice system. Those who believed that the special court should mimic international justice standards spoke of building a repository with 'paradigmatic' cases, whereas those who thought it should be guided primarily by domestic law advocated a focus on 'emblematic' cases. In other words, the former wanted individual cases to be mere illustrations of what had been duly proven as systematic or massive, while the latter wanted individual cases capable of showing more general criminal phenomena.

Eventually, the view emerged within the government team that, once the repository was created (an objective selection), the special prosecutorial committee – with the participation of the Prosecutor General – would select the candidates meeting the threshold of maximum responsibility (a subjective selection) and proceed to issue tentative indictments. The named persons would then have various opportunities to acknowledge their responsibility, or alternatively refute it in accordance with full due process.

But there were also different points of view on specific nuances of the model. Professor Orozco argued, for example, that a first chance be offered so those who wished could 'raise their hands' after the special committee had made the objective selection of crimes, but before it had made the subjective selection of those most responsible. His argument was that once the crimes (but not persons) to be investigated and prosecuted had been selected, those who suspected that they could be called to answer for them could be offered special incentives to say 'it was me', which would have important benefits for the legitimacy and efficacy of the process. Afterwards, during the judicial investigation phase, and while the prosecutorial circle was closing in on those most responsible, at least one more procedural opportunity could be offered to step forward and acknowledge responsibility (with reduced, but nevertheless important, legal incentives on offer). Any sentence would include, as a condition for preserving judicial benefits, the obligation to appear before the truth commission, in the event that it should so request. Orozco said that criminal justice should operate as a lightning rod that would quickly quench the 'thirst for blood', so that the truth commission would be freed from having to operate as an 'adjunct to justice'.

Within the government team, most everyone agreed that there should be justice first and then truth; a sequence that, among other things, would be more appealing and less threatening to actors such as the military. However, the fact that post-conflict justice, even the most expeditious kind, requires significant time to start working, made it necessary to think of an integrated model somewhere between sequential and simultaneous. The idea was that it would need to be set in motion, either before or after signing the final agreement, with early and voluntary gestures of recognition of responsibility by each side, and with amnesties for those who were not considered ultimately responsible and had not committed the most serious and representative crimes. This would buy the time needed to set up the special prosecutorial mechanism and, in due course, the truth commission.

Several members of a small group of transitional justice specialists, set up by Norway in order to have technical exchanges with the FARC's legal advisers, viewed some of the government's thinking with scepticism. One of them, a truth commission expert, believed that truth commissions had been particularly successful when their reports had operated as an 'icebreaker' to clear the way for justice, in contexts where accountability would have initially been impossible because of amnesty laws or the staunch resistance of veto holders. She and other members of the group also supported a 'naming names' power for the commission, since they seemed to doubt the capacity of the Colombian judicial system, believing that there would be a need to rely on the investigations of a truth commission. One of the group's members even suggested a formula of progressive presidential pardons, followed by an assertion of state sovereignty before the International Criminal Court: an approach that was more in line with the guerrillas' thinking than the government's.

The FARC's opposition to the government's vision on sequencing was therefore supported, indirectly, by the views of a number of international experts. Above all, however, the rebels' opposition was based on the desire to agree on a sequence of mechanisms that, in its estimation, would give the best chance possible of having the state appear as the great victimiser. In line with this objective, the FARC had the idea that the initial step should be the Historical Commission, leading to recognition of the righteousness of their rebellion. The role of the truth commission would be to continue this work in the post-agreement period. The calculation was that the truth commission, with the massive participation of human rights organisations and organisations of victims of state crimes, would produce a narrative that would show that the greatest responsibility for the humanitarian tragedy lay with the state. Once this asymmetric picture of 'the Truth' was constructed, both in the sense of jus ad bellum and of jus in bello, the only thing left would be to establish a residual tribunal to judge those maximally responsible.

Forward to the Past?

Ultimately, the sequencing of truth and justice was only partly resolved in Havana. The government team came to the view that, whatever the wording of the final peace deal, in practice the court and the truth commission would end up having to operate simultaneously for much of the time, just as in Sierra Leone. They understood that it would also become necessary for there to be future mechanisms and protocols of cooperation between the bodies, in order to preserve the extra-judicial nature of the commission, and prevent the court from turning it into a simple auxiliary to justice.

Be that as it may, it will take an Olympian effort, and many more years, to overcome the narratives of victims and victimisers that have entrenched in the public imagination. Indeed, even if it is accepted that human rights NGOs confront the state in an effort to strengthen it, while the guerrillas confront it to destroy it, convergence in the means, despite divergence in the objectives, results in an unintentional alliance between human rights NGOs and the guerrillas in the public imagination: disastrous for the former and sometimes also for the survival of the state itself.

Even against their own best wishes, guerrilla groups usually end up being not so much the expression of repressed social movements as an 'anti-social movement'.[9] When guerrillas appear, as they did in Colombia, autonomous

---

[9] Michel Wieviorka, *The Making of Terrorism* (Chicago: University of Chicago Press, 1993).

social movements almost always wither away. Only after the wars end and the repression they are subjected to by all the armed actors ceases can the social movements again begin to articulate themselves autonomously.

In the meantime, Colombia's broad human rights movement has, to an excessive degree, continued to be treated as part of the subversion. For example, in mid-November 2017, during the legislative debates on the statutory law for the JEP, the plenary of the Senate reached the conclusion that experience in conducting human rights cases against the state during the last five years in domestic as well as international courts, would render someone ineligible to become a JEP magistrate. The President of the JEP was compelled, therefore, to issue a statement in which she said that this criterion of ineligibility, if maintained by the plenary of the House of Representatives, would be in violation of the Constitution as it punished the exercise of a "lawful" profession, and the Constitutional Court should therefore declare it unconstitutional.

More ominously, following the demobilisation of the FARC, hundreds of ex-combatants, social leaders, and human rights defenders whose demands touched on unaccomplished state promises derived from the peace agreements (relating to land restitution, political participation, coca crops substitution, victim reparations and so on) have been killed at the hands of criminal gangs, neoparamilitaries, FARC dissidents, and ELN guerrillas as part of a harsh power struggle over who will establish the new rule over the territories. The guarantee of non-recurrence of atrocities – the fourth 'pillar' of transitional justice and an underlying theme of the peace accord as a whole – is being tested every day.

B. ORDINARY VERSUS EXTRAORDINARY JUSTICE

When the writing of this chapter began in mid-2016, the ordinary and the extraordinary were, above all, analytical categories devised by the author and applied to the Havana talks. After the 'No' victory in the October 2016 plebiscite, they became controversial and highly political concepts, and even battle cries in the public debate. If one were to do a statistical analysis of the use of the adjective 'ordinary' in the negotiation documents, as well as in press statements and articles, one would see a sharp jump in frequency after the centre of gravity of the discussion moved from Havana to Bogota. For the FARC, which in Havana had tirelessly repeated ideas to the effect that 'ordinary justice amounts to victor's justice', the resurgence of a more status-quo ideal of justice was especially traumatic. The extraordinary Havana model of justice (endorsed by the government, the FARC, and virtually the entire international community) would have to meet the Colombian opposition's ordinary model halfway, in the post-plebiscite reality of the country.

The ordinary and the extraordinary are ontologically and epistemologically unstable categories. The criteria that allow us to recognise them not only in reality, but also in law, change in space and time. What yesterday was held for extraordinary may be held for ordinary today. What is held for ordinary in one place may be held for extraordinary in another place. What is clearly extraordinary at the macro level (and reinforced by macro-narrative) may become difficult to maintain by way of characterisation at the micro level. In that sense, the following account of the ordinary and extraordinary of what happened before, during, and after the negotiation of the peace agreement between the Santos government and the FARC guerrillas is above all one of heuristic rather than scientific value.

The Ordinary and the Extraordinary in Law and Politics

Despite the clear willingness of both parties to make peace, the Havana negotiations were, almost up until the end, a continuation by other means of the war that they had waged for more than fifty years. Among the issues on this alternative battlefield was the tension between the ordinary and the extraordinary, which played out in the clarification of factual matters before, during, and after the negotiation, as well as in the choice of the legal instruments meant to achieve sustainable peace with justice.

The distinction examined here between the ordinary and the extraordinary exists in socio-political reality as well as in law. The term 'ordinary' often alludes to what is routine, follows the norm, and is expected to continue without change. The term 'extraordinary' refers rather to what is outside the norm, breaks routine, makes us feel insecure, and is expected to be temporary. Being in the world of the extraordinary is a bit like being homeless, exposed to the elements; by contrast, the world of the ordinary is as familiar as being at home.

Overall, the law operates as the regulation of routines that flow through institutional channels. The institutions themselves are channels for the reproduction of normality. It is only when things happen outside what is normal that the law has to go beyond its normal course and make use of extraordinary and highly flexible devices in order to provide an adequate response to an unexpected and turbulent situation. Whereas the ordinary in law presupposes peace and social and political normality, the extraordinary in law presupposes war and social and political abnormality.

In historical-sociological terms, it is often said that the ambit of the ordinary is defined by the reign of structure over agency, and that the ambit of the extraordinary is, on the contrary, defined by the reign of agency over structure. In this regard, those who read political history in linear, progressive fashion may view it as a long road beginning in the convulsed days of Athens in the fifth century B.C.E., and culminating in the highly institutionalised and routine-driven democracies of modern societies dominated by structure.[10] But with civil wars and revolutions, and the authoritarianism they often engender, the extraordinary prevails over the ordinary, and thus agency over structure. In these settings, the future is wide open and those who compete for power interact in ways that are mostly unregulated, and often violent, with little capacity to anticipate and control the causal chains that are set into motion by their interactions. Political leaders in such contexts regularly make life-and-death decisions, without the anchor of a stable, predictable system.

As for politics and law, the logic of the ordinary designates the subordination of the former to the latter. In its idealised form, politics becomes a fully regulated constitutional competition. Such circumstances are described as ones in which law has a 'routine' character. By contrast, the logic of the extraordinary designates the subordination of law to politics, such that law is merely the expression of a discretionary political decision. Such circumstances lead to uses and forms of law that are said to be 'foundational', rather than routine. Leaders can produce such law by gathering, mobilising, and stabilising hitherto-fragmented opinions and interests into a common project. Alternatively, foundational forms of law can emerge after the affirmation of power and domination by a minority or majority over society as a whole, or after a war that ends through negotiation.

The Ordinary and the Extraordinary in Times of Globalisation

In a world where the idea of the sovereign, territorial state was hegemonic, such as in the frail Weimar Republic of 1920s Germany, the distinction between the ordinary and the extraordinary was enshrined in political-legal discussion. The very conservative Carl Schmitt claimed that the sovereign is whoever decides over states of exception – and with it, over who are friends or foes, and who are criminals or upstanding citizens. In response, the social

---

[10] Christian Meier, *Die Entstehung des Politischen bei den Griechen* (Frankfurt: Suhrkamp, 1980).

democrat Hermann Heller claimed that the sovereign is whoever decides over normality and routine. Thus, Heller acted as a theorist of consolidated sovereignty, and Schmitt as a theorist of sovereignty under threat.

In today's highly interdependent, postmodern world, some of this may seem outdated. The secular and highly globalised religion of the liberal-democratic rule of law pretends to have killed the modern state, and especially its sovereign executive. Yet we continue to have to deal with multiple internal and external sovereignties, and with those who try to influence them or act in their name.

Modern Westphalian states were characterised as inhabiting largely pacified territories, on the one hand, while facing potential war between states on the other. Here, domestic law was dominated by ordinary rationales, and made room for the extraordinary as an exception, if at all. Interstate law, by contrast, was perceived as extraordinary from the standpoint of domestic, ordinary law, particularly if it was to be applied in the domestic arena. A dramatic and illustrative example of this occurred in nineteenth-century Colombia, during the collapse of the central colonial state and amid strong political and territorial fragmentation. In 1863, in an attempt to regulate the internal wars that ravaged the country and to facilitate negotiated solutions, the Rio Negro Constitutional College determined that the wars and their resolution had to be regulated following the extraordinary criteria of the law of nations and of political-criminal law, instead of those of ordinary domestic criminal law. This meant resorting to negotiation, amnesty, integration, and reconciliation vis-à-vis the defeated.

By contrast, today's globalised world is transferring the rationales of domestic law to the international sphere, using an ordinary-making logic, to establish what Hardt and Negri refer to as 'Empire': a sort of global super-rule of law.[11] Under conditions of peace and normalcy, this paradigm – at least in constitutional, liberal states – has the capacity to afford benevolent treatment for dissidents and law offenders of all types. However, in times of war and political turmoil, it generally produces discrimination and criminalisation when addressing political deviancy. For example, under stress, the ordinary-based rationale of the global super-rule of law results in extraordinary devices like the PATRIOT Act, used by the US government in the aftermath of 9/11. In the context of highly asymmetrical and irregular wars that confront the global centre and peripheries more generally, it produces a vocabulary of terrorism rather than rebellion.

---

[11] Michael Hardt and Antonio Negri, *Empire* (Cambridge, Mass.: Harvard University Press, 2000).

Rationales leaning toward the ordinary, both globally and domestically, are increasingly anchored in human rights institutions and discourse, and automatically incorporate a strong compulsion for punishment of those responsible for serious crimes. Yet, debates about transitional justice in the post-Westphalian international sphere are unavoidably crisscrossed by the tension between the ordinary and the extraordinary. The ever-changing doctrine and jurisprudence leading to the development and adoption of international standards for the design and application of truth, justice, reparation, and guarantees of non-recurrence is understood by authors like Ruti Teitel as a process of making transitional justice ordinary, with both positive and negative effects.[12]

Amnesty and the Tension between the Ordinary and the Extraordinary

Today's fights over the invocation of amnesties lie at the heart of tensions between the ordinary and the extraordinary. After all, amnesty is usually understood as extraordinary and political par excellence. Indeed, from the perspective of classic penal retributivism, amnesty has to be understood as intrinsically unjust because it destroys the moral necessity of recompensing the crime with a proportional punishment. And yet, it is important to recall that amnesty, even for international crimes and serious human rights violations, is not absolutely prohibited in international law; moreover, it is unlikely that it will ever be.

Among the many functions that are attributed to punishment and criminal law in modern politics, there is none more ordinary than that of deterrence. This applies to both general and specific forms of deterrence; on the understanding that one of the fundamental conditions for punishment to be effective is that the institutions that impose it behave consistently.

However, in those places where, out of inefficiency or for any other reason, the justice system sometimes punishes and sometimes fails to punish those who commit serious crimes, the threat of punishment is not credible to potential criminals and, as a consequence, hardly discourages them from committing misdeeds. In this respect, amnesty plays a crucial role among the factors understood to interfere with the ordinary functioning of justice, keeping it from acting consistently as a credible deterrent whereby punishment follows conviction almost automatically. This being the case, amnesty is unsurprisingly the legal device most often targeted by humanitarian

---

[12] Ruti G. Teitel, *Transitional Justice* (Oxford: Oxford University Press, 2000); Teitel, *Globalising Transitional Justice: Contemporary Essays* (Oxford: Oxford University Press, 2014).

'punitivism'. The fight against impunity is one of the ideals of criminal law, and thus the struggle of ordinary law to eradicate amnesty and other extraordinary devices that resemble it is as logical as it is predictable. In Colombia, there are still many human rights organisations that consider the constitutional tradition of privileged treatment of political crimes and the culture of amnesty as central drivers of political violence and war.

At the international level, the preamble of the Rome Statute of the International Criminal Court (ICC) posits the end of impunity for international crimes as a central means to contribute to prevention. Yet, this prevention-through-accountability logic is particularly problematic for the ICC. In the absence of a planetary government that, analogous to national governments, is able to assert its sovereignty over the globe to create a global rule of law, the ICC must appeal to the principle of complementarity so that individual states, if necessary with ICC support, can create the conditions that make the treaty's ideals possible within the national territory. However, it is well known that the mix of consolidated, weak, and collapsed states that make up the international community can hardly fulfil the function of consistency of treatment across international criminal cases. As such, the ICC's 'ordinary-ist' dream of global justice is far from being achievable.

In that regard, Jon Elster is probably right when he says that the threat of punishment dissuades potential dictators but entrenches current ones.[13] The same applies to rebel leaders: the threat of punishment possibly intimidates those who are still thinking whether or not to start a rebellion, but very surely entrenches and radicalises those who are already in up to their necks. In this sense, it is difficult to ascertain the factual conditions that will make it possible for punishment to fulfil the function of positive prevention; for this presupposes a minimum common denominator of shared values and the existence of local societies (and even of a global society) that are highly homogeneous or at least very coherent – conditions that do not remotely exist in today's world.

Because of these realities, the struggle of the ordinary against the extraordinary in the legal sphere ends up operating as a quest more to encroach and marginalise the extraordinary, than to exclude it altogether. It is understood that where the state and its justice system are weak, the ruling out of amnesty actually leads to its return through the back door, camouflaged as de facto impunity. That is why even international treaties that articulate the state's duty to provide effective remedies or conduct trials for serious human rights

---

[13] Jon Elster, 'Coming to Terms with the Past. A Framework for the Study of Justice in the Transition to Democracy', *European Journal of Sociology* 39, no. 1 (1998): 7–48.

violations or international crimes, such as, for example, the International Covenant on Civil and Political Rights and the Rome Statute, contain formulas that allow room for the extraordinary. They allow for the possibility that in very particular circumstances, after adequately weighing the values, principles, and circumstances involved, actions such as desisting from prosecutorial investigation (e.g., Rome Statute Article 53) or derogating from treaty obligations (the 'public emergency' clause of various human rights treaties) are justifiable. This is notwithstanding the fact that the institutional framework of human rights, in its abstract and general protection of individual rights, largely presupposes peaceful conditions of social and political normality.

However, there has also been a visible trend since the nineteenth century toward judicialisation of the political and politicisation of the judicial. The arena of IHL reflects this. When IHL was initially dominantly anchored to the idea of the reciprocal vulnerability of opposing enemies, amnesty, even in blanket forms, was ordinary in its functionality and normative role within IHL. The emergence of ad hoc international courts created by the UN Security Council as the precarious foreshadowing of the ICC and a global super-rule of law, conveys that the symmetry of IHL no longer depends mostly on the reciprocal vulnerability of enemies but rather on their equidistance from an independent and impartial third party that uses the same yardstick to judge the conduct of each. Under this paradigm, amnesty, especially a broad and deep one, tends to become, even within IHL, an increasingly extraordinary notion. As such, it is unsurprising that the ICRC has ceased to operate merely as an intermediary between parties in conflict and has increasingly become a landscaper of criminal categories as well. This also explains why Article 6.5 of Protocol II to the Geneva Conventions of 1949, according to which the authorities in power are obligated at the end of hostilities to endeavour to grant 'the broadest possible amnesty', has been subject to increasingly restrictive but highly questionable re-interpretations, both by the ICRC and several international courts.

But in the absence of a global super-rule of law, amnesty remains a more ordinary than extraordinary figure in IHL. This is different at the domestic level, where constitutional law is conceived under the premise of territorial sovereignty and the rule of law. There, amnesty is by necessity more extraordinary than ordinary in its conception and function. And yet the balance between the ordinary and the extraordinary, both in IHL and in domestic constitutional law, also depends, in the case of amnesty, on the terms and conditions of the specific law. From the standpoint of both international and domestic law, amnesty for less serious crimes is naturally more acceptable, and thus more ordinary, than amnesty for the most serious crimes; amnesty for foot soldiers is more acceptable, and thus more ordinary, than amnesty for the top echelons; and so on.

In this regard, it is worth recalling that in both the pre- and post-plebiscite versions of the final agreement between the Colombian government and the FARC, the amnesty formulas, which covered all parties involved in the war – albeit drafted under other names in the case of the military – were based on IHL. As to the specific amnesty for the guerrillas, which restored the constitutional tradition of the 'combatant-rebel', it relied on a combination of reinforced IHL and the privileged treatment of political crime. Also, in contrast to the tendency described above to interpret amnesty restrictively, Colombia's 2012 Legal Framework for Peace and the pre-plebiscite version of the final agreement contemplated the possibility of allowing partial amnesty for those responsible for non-systematically-perpetrated international crimes.

This kind of balanced approach precisely coincides with the general practice of states, despite much rhetoric to the contrary. Louise Mallinder, Francesca Lessa, Leigh Payne, and others have described the ubiquitous recurrence of models that combine selective punishment and conditional amnesty in the scope of transitional practice by states, as an indicator that conditional amnesty is a device of justice and not of impunity.[14] The fact of the matter is that selective punishment and conditional amnesty are complementary sides of the same coin. One may even go so far as to say that the ubiquity of the amnesty-plus-justice formula makes it into something highly ordinary, rather than extraordinary.

On the Extraordinary and the Ordinary in Transitions from War and from Dictatorship

Political and legal rhetoric, when used effectively, does not adapt to reality but rather constructs it. It has an almost unlimited potential to qualify a situation as extraordinary or as ordinary and to choose the means – also extraordinary or ordinary – required to address it. Insofar as its users discard the effort to be truthful, they can represent asymmetrical repression, typical of a dictatorship, as if it were a symmetrical confrontation between parties in an armed conflict. Likewise, they can represent reciprocal victimisation between warring parties

---

[14] Francesca Lessa and Leigh A. Payne, eds., *Amnesty in the Age of Human Rights Accountability: Comparative and International Perspectives* (Cambridge: Cambridge University Press, 2012); Louise Mallinder, 'Atrocity, Accountability, and Amnesty in a "Post-Human Rights World"?' (Inaugural Professorial Lecture, Ulster University, Belfast, 23 March 2017).

as though it were an asymmetric and unidirectional victimisation by a dictatorial state.

By contrast, insofar as the users of political and legal rhetoric seek to represent reality truthfully, the diagnoses and policies appropriate to transitions from dictatorship to democracy are best articulated in terms of ordinary rationales and those from civil war to peace as extraordinary ones. To the extent that the transition to a democratic regime presupposes the continuity of the state apparatus that sustains it, what is involved in the transition is restoring ordinary institutions as quickly as possible. In this sense, those who identify with an emerging democracy have no better discourse to distance themselves from their predecessors than to claim the ordinary against the extraordinary, since a dictatorship tends to be rightly interpreted as a state of exception. Transitions from a civil war, by contrast, have presupposed the nonexistence or at least the partial collapse of the state. As such, they can be sensibly executed only by linking them to an extraordinary discourse, in which the full return to the ordinary is usually represented as the end of a long road over which the extraordinary progressively gives way to the ordinary.

In Colombia, it may be observed that those who see national events as taking place in the bosom of an ordinary state and under a constitution that persists largely unaltered – all based on the premise that Colombia hasn't experienced full-fledged internal armed conflict – tend to ascribe no value to *pacta sunt servanda* (i.e., the contractual promise that underlies a peace agreement). By contrast, those who understand Colombia as a country which has lived through decades of war that prevented state-building in vast peripheral areas or caused its partial collapse, see the need for an agreement capable of ushering in a transition from war to peace. While for the former the decisions made by Congress and the ordinary courts are the only source of legitimacy and legal security, for the latter the principle of *pacta sunt servanda* is an enormous source of legitimacy and legal security, requiring a balance between the foundational aspect of the peace agreement and the legal security derived from the ordinary competencies of public authority. This kind of logic underwrote much of the Havana process, as we later explain.

The Ordinary and the Extraordinary in Criminal Justice

In her classic book, *Legalism*, Judith Shklar explains that in order to judge extraordinary and unprecedented crimes such as the Nazis' industrial and mass murder of European Jewry, the law of the Nuremberg trials had to transcend the conventional standards of the international criminal law of its time.[15] As such, the London Charter established new categories of crimes, such as 'crimes against humanity' and 'crimes against peace', and attempted to create new prosecution criteria. Among other things, it put limits on the principle of due obedience, and prohibited *tu quoque* and military necessity as arguments of exoneration. It even allowed for the possibility that entities, such as the SS, could be declared as criminal organisations, thus making individual membership a criminal act.

In the effort to use law to judge the Holocaust, Shklar points out that 'legalism' was subjected to two opposing drives: on the one hand, to embrace the extraordinary by changing the rules in order to account for unprecedented events; and on the other, to avoid deforming law in the process. Lawrence Douglas, in his book *The Memory of Judgment*, and following Shklar, says that in the Nuremberg trials as well as in the Eichmann trial in Jerusalem, the judges aimed to preserve the legitimacy of the trials by responding to the innovative audacity of legislators and prosecutors with great efforts to make the extraordinary ordinary, or at least to give the extraordinary the appearance of the ordinary.[16]

In *Closing the Books*, Jon Elster, closely following Otto Kirchheimer, describes what we might call, in Weberian language, the ideal types of legal justice and political justice.[17] According to Elster, in its extreme form, legal justice is characterised by contingency in results and a strict respect for the rule of law and due process; whereas political justice is characterised by non-contingency in results, restrictions on due process, and political over-determination. One could even say that extreme forms of political justice are not justice at all, but merely politics. Classic examples of the latter include, for example, the administrative criminal justice of the Nazis, the show trials of Stalin's Soviet Union during the 1930s, and the examples of victor's justice after the Second World War in many European countries.

Within the cultural horizon of liberal democratic constitutionalism, legal justice is the ultimate ideal type of ordinary justice. By contrast, political justice – in its less extreme forms – is the ultimate ideal type of extraordinary justice. However, being an extraordinary form of justice, political justice usually suffers from a lack of legitimacy. That is because, among other things,

---

[15] Judith Shklar, *Legalism: Law, Morals, and Political Trials* (Cambridge, Mass.: Harvard University Press, 1986).
[16] Lawrence Douglas, *The Memory of Judgment: Making Law and History in the Trials of the Holocaust* (New Haven, Conn.: Yale University Press, 2005), chaps. 2–3.
[17] Jon Elster, *Closing the Books: Transitional Justice in Historical Perspective* (Cambridge: Cambridge University Press, 2004).

it contradicts ordinary justice's sacred principle of equal treatment for equal cases, and diverges from the idea that criminal trials should serve only the goal of imparting justice to the accused, and not some kind of political or socio-pedagogical goal.

Here, we must contrast the role of judges in ordinary versus extraordinary circumstances. In the former, judges may primarily orient themselves by inputs (legal and judicial precedents) rather than outputs (good results). However, in the latter circumstances, no such luxury exists. In the face of large-scale political uncertainty and in the absence of pre-established normative guidance, the judges who operate in the extraordinary setting of a transition out of war or long-standing authoritarianism frequently have to orient themselves by outputs rather than inputs. When drafting their decisions, they usually are forced to look into the future more than into the past because, like politicians, they have to weigh values without a pre-set orientation at their disposal. In Weberian terms, they have to reflect on the consequences of their decisions as much as on principles.

The legislator in the extraordinary circumstances of a post-conflict peace agreement implementation process bears a similar responsibility to prioritise outputs. In the effort to preserve the legitimacy of justice when it can't avoid being viewed as political (and when it must be protected against those who attack it in the name of the paradigm of legal justice), the legislator has to strive to give it the appearance of ordinary justice, if not making it ordinary altogether.

Here it is worth observing that transitional justice – our main concern in this book – is subject to a double movement towards both the extraordinary and ordinary, integrating various combinations of political and legal justice. For example, during the negotiations in Havana, the FARC's struggle to assert its dignity was mainly a fight for the extraordinary, whereas that of the government – focused as it was on maximising legal security – was mainly a struggle in favour of the ordinary. In the words of High Commissioner Jaramillo, the duck of the peace deal's justice formula had to 'quack'; that is, it had to be recognisable as such, failing which it would be at constant risk of being derailed for diverging excessively from notions of ordinary justice, thus depriving those who passed before it of a reliable verdict.

Yet, the need for this balancing act should not surprise us, especially in the context of a peace process. Negotiation's need for mutual concessions and formal equality – discussed in Part I of this book – organically crystallise in symmetrical models of reciprocal commitment that offer an impartial form of justice to all the parties involved in the commission of serious crimes, under the umbrella of transitional justice's larger transformative aims. By contrast, the law derived from military victory, much like ordinary criminal law (and as affirmation of the sovereignty of the state), usually crystallises in asymmetric models of simple submission to justice vis-à-vis the vanquished party.

Spain achieved its negotiated transition out of Francoism through recourse to an extraordinary, unconditional amnesty of all crimes of the dictatorship. It did so without a transitional court. Later, after the amnesty regime weakened through judicial reviews, Spain ended up having to prosecute certain crimes of the past through ordinary courts. Responding to the extraordinary with ordinary instruments has meant that the struggle for accountability has no end and becomes a permanent and painful companion to ordinary life. Indeed, something similar has happened in Chile. Unlike Spain, Chile employed the extraordinary measure of establishing a truth commission. However, the Chilean transition also involved respect for a broad self-amnesty, dating back to 1978, that covered all prior crimes perpetrated by the Pinochet regime (and others). When the Inter-American Court of Human Rights invalidated the amnesty, it became necessary to judge the crimes of the past; and, just as in Spain, the task was entrusted to ordinary courts. The result has been that a wide range of members of the military involved in the crimes of the dictatorship have had to appear before ordinary courts, with no end in sight for the trials.

Unlike what happened in Spain and Chile, the final agreement negotiated in Havana between the Colombian government and the FARC devised a complex system of transitional justice that included a temporary special court, separated from the ordinary courts. Acting as the first and last word on the matter, the special court was meant to judge, in a comparatively short period of time, the most serious and representative crimes, while resolving the legal situation of all others who had direct or indirect participation in conflict-related crimes. The idea was that extraordinary justice would absorb the full prosecutorial and judicial burden of the war and, in so doing, help decongest ordinary justice, which was highly inoperative and over-burdened.

While the Colombian model is only beginning to be tested in practice, it highlights how, from a short- and medium-term teleological perspective, transitional justice can be understood as a normalisation process (that is, an induced transformation of the extraordinary into the ordinary), through a combination of argumentative and instrumental resources adopted to that effect by the most relevant actors. Let us recall that during the final years of the Weimar Republic, at a time when the concept of transitional justice had not yet appeared, the broad legal-political discussions around how to restore the seriously perturbed public order centred on a debate around the ordinary and the extraordinary. Hans Kelsen argued that in order to preserve and restore peace, Germany's Constitution had to be constructed exclusively upon rationales and devices of ordinary law and, in consequence, without appealing to the idea of states of exception (a relic of the age of absolutism that ought to disappear). Carl Schmitt, his great contradictor at the time, argued that to restore peace and public order, it would be best to allow for an expanded use of presidential powers of exception, even beyond the limits established by the Constitution. Today, with the benefit of hindsight, we know more about such risks and thus should be able to design for better results.

The Ordinary and the Extraordinary: Before, During, and After the Negotiations

In Havana, the tension between the ordinary and the extraordinary was constant. In order to reconstruct the tension adequately, several initial points bear mention:

1. The tension did not begin in Havana. It long predated it.
2. The ordinary and the extraordinary are transversal concepts. They run across other substantive areas of tension in the negotiations, such as the tension between truth and justice, legal security and dignity, and more.
3. Because the tension between the ordinary and the extraordinary is often subtle in its manifestations, we need markers that help identify its occurrences. In the context of the negotiation of Point 5, such markers included the following: (1) what may be considered 'normal' and 'routine', versus that which is neither; (2) what presupposes peace and public order, versus that which presupposes war and disorder; (3) what has precedent, versus that which would be foundational; (4) what apportions responsibilities among all parties, versus that which would amount to the submission of only one side; (5) what is part of the ordinary functioning of the rule of law and the constitution, versus that which could alter it from outside; (6) what is permanent, versus temporary; (7) what applies generally and abstractly in all circumstances, versus that which could apply only in particular situations; and (8) what implies a single standard of judgement and punishment, versus multiple standards.
4. In the area of criminal law, the tension between the ordinary and the extraordinary had additional markers, including distinguishing between (1) the ordinary treatment of an internal enemy using a police-like punitive approach, and the extraordinary treatment implied in a

political-military method; (2) ordinary judgement and punishment, and extraordinary amnesty and pardon; (3) the ordinary prosecution of common crime, and the extraordinary prosecution of mass political crime; and (4) the ordinary approach of ensuring the prosecution of all those who have committed serious crimes, and the extraordinary logic of prosecuting only those considered most responsible for the most serious crimes.
5. The tension between the ordinary and the extraordinary is greater in international law than in national, but in either case unfolds through a process that involves making the ordinary more extraordinary, and the extraordinary more ordinary.
6. To increase the legitimacy of a justice that would otherwise look more political than legal, the ordinariness will usually increase and the extraordinariness will tend to be concealed.

The Ordinary and the Extraordinary in the Recent History of Colombian Constitutionalism

There is much self-deception in believing that the history of humanity – and with it, that of Colombia – has progressed along a line that goes from the primacy of the extraordinary, represented in deregulated decisions and disruptive events, to the primacy of the ordinary and its routines, manifest in more structured behaviours and in the largely smooth functioning of impersonal institutions with their regulated decisions and procedural controls. Reality is otherwise: modern law still struggles to reduce the scope of the extraordinary, to domesticate it and to diminish its frequency.

The Colombian Constitution of 1886, which gave legal form to the 1885 war victory of the regeneration movement, established the 'state of siege' standard in its Article 121. This gave discretionary powers to the President of the Republic to replace the ordinary legislator and to suspend rights and guarantees in extraordinary circumstances of disturbance of public order. The fact that the President had a discretionary power to decide whether the conditions were in place to declare a state of siege, and to determine the instruments that should be employed, favoured the abuse of this constitutional device. The state of emergency became normal, and with it, the replacement of Congress by the government in the task of making laws. Decades later, during the period of the National Front (1958–1974), the existence of the guerrillas in the rural periphery served as a justification, but also as an excuse, for successive governments to maintain the country – including urban centres where life was largely normal – under a state of siege.

The political left, with the support of the nascent human rights movement, eventually succeeded in its aim to re-signify the restricted democracy of the National Front as analogous to dictatorship. Once the National Front period had formally ended, though still under its shadow, the government of Julio César Turbay (1978–1982), facing difficult disturbances – epitomised by the spectacular armed actions of the M-19 guerrillas in major cities – appealed yet again to the state of siege. The 'Security Statute', as it was called during the Turbay government, was a device of repression that, among other things, sharply curtailed civil liberties, criminalised social protest, invested the military with judicial police functions, and handed the administration of civilian trials to military courts. People commonly spoke of the 'Turbay-Camacho Leyva dictatorship' (Camacho Leyva was a military general and the Minister of Defence), thus allowing revolutionary warfare to be reinterpreted and obscured as resistance against oppression. The guerrillas were able to portray themselves simultaneously as victims of a dictatorship and the defenders of other victims.

Under the weight of the arbitrary acts of despotism perpetrated by the military under the Security Statute, the state of siege norm eventually became discredited. This explains why the 1991 National Constituent Assembly opted to replace it with the 'state of internal commotion', a legal norm whose use by the government is controlled by the Constitutional Court. Thus, in the current Constitution, the extraordinary, in the form of states of exception, was not eliminated altogether; yet it was clearly domesticated. It is no longer possible to suspend fundamental rights and guarantees, but only to restrict them, subject to judicial controls and precise deadlines. As a result, governments use it less often, which has in turn lent greater credibility to the ordinary organs of government.

Something similar happened with the ability of Congress to grant the President extraordinary powers in legislative matters. Whereas the 1886 Constitution allowed legislators to grant such powers by simple majority and for all kinds of circumstances, today it requires a special majority, and the powers must be limited to fewer and more precise tasks. In this sense, the change from one constitution to another represented an effort to guarantee the stable, predictable, and routine functioning of an ordinary constitutional logic. Importantly, the 1991 Constitution also created the Constitutional Court as an antidote against the tyranny of the majority.

It would be wrong, however, to affirm that Colombia's new Constitution eradicated extraordinary thinking from its core. Instead, what it did was to establish a new balance between ordinary and extraordinary rationales, in favour of the former. In the new Constitution, the authorities can appeal to the extraordinary only when it is unavoidable, and in all cases impairing the ordinary as little as possible.

However, when a constitution, wanting to realise the Kelsenian dream, is radically ordinary such that it excludes all extraordinary devices to respond to extraordinary circumstances, what it often does is to dig its own grave. Especially in contexts of chronic war and crisis, such as in Colombia during long periods of the nineteenth to twenty-first centuries, the presence of the extraordinary ends up imposing itself and forcing governments and states, even the best managed and intentioned, to respond outside the ordinary law. During the constitutive assembly of his time, Miguel Antonio Caro had already said, in his effort to incorporate the state of siege into the 1886 Constitution, that doing so would prevent the law from becoming the 'king of ridicule' when faced with extraordinary circumstances.[18] Avoidance of such ridicule is also what led the Santos administration, over a century later, to secure adoption of Transitory Articles 66 and 67, which together constitute the Legal Framework for Peace that allowed the constitutional space needed to achieve transitional justice within a peace deal.

Note, in this sense, that transitional justice mechanisms are a contemporary functional equivalent (albeit morally, politically, and legally superior) to the old states of exception and extraordinary powers. As a functional equivalent, they emerged hand in hand with the revolution in human rights and the new humanitarian conscience, in order to make justice possible in a transitional Colombia in response to atrocities committed in wartime. In comparison with the exceptional, the transitional tends to represent a better coupling of the extraordinary and the ordinary in the distribution of functions among public powers. It allows for better balance between reparative, restorative, and transformative approaches, and between looking to the past and looking to the future. But above all, it tends to produce a better compromise between the demands of peace and the demands of justice. As such, it should not be surprising that while states of exception have fallen into disuse, transitional justice has become the order of the day. This is so not merely because it is fashionable but also because it is a much better response to the challenges posed by the extraordinary.

Here it must be recalled that the 1991 Constitution was, itself, born in the context of various peace processes that took place in the late 1980s and early 1990s between the Colombian government and social-revolutionary guerrilla groups such as the M-19 and the EPL, both of which decided to replace

---

[18] Iván Orozco Abad, *Die Gestaltung des Ausnahmezustandes in Kolumbien im 19. Jahrhundert*, vol. 15 (Saarbrücke: Breitenbach Verlag, 1988), 341–345.

bullets with ballots and reintegrate into civilian and democratic life. Given these origins, the Constitution is clearly open to negotiated peace, including to future opportunities for extraordinary peacemaking by negotiation. As such, it was perfectly natural to amend it via Transitory Articles 66 and 67. This act both embraced and reinforced the Colombian Constitution's identity as one that is aspirational and guided by a strong preference for negotiated peace, constructed around ordinary and extraordinary devices held in tension.

The Ordinary and the Extraordinary in the Debate about the Legal Framework for Peace

The heated public debate in 2012 that led to the approval of the Legal Framework for Peace contributed decisively to acclimatising the concept of transitional justice in Colombia. The discussions that preceded and accompanied this constitutional amendment, first in Congress and later before the Constitutional Court, were explicitly informed by the debate around the ordinary and the extraordinary.

The government officials and legislators who submitted the bill began by stating that the implementation of Law 975 of 2005 (i.e., the Justice and Peace Law) had produced serious congestion problems in the administration of justice and was on the verge of collapse. The law in question regulated a macro-judicial process that had already been going on for six years, mainly against the demobilised members of the United Self-Defence Forces of Colombia (AUC), but also against some individual guerrilla members who voluntarily gave up arms and who may have perpetrated international crimes. The advocates of the Legal Framework for Peace pointed out that, through Law 975, prosecutors and judges were investigating and judging hundreds of thousands of crimes perpetrated by the AUC on case-by-case basis, as the ordinary courts might do, and that this produces more, rather than less, aggregate impunity. The prosecutors and judges were failing to establish the underlying systems and patterns of crime, and neglecting to use selection criteria that would allow for the prioritisation and selection of cases. As such, the individuals participating in the law's qualified plea bargaining regime would either withdraw their plea or be released without having resolved their situation before the law. The accusation, therefore, was that the implementation of the Justice and Peace Law had become ordinary in its logic, despite regulating an extraordinary process and caseload.

Based on this diagnosis, the creators and advocates of the Framework asserted the importance of establishing an extraordinary system of transitional justice, which would be separated from the ordinary system and restricted to the punishment of those most responsible for the most serious crimes (as opposed to criminal prosecution of the largest number of persons possible). Acting in this way would allow for qualitative criteria of prosecution to prevail over quantitative ones, relieving the state from the self-destructive burden of prosecuting an infinite caseload left by fifty years of war. Thus, the draft Legal Framework for Peace opened room for amnesties, alternative sentences, suspended sentences, early releases, and so on. Most importantly perhaps, the Framework stipulated that war crimes that were not systematically perpetrated could be excluded from the state's duty to prosecute.

Some advocates of Transitory Articles 66 and 67 argued – even against the Framework's drafters – that it was also necessary to rescue Colombian constitutional traditions and jurisprudence that would, in extraordinary fashion, permit revival of the domestic concept of political crime in order to help balance justice and peace in the negotiation. In that regard, they criticised various rulings of the Constitutional Court that had begun eliminating key distinctions between political and ordinary crime and undermining the needed balance between peace and justice, including a 2010 judgement that reviewed the constitutionality of Law 1312 of 2009 on the principle of plea bargaining.[19] This law had created a new freedom to refrain from criminally prosecuting demobilised combatants who had not committed crimes against humanity; yet the Court knocked it down with the absurd argument that its constitutionality had to be analysed as ordinary criminal policy and not as transitional justice, because the law was not the product of a national peace agreement. So, following the principle of legality, with its idea that all crimes deserve to be equally treated, ordinary justice had to prosecute such cases. Other rulings pointed in a similar direction, determining that the serious crimes perpetrated within the armed conflict could not be treated as political crimes based on the circular logic that they were ordinary (i.e., common) crimes by virtue of their seriousness.

Opponents of the Legal Framework for Peace, such as the Inspector General and the *Centro Democrático* party, which participated vividly in these debates, argued from an exclusively ordinary mind-set. They asserted that a prosecutorial concentration on the persons most responsible for the most serious crimes would violate the 'principle of legality' (i.e., the state's duty to prosecute all international crimes) and the rights of victims. Similar claims were espoused by some human rights defenders and those who spoke on behalf of respecting rigid international punitive standards in relation to all those who are responsible for international crimes, regardless of their role and

---

[19] Constitutional Court of Colombia, Ruling C-936 of 2010.

degree of involvement. In this respect, some of them cited the broadly punitive logic of the Inter-American Court of Human Rights, demanding ordinary treatment for extraordinary situations.

In his intervention as a private citizen before the Constitutional Court during the special hearings on the Legal Framework for Peace, Professor Orozco, still unaware that the secret phase of the peace negotiations was taking place in Havana, defended the Framework's usefulness as an extraordinary device to facilitate negotiated peace with justice. Above all, he promoted the value of ensuring privileged legal treatment for political offenders (something insufficiently reflected in the Framework) and the idea that this should result in alternative and reduced penalties that would be both retributive and reparative.

But if the Legal Framework for Peace was rather miserly in its acceptance of political crime, it was, by contrast, very generous in its embrace of the idea of extraordinariness. Article 66 is explicit in saying that transitional justice mechanisms are 'exceptional' and that they aim towards the 'predominant' goal of achieving peace. As such, it establishes an extraordinary criterion for assigning relative weight, binding for all public powers, not only between justice and the rights of victims and society, but also between these values and peace. Article 66 also (1) establishes that both judicial and extrajudicial mechanisms may be used; (2) orders the creation of a truth commission in the event that peace is reached – a mechanism that is by definition extraordinary but that has become ordinary in the international arena; and (3) links the benefits of transitional justice to the precondition of demobilisation for groups like the FARC.

The existence of the Legal Framework for Peace in the current Constitution is, itself, a reflection of earlier efforts to 'ordinarify' (legalise) the extraordinary. It makes clear that the Constitution is a system of balances between ordinary and extraordinary mind-sets whose relative prevalence should be weighted according to the circumstances in question. In political terms, this has nevertheless meant that the Colombian Constitution has become – before, during, and after the negotiations in Havana – a battlefield for strategic litigation between those in favour and those against the negotiations and the peace agreement itself. More generally, it has become a battlefield between those who, for one reason or another, aspire to the absolute sanctification of either ordinary or extraordinary rationales.

A Brief Comparison

To fully understand where the Legal Framework for Peace sits on the continuum from the ordinary to the extraordinary, it may be useful to distinguish between selection of cases based on the nature and degree of personal accountability (subjective selection) and selection based on the nature and gravity of the crime (objective selection). To draw out the contrast, a comparison may be made with the 2005 Justice and Peace Law, a model of justice lacking in subjective case selection vis-à-vis those who turned themselves in for the commission of non-amnestiable crimes. The model demanded the processing of all those who were responsible for having perpetrated serious crimes, regardless of their role and degree of involvement. Consequently, following the logic of ordinary justice, prosecutors started investigating everyone rather than focusing on those most responsible for patterns of macro-criminal behaviour. Even after legal reforms several years later when the macro-process was on the verge of failure because it had failed to produce any decisive sentences, the Justice and Peace Law largely remained a model of extraordinary justice that operated on a very ordinary rationale.

The Legal Framework for Peace, with its penchant for extreme subjective case selection, was premised on the very different rationale that only those most responsible for systemic international crimes would be judicially prosecuted. This is an example of radical 'extraordinarification' of domestic justice. In a robust but controversial exercise of the principle of complementarity, which lies at the foundation of the ICC's Rome Statute, the Framework effectively reproduces a domestic clone of the ICC's approach in its special prosecutorial focus on the 'big fish'.

Faced with the options of radical 'ordinarification' of transitional justice manifested in the 2005 Justice and Peace model, and radical extraordinarification manifested in the 2012 Legal Framework for Peace, the final model agreed between the Colombian government and the FARC, post-plebiscite, takes the middle ground in terms of subjective case selection. Neither too many, nor too few, should appear before the Special Jurisdiction for Peace (JEP). This constituted a change from the JEP model adopted in the pre-plebiscite agreement, which resembled the Justice and Peace model more than the Framework; following ordinary rationales, it aimed to prosecute all serious violations perpetrated in the context of the armed conflict, including non-systematically-perpetrated war crimes. In that regard, it was more in keeping with prevailing human rights orthodoxies. By contrast, by allowing impunity for non-systematic war crimes, the Framework for Peace went against such orthodoxies.

Leveraging the Ordinary and the Extraordinary in the Havana Talks

The fact that the Havana talks involved two undefeated sides prepared to negotiate a transition from war to peace served as support and justification for the establishment of extraordinary, and specifically, foundational formulas. At the same time, because the negotiations took place in a context of constitutional rule of law that was largely continuous, robust, and articulated around the principle of the division of powers, the parties (but especially the FARC) had to submit in significant ways to the rationales, devices, and routines of ordinary constitutionalism. Such were the contextual premises that supported the extraordinary and ordinary rationales that would have to be reconciled.

Despite the enormous power asymmetry that characterised the confrontation between the state and the guerrillas in favour of the former, the parties negotiated under the dual premise that the state could not defeat the guerrillas in a reasonable time frame and with reasonable humanitarian and financial costs, and the guerrillas could not take control of the state by force. The equality derived from this negative stalemate embodied a kind of necessary fiction that gave the guerrillas a power they lacked in any armed confrontation with the state. In this light, it is understandable that the FARC wanted the centre of gravity to be the negotiating table in Havana, rather than the democracy back in Colombia. This was its best option for gaining advantages and preventing future breaches of the deal by the state.

Yet, the reality is that the FARC was negotiating with a democratic and constitutional state that functioned relatively well in key parts of its territory (especially the large urban centres where most of the population is concentrated) and with a bona fide division of powers involving not only the executive branch but also a Congress, several high courts, and independent oversight bodies like the Inspector General. As such, it was guaranteed that the parties would eventually relinquish control over whatever they agreed in Havana; any agreement reached was necessarily subject to the contingency of independent review by state bodies and Colombian society. In that sense, what was agreed by the parties was only ever valid *ad referendum*, that is to say, up until it was finally endorsed: by the citizenry, which, it was agreed, would have to ratify the accord by plebiscite; by the Constitutional Court, which would have to ensure that any accord conforms to the minimal norms and exigencies of the Constitution; and by the ordinary legislator, which would have the function of turning the Constitutional Court's rulings on the peace accord into law. In addition, insofar as the Colombian Constitution incorporates ratified international treaties as part of its ordinary law, the uncontrolled contingencies went further: the final accord could potentially be reviewed, among others, by the Inter-American Court of Human Rights. The ICC and foreign prosecutors, not least in the United States, were also beyond the strict control of the Havana negotiating table. All of these contingencies were enumerated repeatedly by the government delegation in explaining why certain FARC proposals were untenable.

It is likely that, by holding the negotiations under conditions of confidentiality and geographic isolation, the FARC may have felt freer to make exaggerated demands and take an excessively foundational (extraordinary) stance on questions of law. Yet, the fact that the parties had committed themselves to submit the final agreement to some form of popular ratification helped to curb even worse excesses, while allowing the government –and ultimately both parties – to adopt a more ordinary stance. After all, the majorities who vote in Colombia are urban majorities living in circumstances of general constitutional routine. Compared to their fellow citizens in the country's interior, these majorities also did not suffer as directly from the war. As such, they tended to put a lower ceiling on any extraordinary pretensions that might emanate from the Havana process. This may be what explains why the FARC eventually gave up their insistence that the final agreement be submitted to approval by a national constituent assembly – an idea that would have embodied an excessive extraordinarification of the peace agreement, making it unviable before a public with more ordinary expectations. For this and many other reasons, the government forcefully and consistently opposed the FARC's proposed constituent assembly.

The Competing Pulls of Havana and Bogota

In reflecting on the negotiation of Point 5, it is evident that the parties' different views on the characteristics and magnitude of the Colombian armed conflict underwrote their respective uses of political-juridical rhetoric about the extraordinary and the ordinary. The FARC started from the premise that the negotiations were meant to put an end to a war whose social and political origins could be traced back at least to the 1930s. The government, by contrast, operated from the premise that the agreement would put an end to an internal armed conflict that had its origin in the emergence of the FARC as a military and political apparatus in the early 1960s, during the National Front era. Meanwhile, back in Bogota, the opposition to the negotiations – led by former President Uribe – replicated the 'democratic security' discourse that had served as the ideological foundation of his two administrations. Uribe insisted that there was no armed conflict in Colombia, much less a civil war, but simply a narcoterrorist threat against a legitimate democracy.

The notion of a great war, which the FARC took for granted, led to their extraordinary and foundational mentality vis-à-vis the negotiations. At the opposite extreme, Uribe's thesis of the non-war and of the FARC as a terrorist threat, gave rise to a rhetoric of affirmation of the sovereignty of the state and the routines of the Constitution and ordinary law. The government, with its notion of an internal armed conflict somewhere between the FARC's great civil war and Uribe's non-war, followed a rhetoric halfway between the mentality of the extraordinary (and foundational) and that of the ordinary (and sovereigntist). But the differences were not merely ideological. In the relative isolation of Cuba, the government and the FARC did not pay the same heed to Uribe's views as they eventually would need to, following the triumph of the 'No' vote in the 2016 peace plebiscite.

A quick look at the ritualistic communiqués read at eight o'clock each morning by the FARC delegation makes clear how their rhetoric appealed recurrently to the extraordinary as foundational. They often reminded their audience that they had reached the negotiating table after a long war that brought together deep and just historical causes such as the usurpation of land from the peasantry and the criminalisation of social protest. Likewise, at the negotiating table, their foundational vision projected itself in the form of their insistence on creating a national constituent assembly, and their proposal that the negotiating parties be the ones to draft the implementing legislation in lieu of Congress. But their demands for the re-founding of the state reached their inflationary peak with the idea that the final agreement should be treated as a sort of international treaty that would somehow be integrated into the constitutional bloc.[20] Like so many such notions, this one had to be abandoned in favour of a more pragmatic and transactional formula that entailed subjecting the final agreement to Congressional approval as a law, with judicial review by the Constitutional Court.

Nevertheless, as later events would reveal, even the non-foundational formulas finally agreed in Havana did not sufficiently reinforce the paradigm (or expectation) of ordinariness held by many in Colombia – a country where a legalistic Kelsenian positivism pervades. Indeed, a whole series of elements operated as perfect instrumental allies for everything the 'No' result expressed through the votes of those who inhabit the routines and normality of urban life in Colombia: the Kelsenian disregard of war; the understanding of the law as the keeper of a presumed peace and not the maker of a missing one; the purification of the ordinary constitution and removal of any vestige of extraordinary institutions or tools; the reduction of the idea of justice to one of

---

[20] The constitutional bloc – addressed in Law 734 of 2002 – refers to norms and rules agreed in international human rights treaties and International Labour Organization conventions that occupy a shared normative hierarchy with the Colombian Constitution. More information is available at www.corteconstitucional.gov.co/relatoria/2003/c-067-03.htm.

ordinary criminal law; and the inability to offer differential treatment to political and common criminals.

The Inspector General and the Defence of the Ordinary

Few defended the idea of ordinary justice in relation to the Havana talks as much as Inspector General Alejandro Ordoñez. His continuous public statements from Bogota became a sort of background music that accompanied the negotiations for the duration of Point 5. He purported to speak neutrally on behalf of the Constitution, society, and victims all at once.

In September 2015, while the composite deal on Point 5 was still being negotiated, Ordoñez accused the government of pursuing a deal with the FARC that would place the legal interests of state agents, including military and police, and third parties, in the hands of a special jurisdiction located outside the constitutional order.[21] He would repeat this claim often, despite consistent refutations by the government delegation. In his ordinary understanding of the Constitution, Colombia's supreme law did not allow for a model of apportionment of responsibilities between all categories of conflict actors; instead, it only allowed for the possibility of judging the illegal FARC.

Ordoñez also issued communiques and public statements in which he asserted that any penalty, to be understood as such by domestic and international criminal law, had to be proportional to the seriousness of the crimes; and that for those most responsible for crimes against humanity and in general for international crimes, the appropriate punishment could only be that of 'imprisonment', accompanied by a lifetime ban from public office. He thus rejected the reparative and restorative functions of punishment, considering them merely symbolic and thus farcical; and he warned that the ICC held the same view. He demanded, instead, that 'real and effective' justice be done.[22]

His objections revolved around the claim that what was agreed in Havana in terms of political crime would have to follow the patterns already established by the Constitution, by the Congress, and by the courts. As such, he rejected, among other things, any possibility of an exonerating political connection between the act of drug trafficking and the act of rebellion. Ordoñez argued that drug trafficking was a common crime that had served the FARC to

---

[21] 'Existen Sectores Que Parecen Más Preocupados Por La Impunidad Que Por La Justicia: Procurador', 90 Minutos (2015), https://90minutos.co/existen-sectores-que-parecen-mas-preocupados-por-la-impunidad-que-por-la-justicia-procurador/.
[22] 'Los Riesgos Del Proceso De Paz En La Habana, Según El Procurador', *El Tiempo* (2015), www.eltiempo.com/archivo/documento/CMS-16474621.

accumulate land and wealth, and that treating it as connected to rebellion could only serve the dark purpose of shielding its perpetrators from extradition, making it tantamount to giving a drug-trafficking organisation the right to govern Colombia.[23] Paradoxically, he also complained that the agreement with the FARC reduced the amnesty of IHL to an amnesty for political crimes, and with this, it served no other purpose than to exclude the military from such benefit, contrary to the principle of symmetrical treatment agreed by the parties.[24] By the time the full text of the final agreement had been published, along with bill creating the fast-track procedures and extraordinary powers of implementation for the President, Inspector General Ordoñez saw fit to describe the various measures as 'time bombs against the Constitution'.[25]

The Ordinary and the Extraordinary in the Discussion on Truth, Justice, and Amnesty

If the Inspector General represented an extreme defence of the ordinary, the FARC came closest to representing an extreme defence of the extraordinary. Before the negotiation of Point 5 got into full swing, the FARC first proposed an international tribunal, overseen by UNASUR, as the instrument for judging the war's actors. They wanted to leave nothing in the hands of ordinary justice. Failing that, they wanted to have a South African–type truth commission, or a special domestic court that didn't resemble a criminal court. Meanwhile, as already noted, the critics of the Havana negotiations, represented with particular vehemence by the Inspector General and former President Uribe, persistently advocated an ordinary stance, affirming the routines of the rule of law and the Constitution. For them, the solution was simple: the FARC leadership had to submit to an ordinary legal justice system and settle their debt to society with ordinary imprisonment, proportional to the seriousness of the crimes perpetrated, and a lifetime ban from office for those most responsible. Regarding the military, they appealed to their differential legal status and demanded that they be judged by ordinary military tribunals on the basis of the presumption of legality of their acts. As such, in practical terms, their position amounted to a rejection of the negotiation as a whole, but for their

---

[23] 'A Los Capos De Las FARC Los Quieren "Blindar" De La Extradición', *Semana* (2015), https://www.semana.com/nacion/articulo/procurador-dice-que-quieren-blindar-de-la-extradicion-las-farc/411063-3.
[24] 'Existen Sectores Que Parecen'.
[25] 'Ordoñez Anuncia A Colombia Que "La Constitución De 1991 Ha Muerto"', *El Nodo Colombia* (2016), http://elnodo.co/mensajeordonez.

validation of the need for a demobilising amnesty for the guerrilla rank-and-file not involved in serious crimes.

In these circumstances, the government understood correctly that its task was to find a reasonable balance between the ordinary and the extraordinary. After all, it was engaged in a two-way negotiation to end a war, with a rebel group that had been dramatically weakened but not defeated.

Early in the discussions on Point 5, the FARC began its hard push for the Colombian transitional justice model to reproduce the South African one, especially as regards its central device: individualised amnesty for politically motivated offenders willing to confess. Colombia's own Justice and Peace model had been built upon a similar trade-off, but with key differences: what was on offer was a reduced sentence, rather than amnesty; and confessions need to take place before a special criminal tribunal (attached to the ordinary justice system), rather than the special committee of a truth commission. In any case, the FARC wanted to replicate the South African model, giving the truth commission the authority to amnesty political crimes and connected offences (even if international in nature), provided that the confession given was complete.

The government delegation in Havana had very different ideas. It favoured an intermediate amnesty in a judicial setting, one less imbued with the tenor of political crimes and more with that of IHL. It also believed that, for top ranks accused of international crimes, there had to be a mechanism for the administration of criminal justice because that is what Colombians demanded. It argued that leaders of both sides would benefit from a special justice regime, but only under the condition that (1) a person recognise his or her responsibility and contribute to the truth, and (2) a court and not a truth commission decide the special treatment.

Naturally, the FARC pushed hard against this, insisting, publicly as well as privately, on a more amnesty-driven formula, based on recognition of the political character of the armed insurgency in the exercise of their right of rebellion. But their push was in vain. Over time, the government delegation became adamant that a 'justice component' was a minimally necessary aspect of any viable agreement, complaining that the FARC, in its documents and proposals for most of the negotiation of Point 5, failed to mention justice at all. The government also opposed any overly broad amnesty, which it considered unsustainable both domestically and internationally. It said that there had always been limits to amnesty, that those limits had become clearer, and that a 'forgive and forget' approach offered no legal security.

But the government delegation ran out of time to make its case fully, and in mid-2015 was provisionally displaced by an ad hoc legal committee, composed of three legal representatives appointed by each side, which had the task of wrapping up the details of the justice element that the FARC finally accepted as necessary to consummate the deal on Point 5. By this time, however, the conditions and strategy of the negotiation had already changed dramatically, with speed of results being the number one priority of President Santos in light of the increasingly adverse state of public opinion about the talks.

The government delegation in Havana reacted to the first drafts agreed by the government members of the ad hoc legal committee by reminding them that it was essential that the justice model agreed be 'recognisable'. That justice had to be recognisable as such was important for a number of reasons: because it provided the parties legal security; because it allowed state agents to have their uncertain legal situations resolved by a court; because the parties had already agreed that the truth commission would act as a complement and not as a substitute for justice; because without justice for those most responsible, it would be impossible to justify the acquittal or lenient treatment of the vast majority, as the Legal Framework for Peace intended; and, finally, because it was what Colombians had consistently demanded. In short, the government delegation was guided by the intuition that the more clearly defined justice was – following the easily recognisable ideal type of legal and ordinary justice – the greater the political legitimacy and legal security of the model would be.

Ultimately, the FARC ended up much closer to the government position than its own. In December 2015, in its closing message about the JEP, the FARC proclaimed that in the face of the crisis of the state's ordinary justice system, an autonomous judicial mechanism had been agreed for all, and that this honoured Colombia's international commitments and their own emphasis on the centrality of truth. Thus, the FARC had gone from seeking that the issue of justice be resolved within an extrajudicial truth commission, to proclaiming as an achievement that truth lay at the heart of the justice mechanism. But let there be no doubt: this shift would not have happened but for the fact that the JEP covered all conflict actors, and operated according to the logic of reduced punishment for voluntary confessions.

While the FARC may have continued to believe that it would have been possible to employ a variation on the South African model, for the government delegation this was always going to be a non-starter. Ultimately, for a final deal to be reached, the FARC had no alternative but to accept the need for a comprehensive system of transitional justice that included an extraordinary tribunal with enough ordinary attributes to be identifiable as an authentic dispenser of legal justice.

Ordinary Justice as the Enemy's Justice

Notwithstanding the accords that were reached, criminal justice was almost by definition humiliating for the FARC. If it could not be avoided, it had to be transformed or blurred in some way.

For the guerrillas, ordinary Colombian criminal justice had been, especially during the last decades of armed confrontation, 'the enemy's justice'. Prompted by public outcry as the armed conflict escalated and degraded, both Congress and the upper and lower courts, as organs of the ordinary Constitution, had enacted laws and issued rulings that criminalised the guerrillas. The category of 'political crime' had been voided of its content, as members of Congress and the judiciary had dismantled, step by step, the connection between political crime as an end in itself, and associated crimes meant to advance that end. The latter had ceased to be eligible for amnesty, and the guerrillas were no longer being tried and convicted for the crime of rebellion and connected crimes. Instead, they were being increasingly prosecuted and convicted for aggravated conspiracy, kidnapping, terrorism, and so forth. As such, if facing justice was going to be inevitable in the negotiation, the FARC needed to secure a mechanism that would stand as far as possible from ordinary domestic justice, in terms of both the composition of the tribunal and the applicable criminal law regime. This helps explain why the FARC delegation, at times, analysed the possibility of establishing, under the aegis of UNASUR or the UN, an international tribunal that could do the job.

The flight to the extraordinary through an international tribunal was eventually abandoned because, among other things, the FARC became convinced that such a tribunal would be very difficult to create and implement; that it would entail an excess of heteronomy and unpredictability regarding the type of justice it would impart; and that it would neither be acceptable to the government nor legitimate in the eyes of Colombian society. In a world in which punitive-humanitarianism pervades, and where foreign and supranational courts of justice hunt down perpetrators of international crimes, it was ultimately a bad option to put themselves in the hands of an international tribunal. As such, the middle ground between the extraordinary and the ordinary was, in the end, a national court created separately from ordinary justice with the participation of a few foreigners and operating on the basis of a blend of international and domestic criminal law, with jurisdiction extending over all crimes perpetrated in the course of the war.

But if ordinary domestic criminal law was viewed by the FARC as the enemy's law, invoking it nevertheless offered many potential advantages for them. For example, domestic law could facilitate a constitutional reform to restore the tradition of privileged treatment for political crime and its connected offences, as well as ensuring that there were no regulatory gaps in prosecuting crimes that were not codified until well into the decades-long war. International law, by contrast, has little to no flexibility in terms of amendments, and reflects generic ideals that may or may not resonate with the exigencies, constraints, and dysfunctions of particular contexts. On top of this, some of the treaties – not least the Rome Statute of the ICC, in force for Colombia as of 2002 for crimes against humanity and genocide, and as of 2009 for war crimes – have institutions attached to them which are capable of making highly unpredictable decisions. Nevertheless, the FARC recognised that adopting the standards of IHL, and international criminal law in general, would grant greater legal certainty to post-conflict judicial decisions.

The Discussion on the Ordinary and the Extraordinary within the Technical Committee

As noted earlier, the government's internal discussions about transitional justice took place along two parallel tracks: in Havana, within the negotiating team, and in Bogota, within the framework of the Technical Committee. The latter – whose composition is described below – was created to contribute to the construction of the government's official position on transitional justice for the Havana discussions on Point 5. It was a fundamental forum in which the tension between the ordinary and the extraordinary was omnipresent.

To put things in context, it is important to note that the field of IHL is articulated around the dispute between two theses: that of convergence between IHL and human rights, and that of partial divergence.[26] Although it is often said that neither of the two sources prevails over the other, one could say that the first thesis tends, from an ordinary stance, to subordinate IHL to human rights and to presuppose a state of peace. By contrast, the second tends, from an extraordinary stance, to separate IHL and human rights, entrusting the former with regulating war and the latter with regulating peace.

Both theses conceive relations between military criminal justice and ordinary civilian justice and, with it, the extent of military jurisdiction, in very different ways. The first thesis (convergence) understands IHL as a body of law that limits rather than authorises certain conducts, conceiving military

---

[26] Pablo Kalmanovitz, 'Entre el deber de protección y la necesidad militar: oscilaciones del discurso humanitario en Colombia, 1991–2016', *Latin American Law Review* 1 (July 2018): 33–60.

jurisdiction in a very restricted manner. By contrast, the second (partial divergence) understands IHL as a body of law that authorises rather than limits troops' actions in situations of armed confrontation, allowing broad scope for military jurisdiction and comparatively narrower scope for ordinary civilian justice.

Following the first thesis, military jurisdiction is usually understood by human rights defenders and courts (including the Inter-American) not as an extraordinary privilege bestowed upon the military, but as a specialised judicial device to punish soldiers who commit crimes of military indiscipline. The argument is that the law regulating military conduct in armed confrontation should be restrictive; there should be broad civilian jurisdiction to address any war crimes perpetrated by them. This is a way to guarantee oversight of the military by a truly independent and impartial third party and, with that, to encourage restraint among the troops as they engage the enemy. Defenders of this approach fear that, without such oversight, the esprit de corps and the hierarchical subordination between military judges and high commanders would create an incentive for degraded behaviour by the army in times of war, especially an irregular one.

Those who defend the second thesis have sought in recent decades to construe IHL as a *lex specialis* applied preferentially over human rights in contexts of war; as a body of law that authorises, instead of limits, military action in circumstances of armed confrontation. When defending this thesis, the military usually notes that civilian judges do not (and cannot) understand war because they have not lived it, and that they lack the technical knowledge required to judge it adequately. Claiming that IHL shouldn't be interpreted with a peacetime logic, they say that issues such as deciding what is a legitimate target, determining the need and proportionality of attacks, and assessing the collateral damages permitted in the quest for military advantages are technical matters that go beyond the knowledge of civilian judges.

In Colombia, the military usually also claims that civilian judges bear a lot of animosity towards them. Sociologists have thoroughly studied the separation between civilian and military worlds, and this separation is partly responsible for the long history of poor relations between civilian and military judges in Colombia. Starting with the tragedy of the Palace of Justice in 1985, this feud continued in the aftermath of the La Rochela massacre in 1989 and other episodes in which prosecutors and judges were victims of soldiers who felt threatened by justice and, fixated on impunity, made alliances with paramilitaries to silence it. Arguably, the story reached its rhetorical zenith in the confrontation between the Uribe government and the superior courts on account of the 'parapolitics' trials.[27] The episode and its antecedents led many soldiers to the conviction that they are targets of a 'judicial war' waged by civilian judges. President Uribe's *Centro Democrático* party, together with right-wing intellectuals and military retiree associations, fuelled this belief.

In this context, and perhaps as an expression of the relative rise of the thesis of partial divergence – which had already borne its first major fruit in the military operation manuals drawn up during the Uribe and Santos governments – in 2012 the Congress passed Law 192. It established a very broad military jurisdiction, allowing military judges to hear cases of serious war crimes constituting human rights violations, such as extrajudicial executions and sexual violence; and it established that only in exceptional cases would civilian judges be involved, and only for a narrow list of violations. This was, without a doubt, the legal framework with which the military and police forces wanted to face the end of the conflict and the negotiated peace.

But the broad military jurisdiction of Law 192 was struck down by the Constitutional Court in ruling C-740 of 2013. The Santos government, which had initially supported the initiative of a broad military jurisdiction, decided to back down – perhaps frightened by strong reactions by the human rights community. Congress, following the government's initiative, enacted a new law in 2015 that established a more restricted military and police jurisdiction, which was approved by the Constitutional Court in 2016. Despite allowing some concessions to the military – such as requiring IHL knowledge by ordinary civilian judges hearing cases involving the military – the Court, through ruling C-084 of 2016, resurrected the convergence thesis. Civilian judges, not military ones, would try those cases considered most serious.

As it would happen, the Technical Committee was created and operated within the period framed by these two critical judgements. It included, among others, the Minister of Justice, the Prosecutor General, the chief of the government delegation in Havana, the High Commissioner for Peace and his closest aides, members from each branch of the Armed Forces and the National Police, civilian officials from the Ministry of Defence, and various external advisers. When the Technical Committee began to work, Law 192 – the military's 'Plan A' – had already been overturned by the Constitutional Court. This may explain why during the first meetings of the Technical Committee, the advisers of the Ministry of Defence began by proposing that when the armed conflict with the FARC ended, and regardless of what was

---

[27] Parapolitics refers to the political scandal generated by the revelation of linkages between politicians and paramilitaries – heavily involved in narcotrafficking – after the demobilisation of the United Self-Defence Groups of Colombia (AUC) that ended in 2006.

agreed in Havana, the prosecution of war crimes perpetrated by the military during the armed conflict should be conducted by ordinary civilian justice rather than a special transitional tribunal. As such, the military had turned to a 'Plan B'.

The positions among those who in one way or another represented the military establishment in these early meetings were not uniform. They were implicitly divided between supporters of the convergence thesis and supporters of the partial divergence thesis, and between those who for technical or political reasons trusted or distrusted the ordinary civilian judiciary. For all of them, however, it would be a tall order to embrace the kind of special transitional and extraordinary jurisdiction being conjured in the Havana talks.

In addition to the military's constitutional mandate to refrain from participating in politics, and its subordination to civilian power, the factors that may explain why the military ultimately acceded to the extraordinary Havana model include that (1) the road back to a broad military jurisdiction had been blocked; (2) many believed that ordinary judges had more sympathy for the enemy than the military; (3) the ordinary justice system was heavily backlogged and the trials against members of the military for violations of human rights were stalled or adrift, while the defendants remained incarcerated and thus victims of an injustice; (4) the new special jurisdiction would allow a prominent role for experts in IHL; (5) the special jurisdiction would be able to review prior convictions of military personnel by civilian courts; and (6) the system would be governed not only by the principle of differential processing of military and guerrilla fighters, but also by the principle of symmetric legal benefits.

That the Technical Committee agreed that differential but equitable treatment would be the dominant principle reflected a kind of compromise between the convergence and partial divergence theses, and one that was entirely appropriate in light of the reality that Colombia would be entering a transition out of war, not dictatorship. After all, the first implication of the convergence thesis is the notion that the state's agents always bear the greatest responsibility. The thesis of partial divergence, by contrast, opens up the possibility for more equal legal treatment between the parties in conflict, typical of the old tradition of symmetrical wars.

This last issue of differentiated yet symmetrical treatment was the subject of important discussions within the Technical Committee during its first sessions. For reasons of dignity and legal security, some insisted that the military bore duties and responsibilities that the guerrillas did not, and that these should be reflected in a higher willingness to submit to justice, assume responsibility for omissions (and not just actions), and serve jail time for proven serious crimes. However, in a final pragmatic move, the Committee accepted that the principle of differential treatment should be complemented by the principle of symmetrical benefits. Within the Committee, it was often heard that Colombians would not countenance the fact that while a demobilised M-19 guerrilla served as Mayor of Bogota, the soldiers who had defended the country's institutions and citizens languished in jail.

Another factor that led members of the state's security forces (and in particular the military) to accept the idea of a special post-conflict jurisdiction was the conviction, informed by the interventions of the Prosecutor General, that his office had better information to indict guerrilla leaders than top military brass. The statistics offered by the Prosecutor General on the number of convictions and investigations opened against members of the FARC compared to members of the military were overwhelmingly favourable to the latter. Moreover, the Prosecutor General reportedly observed that regardless of whether the cases were to be brought before ordinary courts or before a special jurisdiction, a model of attribution of responsibilities for systemic crimes (through concepts like the one developed by Claus Roxin based on indirect perpetration through hierarchical control) would be more easily applicable to the guerrilla leaders than to the generals.[28]

Meanwhile, Professor Orozco reflected backstage in light of these statistics and messages of reassurance to the generals, that following the rationale of the sovereign rule of law, state agents enjoy a powerful political-epistemic privilege according to which the ordinary justice system's top prosecutor tends to focus on the guerrillas and not state agents. Whereas the guerrillas act in the shadow of the presumptively criminal nature of their actions, the state acts in the shadow of the presumptively legal nature of its own. Yet, inverting this line of thought, Professor Orozco realised that the state's monopoly on the legitimate means of violence – when combined with its unquestionable military superiority vis-à-vis the guerrillas – is tantamount to presupposing peace. In such circumstances, orthodox human rights groups are more likely to incline toward an ordinary mind-set, in which they hold the state more accountable than those who took up arms illegally. In spite of this, human rights NGOs lack the technical and legal resources that would allow them to compete with the Prosecutor General in the task of building cases for indictment; it could therefore be expected that although both sources could inform the first phase of case selection in the future special jurisdiction (where the conflict's major

---

[28] On authorship and participation in criminal law, see Claus Roxin, *Täterschaft and Tatherrschaft* (Berlin: Walter de Gruyter, 1984).

crimes would be assessed for indictment), their contributions would be very unequal in terms of their incriminating capacity.

All told, the military establishment was eventually able to accept the Special Jurisdiction for Peace (JEP), as reflected in an agreed 75-point text (hereafter 'D-75') on justice announced on 15 December 2015 by the negotiating parties.[29] The accord included the guarantee that the JEP would have primacy of jurisdiction over all those who had participated directly or indirectly in the armed conflict and over all crimes perpetrated therein. Furthermore, Paragraph 48 of D-75 states that all ordinary jurisdictions (administrative, civil, criminal, military, etc.) would be obliged to send their internal case files to the initial reception chamber of the JEP (*Sala de Reconocimiento de Verdad, de Responsabilidad y de Determinación de los Hechos y Conductas*), so that it would be the one to decide on the connection of any crimes with the armed conflict and on the cases to be prosecuted. Later, in accordance with the provisions of the final agreement, it was stipulated that the JEP's special chamber for resolving legal issues involving state agents (*Sala de Definición de Situaciones Jurídicas*), rather than the ordinary military jurisdiction, would be the one to decide, among other things, whether or not defendants were eligible to receive the special treatment afforded to public servants (following the principle of differential treatment). If they were deemed ineligible, the case would be turned over to a criminal chamber within the ordinary military jurisdiction. However, in accordance with the provisions of Paragraph 44 of D-75, the JEP would be required, in its decision-making, to take into account the operational manuals of the Armed Forces as a special law, and not merely rely on the applicable international and domestic criminal law. The provision implies that the JEP interpret IHL not only as law that imposes constraints but also as law that authorises, representing a concrete victory for the partial divergence thesis in the midst of its overall defeat.

The Technical Committee and the 'False Positives'

The ghost of the 'false positives' – military-sponsored murders of civilians that were falsely presented as rebel crimes in order to inflate war figures – gravitated around the Technical Committee from the beginning to the end. The question was, who should judge these cases – the ordinary courts or the special transitional jurisdiction? This depended not only on the constitutional competences assigned to one jurisdiction or another, but also on what the 'false

---

[29] See www.pazfarc-ep.org/comunicados/acuerdo-sobre-victimas-justicia-especial-para-la-paz.html.

positives' actually were and how they should be interpreted in their very heterogeneous manifestations. It was one thing, as in the cases from Soacha, to dupe and murder neighbourhood boys and pass them off as guerrillas killed in combat to collect awards and employment benefits out of selfish private interest, and quite another to kill suspected collaborators and dress them up as guerrilla fighters to make them appear as such. Both things were reprehensible. But while the former was not in any way part of the counterinsurgency struggle, the latter was at least partly so.

The questions swirled within the Technical Committee: Would the thousands of reported cases and the hundreds of false positives already investigated by the ordinary courts be shifted to the special jurisdiction? Would the decisions about such shifts depend on the nature of the crime in question, and in any case, who would decide? Was the body-count methodology, developed under Uribe's government and its onetime Minister of Defence, Camilo Ospina, responsible for producing the perverse effect of encouraging mass war crimes and serious human rights violations within its flagship 'democratic security' policy? Could it be said that false positives were a crime against humanity for their systematic nature, or for being perpetrated en masse?

When the false positives scandal was first uncovered in 2008, the government reacted immediately by removing dozens of high- and middle-ranking officers, as well as enlisted soldiers. Nonetheless, the country remained in the sights of human rights organisations and the ICC, all of which demanded justice on behalf of the victims. The ICC Prosecutor pressured the government to try false positive cases in ordinary, rather than military courts, and to investigate up the chain of command in light of the massive scale of the crimes. As such, the issue of false positives required attention. In a sense, a solution was found in Paragraph 44 of D-75, which states that, when determining the responsibility of a superior officer, rank alone is insufficient; the JEP must prove that whoever was in charge had effective control and knowledge of what happened and the means required to prevent or punish it. However, with the collapse of the initial version of the final agreement following the plebiscite, Paragraph 44 collapsed with it. In the renegotiated agreement signed by the government's De La Calle and the FARC's Timochenko, and made public from Havana on 13 November 2016, the terms that regulated a superior officer's responsibility were changed. The new formula seemed to refer indirectly to the standard of the Rome Statute, and senior military officers, both active and retired, were vehement in their rejection of the amendment. General Mora, who had been part of the government's negotiating team, let it be known that he had not participated in this renegotiation and that the change had taken place behind his back.

The Ordinary and the Extraordinary in D-75

D-75 – and the final agreement on Point 5 as a whole – reflected the crystallisation of a balance between ordinary and extraordinary mind-sets in tension through much of the Havana talks. The ordinary mind-set prevails in the design of the Colombian Constitution, such that the flight towards the extraordinary is restricted to a few windows that should be opened only when the extraordinary bursts into national life. By contrast, because it was born in the extraordinary context of a peace negotiation, the weight of extraordinary devices was comparatively higher in the final agreement that emerged from Havana.

The JEP model had to balance these two realities. It was 'political' and extraordinary insofar as it was the product of a peace negotiation, and was 'legal' and ordinary insofar as it was clearly recognisable as a justice device, despite its extraordinary peculiarities. This balance was decisive because it meant that those who submitted to it would have a minimum of legal security. Indeed, people are quite conservative when it comes to how criminal justice should appear, in order to merit the moniker of justice. Initial claims that a truth commission should fulfil this role, as well as subsequent claims that the JEP should itself be a heterodox justice device, were defeated in no small part because of this reality. In the battle to preserve a recognisable form of criminal justice, the government negotiators' sense of responsibility – reinforced by the pressure of public opinion polls, the political opposition in Bogota, and the gravitating presence of the ICC – militated in favour of the ordinary.

Yet, the JEP was also the crystallisation of an extraordinary mind-set in which the ideas and interests of both the FARC and the Santos government converged. The following non-exhaustive list covers some of the extraordinary elements that most strongly contributed to the accord on the JEP:

1. *Its status as a non-permanent tribunal, independent of the existing judicial structure.* There are no better indicators of the ordinary than the vocation of permanence and institutionalisation. The JEP model rebelled against both.
2. *Its rooting in a model of apportionment of responsibilities across all conflict actors, rather than a model of exclusive submission of the rebels to ordinary justice.* The ideal of the ordinary involves a sovereign state in which the public officials in charge of prosecuting crime have a differentiated status, such that, due to the presumptive legality of their actions, they enjoy a kind of political-epistemic privilege that protects

their legal and administrative determination of who to prosecute. By contrast, the justice of apportionment is far from ordinary; it is meant to limit prosecutorial discretion.

3. *The principle of symmetrical treatment.* On the understanding that the sovereign and ordinary rule of law is underpinned by the recognition of a differentiated status for public officials – which leads, on the one hand, to the presumption of legality of their actions and, on the other, to their greater responsibility in the event of serious violations – nothing is so extraordinary as complementing this differentiated status with the principle of symmetrical burdens and benefits for all sides. In the case of the JEP, this symmetry is associated not only with the fact that IHL operates as a common yardstick to judge war crimes perpetrated by all parties, but also with the idea of granting equivalent legal benefits to guerrillas, military, police, other public officials, and civilian third parties. This explains why, for example, amnesty for certain guerrilla crimes was matched by a rule of non-prosecution of military personnel for the same crimes.

4. *The use of strong subjective selection.* The ordinary principle regarding the subjective imputation of responsibilities for serious crimes – at least in civil and human rights law traditions – is that victims must be guaranteed equal rights to truth, justice, and reparation for equal crimes. For this reason, serious crimes must always in principle be prosecuted. The Inter-American Court and Colombian domestic courts agree on this point. Thus, the selection of those bearing greatest responsibility for serious crimes (and with it, the non-selection of those bearing lesser responsibility for the same crimes) is understood as contrary to the ordinary guarantee of equal access to justice, as well as to the objective of persistently combating impunity in a way that satisfies both specific and general deterrence. D-75's prosecutorial focus on those who had a 'decisive participation in the most serious and representative crimes' was, in this respect, an extraordinary device running against the ordinary principle of equal access to justice for victims.

5. *The device of voluntary submission to justice.* Ordinary justice is founded on the idea of a third party administering the law independently and impartially. A system centred on broad incentives for voluntary self-incrimination and self-regulation by defendants is, in this regard, contrary to the norm and reflective of an extraordinary mind-set.

6. *Use of reparative and restorative penalties.* For acts amounting to international crimes, the ordinary response is for the judge to impose a penalty involving some form of deprivation of liberty, normally prison

time. In Colombia, opinion polls have shown for a long time that the average citizen wants jail cells for those who have perpetrated crimes against humanity, major war crimes, and, in general, any very serious offence. However, applying the logic of extraordinariness, the JEP system offered the prospect of reparative and restorative sanctions for those willing to confess to serious crimes, a model justifiable only to the extent it is able to facilitate the end of a war.

7. *The weight given to the international.* The ordinary thing in the realm of sovereign rule of law is for domestic legislation to be applied to judge crimes perpetrated within the state's territory. But for a state like Colombia that participates in the ICC and Inter-American treaty systems, it is normal for international criminal law to be applied in a harmonised way with domestic criminal law. In that sense, following an internationalised and extraordinary rationale, the JEP model presented in D-75 was very closely tied to the standards set by IHL and international criminal law, and open to having foreign judges.

8. *Using the category of political crime.* In spite of its inclination toward a model in synch with international law, D-75 restored an important domestic tradition: namely, the privileged treatment of political crime as compared with ordinary crime. Based on a long-standing but partly repealed Colombian constitutional tradition, the category of political crime is an exception to the ordinary rule of having a single standard for common and political crimes. It opens a window for ending wars through political arrangements, as opposed to reaffirmations of the sovereign rule of law and the pursuit of bandits by the police. D-75 rescues the category, thus allowing privileged treatment of political crime for the purposes of determining punishment, eligibility for amnesty, extradition bans, and the possibility of participating in politics.

9. *Legal leniency.* D-75 includes a broad amnesty for political crime and connected crimes (including transnational crimes such as drug trafficking). It also includes the use of functional equivalents to amnesty, such as waving criminal prosecution, vis-à-vis public officials and third parties who have not committed crimes against humanity, genocide, or serious war crimes. This was extraordinariness at its purest and riskiest. Even the implementing law of late December 2016 that brought the modified amnesty into force preferred to be explicit and comprehensive about the crimes that were eligible, rather than risking any ambiguity that could put the leniency at additional risk from ordinary legal logics in future.

10. *Special international legal status.* The negotiating parties in Havana opted to invoke a rarely used reference in Article 3 of the Geneva Conventions of 1949 that, in symbolic terms, allows warring parties to create so-called 'special agreements'. With the aim of giving international standing to the final agreement, the parties made use of this provision, with the declared intention of depositing an original copy with the Swiss Federal Council in Bern 'or with such body as might replace it at a future date as repository of the Geneva Conventions'. Nothing was so strange and so extraordinary in the attempt to protect the justice deal as this provision, which landed like a bomb in Colombia's constitutional living room.
11. *The plebiscite.* The agreement to hold a special plebiscite, while lowering the participation threshold established in the Constitution, was yet another reflection of the extraordinary. But it was a necessity; the justice deal, in particular, needed the stamp of popular legitimacy that the plebiscite was meant to bring about (but ultimately did not gain).

One final, indirect element of extraordinariness was the commitment to the creation of a special legislative procedure and special powers for the President to implement the final agreement expeditiously (albeit without modifying the ordinary timetable of Congress). In mid-September 2015, while still deep in the negotiation of Point 5, the government submitted to Congress a draft bill establishing *fast-track* powers and seeking to elevate the eventual final agreement to the constitutionality bloc. The FARC did not accept the initiative at the time, but reportedly it was Senator Roy Barreras who, during the first months of 2016, finally convinced the guerrillas that this reform was necessary. However, with the 'No' victory in the plebiscite that same October, the reform entered into a legal limbo because a positive plebiscite outcome had been legislated as the precondition of implementing it. It was saved from oblivion only when the Constitutional Court and the Congress subsequently came to the rescue in 2017, through rather desperate legal formulations.

The Plebiscite Result and the Rise and Fall of Extraordinary Rhetoric

In the period that elapsed between the international signing ceremony in Cartagena on 26 September 2016 and the holding of the plebiscite six days later, there was a sudden rise and subsequent free fall of the extraordinary mind-set, crushed by the weight of the ordinary.

Many heads of state and international personalities were invited to the ceremony in Cartagena. In a foundational mind-set, the accord between the government and the FARC was given the aura of an international treaty, analogous to a peace agreement between states. The speeches by President Santos and the FARC's Timochenko also took a foundational tone. Quoting the national anthem, with its bombastic phrasing and allusions to the heroes who founded the new republic after the wars of independence from Spain, President Santos told Timochenko and the Colombian people that 'the horrible night has ceased'. Timochenko also gave his speech a clear tinge of foundational epic, affirming that the peace agreement would bring to future generations a 'second chance on earth', akin to that other fictional epic, *One Hundred Years of Solitude*. Aimed at creating a climate of euphoria for the plebiscite that would take place days later, the ceremony was staged in spectacular fashion.

But to everyone's surprise – and fuelled by a campaign involving active misinformation by some leading opponents of the peace deal – the 'No' vote won by a difference of less than one percent, and with a total abstention rate of 63 percent of eligible voters. To his credit, President Santos was quick to make a statement in which, in addition to affirming that he remained the President of all Colombians, he reiterated the validity of the bilateral ceasefire and expressed his willingness to launch a great national dialogue. For his part, Timochenko helped to calm the situation by saying that the FARC remained committed to using nothing but words as their weapons from now on, urging former President Uribe, the big winner of the day, to declare that he and his party would engage in the proposed dialogue. But for Uribe and his followers, the 'No' result amounted to a political-military victory over the FARC and thus a new capacity to make demands.

To wit, the plebiscite led to a renegotiation of key parts of the justice package in the final agreement, all in the direction of the ordinary and away from the extraordinary. For example, the forms of punishment were tweaked to become more prison-like, involving more restriction of movement; the FARC agreed, explicitly, that its reparation undertakings encompassed the obligation to deliver an inventory of all its goods and assets; the JEP would have to be composed exclusively of Colombian prosecutors and judges, and subject to the ordinary system's primacy in the event of any conflicts of jurisdiction; Colombia's criminal code would have to form part of the material competence of the JEP; the full agreement would no longer enter automatically into the constitutional bloc; and the connectedness of drug trafficking with political crime would be partially suspended and postponed until Congress legislated on the matter.

Yet, even the night before the signing of the renegotiated deal, sabres rattled. The government reportedly had wanted the responsibility of the chain of command to be regulated in the terms of Article 28 of the Rome Statute, thereby contravening what was agreed with the military during the internal government discussions prior to the plebiscite. In the heat of the renegotiation, this is precisely what was accorded, until the military quickly forced the government to back down and issue an erratum, which for many has remained a major stain on the final document.

By early 2017, the same law by means of which Congress ratified the renegotiated peace agreement also authorised the fast-track procedure, which had been in a state of suspended animation since the 'No' victory. Having been conceived as an extraordinary device, but within the Constitution, the fast-track mechanism granted the government extraordinary powers to issue, through an abbreviated procedure, executive decrees with the force of law, and to lead the legislative process (also abbreviated) to flesh out the agreement within the law.

Making full use of the fast-track procedure, which still preserved its full original legislative power, the governing National Unity coalition in Congress steamrolled over the opposition of the *Centro Democrático* party and of some sectors of the Conservative party. During the first months of 2017 it issued Legislative Act No. 1 of 2017, which created the comprehensive transitional justice system; promulgated Legislative Act No. 2, which, among other things, gave legal force to the renegotiated agreement; made the agreement binding on the three subsequent administrations; authorised the FARC, once demobilised, to become a political party; created the ten Congressional seats that the new FARC political party would receive for two terms; and issued the amnesty law, which acted as a broad safety net for the FARC to complete its somersault from illegality to legality.

Only the question of the legal treatment for members of the security agencies bucked the trend towards the ordinary unleashed by the 'No' victory. In an attempt to exclude the military leadership from the ICC's jurisdiction, Legislative Act No. 1 of 2017 established that the sources of law that would regulate the responsibility for chain of command would not include international criminal law. In addition, it established an evidentiary standard for command responsibility so high as to make it almost impossible to prove. The legislation also granted jurisdictional privileges to the military and the police that, more generally, entailed superior treatment to the demobilised FARC.

Compared to the criminal liability standard used in constitutional democracies today, which is articulated around the idea of greater responsibility for state agents vis-à-vis private individuals in matters of human rights, Legislative Act No. 1 of 2017 represented the return to a pre–World War II standard founded in the recognition of the greater dignity of state security agencies, the presumptive legality of their acts, and their privileged criminal treatment as guarantors of sovereignty. Even the Constitutional Court accepted, without any objection, the most extraordinary demands of the military on this occasion.[30] The normally asymmetric treatment against them driven by human rights constitutionalism had been replaced by an asymmetric treatment in their favour.

But the trend towards the ordinary that began with the 'No' victory was the greater force. Towards mid-2017, the Constitutional Court declared unconstitutional some key pieces of the fast-track procedure. In the name of defending the ordinary constitutional powers of Congress, the Court released it from having to vote on the constitutional reform and legislative initiatives presented by the government to implement the agreement as a single block. With this ruling, the Court empowered the ordinary legislator, disempowered the government and empowered itself. With a special legislative procedure partially made ordinary, and the government coalition in Congress partially dissolved, the Congressional representation of those who opposed the agreement gained strength, and the parliamentary discussions, in addition to being slow and difficult, continued to drive the JEP further into ordinary ground. By excluding third parties from being obliged to submit themselves to the JEP if suspected of being those most responsible for serious crimes, the original idea of the JEP received a great symbolic blow that seemed to anticipate a third-rate burial. However, the risk of the transformation of the JEP into a model for the exclusive subjection of the FARC couldn't be completed only because, after Iván Duque's presidential victory in mid-2018, when the new political coalition in Congress tried to remove the military from the JEP, the military itself opposed the move.

All told, the JEP continued to entail a certain balance between the ordinary and the extraordinary. Its extraordinary character is still evident in the fact that it is a body separate from ordinary justice, and its alternative penalties, for those who voluntarily acknowledge truth and responsibility, are restorative and do not involve incarceration. But in the fragmented Congress elected in 2018, the legislative struggle over the institutional design of transitional justice will remain difficult.

Post Scriptum

At the end of February 2018, Prosecutor General Martinez made public his intention to prosecute the Mora Urrea brothers, owners of a major regional

---

[30] Constitutional Court Judgement C-674, 14 November 2017.

supermarket chain, as FARC frontmen. This public indictment led to acts of vandalism and looting in the town of Fusagasuga, near Bogota, where several of its stores operated. Making use of a great media display, and in the assertive tone of someone pronouncing an early sentence, the Prosecutor General explained that the Mora brothers had begun their career as merchants, providing logistics for the FARC bloc that operated in the Sumapaz region. Later they became informants in charge of selecting the people who should be kidnapped by the FARC, before completing their meteoric rise to the status of big businessmen and frontmen for Commander Romaña.

This prosecutorial action represented a heavy blow by ordinary justice against the political future of the organisation. Alias Romaña was an experienced, highly charismatic, mid-level guerrilla commander who participated actively in the Havana negotiations and later became an important figure of the new political party. In the inventory of assets that had to be disclosed under oath to be able to access the benefits of the transitional justice system, Romaña did not register his alleged share in the immense fortune of the Mora Urrego brothers. This apparently meant that, unless he later came to recognise his responsibility before the JEP, the former guerrilla would be turned over to the ordinary courts. This would hardly have displeased many Colombians, for whom Romaña symbolised the most hated form of kidnapping practised by the guerrilla in its long criminal history: an appalling form of collective abduction known as 'miraculous fishing'.

One month before the completion of this essay, in a sting operation conducted by the DEA with the support of the same Prosecutor General, Jesús Santrich, one of the heads of the negotiating team of the FARC, was captured in Havana. Santrich, by then a House representative under the special arrangements provided for in the final agreement, had been requested in extradition by a US judge on charges of conspiracy for drug trafficking. This was how the most resentful and the least regretful of all the guerrilla leaders was subjected to the greatest humiliation. He was detained by the ordinary system's top prosecutor, pursuant to an international arrest warrant issued by Interpol, for his apparent recidivism in ordinary crime, perpetrated after 31 December 2016, awaiting the decision as to whether or not he should be extradited. For his part, Iván Márquez, the former head of the FARC delegation in Havana, anticipating the possibility that he too could be requested in extradition and captured, announced publicly that he would not take possession of his seat in Congress, instead taking refuge somewhere in the jungle frontier.

In such circumstances, it may be worth thinking in the same terms as Martti Koskenniemi, who in turn follows the controversial French jurist Jacques

Vergès.[31] The former asserts that justice tends to unfold through 'defences of connivance' in ordinary societies in which there is a ceiling of shared values and narratives and, with that, forms of judicial truth and historical truth that operate in relative harmony. In such highly consensual societies, there is little tolerance for those who defend or justify actions of political violence and strategies of rupture. By contrast, in the extraordinary circumstances of a divided society, in which the ceiling of shared values and narratives has collapsed, the deep political-ideological differences that fracture them are manifested through an abysmal cleft between judicial truth and historical truth.

Having this in mind, it remains to be seen whether in Colombia, when the first public hearings take place in which former FARC guerrillas are expected to acknowledge their responsibilities in serious crimes perpetrated within the war, they will portray themselves as heroes and martyrs (as their codes of honour as political rebels might dictate) or as humiliated and repentant villains (as a majority of Colombian society demands), and whether they will be applauded or repudiated, and by whom. Upon their actions, more than anyone else's, depends the credit or discredit of extraordinary justice in Colombia.

C. DIGNITY VERSUS LEGAL SECURITY

Among the multiple tensions around which the negotiation of Point 5 unfolded, perhaps there is none like that between the parties' interest in legal security and in dignity. Issues related to this tension had unparalleled power to determine the pace and intensity of the internal discussions within the government delegation and of the external discussions with the FARC delegation.

In the context of transitional justice, the term 'legal security' (discussed briefly in Part I) refers to the finality of a legal act that cannot have its effects reversed by any domestic or international court. The concept is closely linked to the idea of res judicata. But it also has a political component, as the greatest factor of insecurity in democracies is the shifting positions of successive governments and, in general, of the majorities that pass or repeal, ratify or revert, any agreements. Legal security, in this respect, extends well beyond decisions of the court system.

As for the term 'dignity', it has a close connection with modern individual morality and links with the idea of recognition of the intrinsic value of the

---

[31] Jacques Vergès, *De La Stratégie Judiciare* (Paris: Les Éditions de Minuit, 1968). Martti Koskenniemi, The Politics of International Law (Oxford: Hart Publishing, 2011), at 190–194.

human person. However, in this book we also use it to signify 'honour', because this is the meaning that prevailed in Havana. The concept of honour is older than dignity; since classical antiquity, it was attached to the values of war castes and military organisations. It is related mainly to the idea of the preservation of self-esteem in one's eyes and those of the 'other': a generalised other held in high regard and who can be the abstract representative either of the community of reference (e.g., the guerrillas) or society at large (e.g., the Colombian people). Honour can be lost, among other reasons, if one surrenders to the enemy and its representative institutions.

As this chapter reveals, balancing the tension between legal security and dignity was especially difficult in relation to criminal justice questions. And while this tension is at the heart of many continuing debates in post-plebiscite Colombia, the focus of this chapter is on what took place during the negotiations in Havana.

About the Tension

There is a perception that the tension between legal security and dignity, so central to the discussions on Point 5, was a relentless zero-sum game centred on whether or not there should be punishment and, if so, whether or not it should involve jail cells and striped uniforms. If there would be a prison, there could be legal security but no dignity. If there would not be prison, there could be dignity but no legal security.

While this perception exaggerates reality significantly, it is nevertheless true that the issue of punishment, because of the complex game of reason and passion that concentrates around it, tends to dramatically polarise negotiations and society as a whole. The fact that punishment lends itself to a binary, clear and simple formulation in terms of black or white, and all or nothing, made it easy, in the case of Colombia, for adversaries of the peace talks to put the issue at the centre of public debates about the legitimacy of the Havana process and its agreements. But independent of that, the issue produced its own tensions and forms of tactical manipulation between the negotiating parties seated around the table.

Prison was not the only source of tension between dignity and legal security inside the process. Other issues associated with transitional justice, such as the use of privileged treatment for political crime, were also battlegrounds. However, the dichotomy wasn't as stark as in the discussion on punishment, making the competing interests less mutually exclusive and more amenable to nuance and reconciliation. Political crime, provided it isn't used to support amnesties for international crimes, isn't prohibited by international human rights law. It can facilitate criminal accountability, so that its use, at least from the perspective of international law, doesn't threaten legal security. Just as importantly, because political crime dignifies the convict to whom it applies, it offers important incentives to negotiate.

In Havana, the government and the FARC vied for their versions of dignity and legal security, proposing both ordinary and extraordinary instruments. As noted in the previous chapter, the FARC's interest in affirming its dignity often led it to make foundational and extraordinary arguments; the political right that opposed the negotiations almost always found its best ally in arguments of constitutional continuity and ordinariness; while the government was caught between the need on one side to open space in the Constitution for a peace deal encompassing an extraordinary justice component, and the need on the other to keep close to the ideal type of legal and ordinary justice. This balancing act was necessary in order to preserve the legitimacy of the agreement, and thus be able to guarantee everyone involved a minimum of legal security.

As we will see, legal security and dignity interests were pertinent for all participants in the conflict and not only the guerrillas. More surprisingly, discussions were sometimes more difficult within the government (and with third parties) than with the guerrillas.

A Brief Comparison between the Legal Framework for Peace and D-75

To understand the manner, pace, and intensity in the evolution of the tension between legal security and dignity, both in the discussions that took place within the government delegation, and between the parties at the table, there is no better place to start than by comparing the Legal Framework for Peace, which guided the position of the Santos government for at least one full year of the negotiation of Point 5, and document D-75, which emerged thereafter and constituted the substance of the justice component of the final agreement put to plebiscite.

To begin, we recall that the government, for reasons related to the preservation of the dignity of the state and its military and police forces, generally refused to allow discussion in Havana about the legal treatment state agents would receive. Indeed, D-75 refers to this only tangentially and for the purpose of guaranteeing the inclusiveness and symmetry of the justice model's benefits. The guidelines and principles meant to regulate the treatment of the military and civilian third parties within the JEP were however subject to internal negotiations inside the government, in which the FARC did not participate. Nevertheless, since both the FARC and the Armed Forces were meant to appear before the same tribunal and since the differential treatment that would be given to them would be controlled by the principle of symmetry, the *Centro Democrático* and the political right promoted the idea that such an arrangement would be humiliating for the military, by equating them with terrorists.

The Philosophy of the Legal Framework for Peace

The Framework for Peace (i.e., Transitory Articles 66 and 67 of the Constitution) faced mostly outward rather than inward, and was structured around the tension between legal security and efficiency, rather than legal security and dignity. The drafters of the Framework were particularly eager to ensure that, despite the introduction of prosecutorial case selection criteria that contradicted, at least in appearance, the principle of the equal right of all victims to justice, the form of transitional justice adopted should grant defendants adequate legal security.

The public debate that accompanied the proposed Framework for Peace was mainly one about selection criteria. It revolved around whether current international standards regarding the prosecution of international crimes authorised only prioritisation, or whether they also authorised selection. The government started its diagnoses with the premise that the poor performance of the Justice and Peace process for the demobilisation of the AUC paramilitaries was largely due to the fact that all those involved in the most serious crimes had to be prosecuted, and it wasn't possible to select them according to their degree of responsibility. With good reason, the drafters of the Framework thought that after more than fifty years of war involving over seven million victims (including six million displaced, hundreds of thousands killed, tens of thousands disappeared, tortured, kidnapped, etc.), only a post-conflict justice based on narrow selection of those most responsible for the most serious and representative crimes would be negotiable in practice and viable in implementation.

Unsurprisingly, within the human rights movement, there were many who argued that applying very tight selection criteria would be contrary to the state's international duties and the rights of the victims to prosecute all international crimes. However, the greatest concern of the drafters of the Framework was how to justify a high degree of selection that avoided the collapse of the justice system under the overwhelming weight of the criminal legacy of a long war, but without compromising legal security (that is to say, without creating the risk that the pressure coming from human rights NGOs and the victims themselves would lead courts, several years later, to overturn cases in the name of the duty to combat impunity for international crimes).

In this context, the ICC and even the Inter-American Court of Human Rights were presented as two threats against the Framework's selection formula. Yet, many national and international experts supported the Framework's drafters in their effort to demonstrate that, ultimately, the selection of those most responsible for the most serious crimes – and the wide use of exoneration devices for those not selected – was a better way to combat impunity than to try to judge everyone, only to fail to live up to such promises.

The drafters of the Framework were so immersed in the debate on the tension between efficiency and legal security that comparatively little attention was given to the problem of dignity and political crime. The drafters thought that the constitutional tradition of privileged treatment of political crime had lost many of its regulatory capacities due to the restrictions imposed by legislators and judges in recent decades, and that the important thing in terms of recognising the dignity of the guerrillas was the act of negotiation itself, which involves sitting as equals, recognition as political subjects, and the promise of becoming a political party.

Article 66 of the Constitution, the justice-focused component of the Legal Framework for Peace, entered into force on 31 July 2012. Among other things, it was meant to guide, as a core input, the initial position of the government towards the FARC on issues of transitional justice in general, and criminal justice in particular. It was a device that had been conceived above all through the lens of the law, the courts, and the international community, and was mainly intended to try to guarantee legal security for all those who participated directly or indirectly in the armed conflict – notwithstanding the wager it represented in terms of its extraordinary case selection criteria. Yet, from the perspective of the guerrillas, Article 66 was disdainful of their dignity – not only because it constituted a unilateral legislative initiative by the government, but also because of its content.

The issue of guerrilla dignity was not given any place in the judicial arena that Article 66 regulated. Instead, its place was in Article 67, which contemplated, except for crimes against humanity, the possibility that many of the crimes perpetrated by guerrillas within the armed conflict could be recognised as connected to political crime, but only for purposes of participating in politics, and only after turning in their weapons and meeting certain conditions. However, Article 67 was separated from Article 66, and did not stipulate how it would be viable for the guerrillas to serve their sentences and also participate in politics after laying down their arms. This would be something for the negotiation in Havana to work out.

Another notable omission from the text of the Legal Framework for Peace was the question of amnesty, despite the fact that amnesty is explicitly referenced not only in Protocol II of the Geneva Conventions of 1949, but also in the 1991 Constitution, which contemplates amnesty and pardon for rebellion and its connected crimes.[32]

The Framework's drafters started from the fact that IHL, as part of the new globalised international law, is better adapted technically to the reality of war, offering more precise definitions and connectedness criteria than the old-fashioned and anachronistic category of political crime (especially taking into account the jurisprudential developments of recent years at the international level). Despite the fact that the Framework defined transitional justice as 'exceptional' – thus opening the space for judges to break with the ordinary jurisprudence of political crime – the drafters didn't encourage the courts to revive the tradition of privileged legal treatment in the name of negotiated peace. Instead, they preferred to give it up for lost, thus assigning it a very minor role.

In this context, it is worth mentioning Article 13 of Law 40 of 1993, the so-called anti-kidnapping law. Arising at a time when abduction rates had increased sharply, the law eliminated the possibility of amnesty for such crime. Ruling C-069 of 1994 then affirmed the constitutionality of the law, suggesting that abduction was a crime against humanity (though four out of the nine justices added that a different logic might apply in a scenario of extraordinary termination of the armed conflict). In any case, for purposes of determining amnesty eligibility in future, laws and jurisprudence subsequently came together to asphyxiate the connection between political offences and any crime considered very serious. Judges folded further and further to the decisions of the legislator, and the caveats in their rulings grew scarce.

As such, part of the drafters of the Legal Framework for Peace's disdain for political crime was based on the way that legislators and the courts had eviscerated the connection between various serious crimes and politically motivated crimes. As a consequence, they did not take into account the different possible applications of connectedness. As the Colombian jurist Rodrigo Uprimny often argued, the fact that the courts had ruled that certain crimes could not be recognised as connected for purposes of amnesty did not imply that they couldn't be so recognised for other purposes (such as determining the type and harshness of a sentence, or the avoidance of extradition).

---

[32] The 1991 Constitution contains eight articles that regulate the treatment of political crime. Article 35 regulates extradition; Article 150, Paragraph 17 and Article 201, Paragraph 2 regulate amnesty and pardon; and Article 179, Paragraph 1 and Articles 232 and 299 regulate access to public office. Additionally, Transitory Articles 18 and 30 relate to amnesty.

The exclusion of political crime and amnesty from the judicial arena had another advantage in the minds of the Framework's drafters: it would save the judges of any post-conflict court from having to determine which crimes were connected to rebellion and which were not. This matter was considered to be especially anti-technical because of how difficult it could be to uncover, through observation, the internal subjective intentions that might constitute an identifiable political motive underlying any serious crime. Just as importantly – and in this, the drafters of the Framework were right – even the broadest amnesty for the guerrillas wouldn't solve the separate needs and expectations of the other side of the conflict theatre, namely, the military and third parties. Thus it was that other sorts of devices were envisaged in the Framework, such as refraining from criminal prosecution, using totally or partially suspended sentences, creating alternatives to prison, and allowing conditional sentence reductions – all of which could now be extended to serious crimes.

Yet, for the FARC, the terms of Article 66 remained offensive. They understood it as a plan to have their leaders appear before prosecutors and judges as part of a humiliating procedure that would expose them to public derision for having committed all sorts of atrocious, systematic, and widespread crimes. Following that, they imagined that their leaders – presumably the same people who would be negotiating on behalf of the FARC in Havana – would be expected to serve prison sentences that could not be fully suspended, in accordance with the provisions of the Constitutional Court's jurisprudence that endorsed the constitutionality of the Framework. Only after having undergone this humiliation – which would purportedly be understood, by most victims and by society, as a purifying and re-dignifying ritual – would the FARC leaders enjoy the privilege of being able to participate in peaceful politics (unless they were convicted of crimes against humanity or genocide, in which case, in accordance with the provisions of Article 122 and Transitory Article 67 of the Constitution, a lifetime ban from political office would apply).

Understanding D-75

A quick reading of D-75, the text articulating the basic elements of the JEP model negotiated in Havana, reflects a clear compromise between the parties. It ensured a justice arrangement with the greatest possible degree of legal security, while fulfilling the competing demands for dignity on the part of the guerrillas, and on the part of the military and the police.

Among other things, legal security was required in order to help reduce the risk that an international, foreign, or domestic court, or a future national government, could blithely overturn the agreement on transitional justice. As such, D-75 precluded amnesty for ICC crimes and established that there would be a special, independent, and impartial criminal court, subject to the principles of due process, with responsibility for investigating, prosecuting, and sentencing those who had a decisive role in the most serious and representative of such crimes. Equally important in terms of legal security was the fact that D-75 established that the JEP should be a court with exclusive and superior jurisdiction over crimes perpetrated in the context and by reason of the armed conflict, by any party that had direct or indirect participation in it. The JEP's final judgements would acquire the status of res judicata, precluded from being reopened by any other national jurisdiction.

Of additional significance was the fact that D75 established that the JEP would be part of a comprehensive system of transitional justice, geared towards the fulfilment of victims' interdependent rights to truth, justice, reparation, and the guarantee of non-repetition. The system would include a truth commission, a special unit on missing persons, an expanded reparation plan (to reinforce the massive existing one), and more.

As regards the requirements of dignity, especially those of the FARC, the following features of the JEP model are among those that stand out:

1. The fact that the JEP was conceived as separate and different from the ordinary justice system was considered dignifying by the FARC insofar as it avoided the requirement to 'submit' to judgement by the existing system, which it characterised as 'the enemy's justice'. The FARC felt that ordinary criminal courts, including the Supreme Court, equated them with common criminals, drug traffickers, and terrorists.

2. The guerrillas found dignifying the euphemistic erasure of categories that conventionally serve to denote the functions of justice and to qualify deviant behaviours as crimes. While they were pragmatic enough to understand that avoiding justice altogether was impossible – lest the legal security of any agreements reached be jeopardised – they fought to ensure that the type of justice that finally applied mimicked ordinary justice as little as possible in its language. In this regard, it is striking how the FARC and the government ultimately turned to expressions such as 'resolutions of conclusions' as opposed to 'indictments', for the JEP's initial case processing chamber; 'serious deprivation of liberty' as opposed to 'kidnapping'; and, as the crown jewel of euphemisms to save the dignity of the guerrillas without affecting the substance of the justice that would apply, 'sanction' instead of 'sentence'.

3. On the understanding that the most dignified and least humiliating legal accountability option would be one founded on collective and voluntary

recognition of wartime offences, the FARC adopted and radicalised a line of thought that had originated in previous governmental suggestions. Specifically, it proposed that the main way to submit to justice should be through a voluntary system of collective and individual statements. For the FARC, but also for the government, the dignity of the approach lay in the fact that the incrimination did not appear to be the result of an exercise of authority imposed downwardly by an independent third party, but as an upward exercise of free will (albeit one that, ultimately, would be subject to impartial evaluation by the JEP's magistrates).

4. The possibility envisaged in D-75 that truth and responsibility acknowledgements should be, at least in the beginning, collective and in writing – except where the relevant JEP chamber required otherwise – attenuated what would otherwise have been a more systematically public, and thus more humiliating, judicial ritual.

5. The substitution of the 'most responsible' concept at the centre of Article 66 and of the government's negotiating position on justice, with the term 'decisive participation', is also explained, in part, by the lower cost in terms of dignity for those who would one day be judged. The substitute term diluted the subjective imputation of responsibility and made it less humiliating for any particular individual. Contrary to the idea of 'the most responsible', which is generally applied to hierarchically organised armed groups, the concept of 'decisive participation' can also apply to civilians, who aren't part of an army but who may have played an important role in the commission of a serious crime. Ironically, this represented a de facto convergence of interests between military and guerrilla leaders, on one side, and the defenders of international standards of justice, on the other. All of them shared an interest in avoiding the kind of radical subjective selection established by the Legal Framework for Peace: the former to escape the humiliation of an excessive concentration of responsibilities on their heads, and the latter to prevent civilians and low-ranking individuals who were nonetheless involved in international crimes from enjoying impunity. None of them was persuaded by the Framework's thesis that, in order to avoid a collapse of the justice model, the best approach was a narrow case selection focused on persons who bore the greatest responsibility.

6. Former President César Gaviria stated that the inclusive nature of the JEP's personal jurisdiction (i.e., its authority to sanction parties from all sides of the war) had less to do with an interest in dignity and more to do with a common interest in ending the conflict as definitively and completely as possible. Yet, for the guerrillas, the dignity associated with having all parties submit to the JEP was considerable. As for the military, it had an ambivalent

view about the JEP's inclusive jurisdiction and about the related principle of symmetric treatment. On the one hand, this assured state agents an equivalent legal leniency to that being accorded the FARC; on the other, it risked equating them, in undignified form, with the guerrillas. This distasteful notion was only partly overcome by recourse to the dignified banner of having a higher set of legal responsibilities, by virtue of being the state.

7. The Legal Framework for Peace stipulated the need for some form of punishment for those most responsible for the most serious and representative crimes of Colombia's armed conflict, together with their exclusion from politics if ever convicted of crimes against humanity or genocide. By contrast, D-75 consecrated, for those who voluntarily recognised their decisive participation in the commission of international crimes, a sanction whose function should be reparative and restorative, more reconciling and dignifying than humiliating, with little or no restriction of the political rights of the convict. D-75 nevertheless preserved the risk of humiliation: using a fundamentally ordinary rationale, it provided for retributive incarceration for those who choose not to recognise their responsibility for serious crimes and who are unsuccessful at trial.

8. The government's initial position, crystallised in the Framework, was to avoid giving political crime a prominent role, and thus limit the risk of it being used as a pretext to amnesty any connected crimes of a serious nature. D-75 consecrated a very different formula. It closed the door to the possibility of connecting rebellion with the most serious international crimes, but opened it to the connection with less serious war crimes and many common crimes, including those that would have been perpetrated to 'finance' the ostensibly revolutionary war effort, such as illegal mining and all crimes associated with the economic cycle of illicit drugs. To understand the political importance of recognising a connection between drug trafficking and rebellion, it suffices to note that its recognition determined, to a great extent, whether the FARC could be judicially characterised not as mere drug traffickers and narcoterrorists, but as political fighters who financed their revolutionary effort with illegal activities. If the latter theory were accepted, the Colombian war could be interpreted as the last expression of the 'Cold War' in Latin America, and not as a criminal, non-ideological 'new war' of the type described and denounced by Mary Kaldor in her writings on old and new wars.[33] Fortunately for the FARC, the theory was allowed; and in this, the support of the Obama administration was a critical factor in overcoming the opposition of broad

---

[33] Mary Kaldor, *New and Old Wars: Organized Violence in a Global Era* (Stanford, Calif.: Stanford University Press, 2001).

political sectors within Colombia. However, D-75 did not release the judges of the JEP's amnesty chamber from the obligation to decide, case by case, which conducts are related to rebellion and political crime and which are not. In that, they can act with the assurance that drug trafficking is a transnational crime but not an international one; its amnestying is not prohibited.

9. D-75 established a rule of non-extradition for those who had been or were being judged by the JEP for conflict-related crimes. For the FARC, this rule was important for legal security and dignity alike. It had the benefit that it implied putting themselves out of reach of the 'great empire' that, in their view, had largely shaped and funded the war. Non-extradition meant the FARC would avoid having to be humiliated by a justice system that uses high-security prisons, relies on snitching, and can issue multiple life sentences. Their fellow rebel, Simón Trinidad, extradited for drug trafficking during President Uribe's government and whose release the FARC demanded throughout the negotiation in Havana, is a good example of the importance that the guerrillas attributed to the non-extradition of members accused of crimes like drug trafficking or terrorism.

Yet, for the FARC, the greater dignity offered in D-75 as compared to the Legal Framework for Peace (and especially Transitory Article 66) would have meant little if it did not also provide a high level of perceived legal security. As discussed later in this chapter, early versions of D-75 had in fact veered dangerously off the road of legal security for guerrillas and state agents alike. Ultimately, the government's core negotiating team had to 'play with the black pieces' (a chess metaphor for losing the initiative and playing defensively) in the internal negotiations with its presumptive allies in the ad hoc legal committee, managing to avoid yielding so much in the name of the recognition of the FARC's dignity interests that the legal security of the whole agreement would have been jeopardised.

Remains of the Legal Framework for Peace

Not much was left of the underlying vision of the Legal Framework for Peace after D-75 came about. Suffice it to note that the constitutionalising of D-75 (partially thwarted in the end) and of the entire final agreement in 2016 entailed a kind of semi-burial of the Framework, especially in terms of the partial defeat of the figure of the 'most responsible' and the resurrection of the tradition of the privileged treatment of political crime and connected crimes. Nonetheless, the Framework survived as a sort of tool box that defined transitional justice as exceptional, and as primarily aimed at achieving peace. This is itself very rich in implications, because it upholds the proposition that justice ideals and pursuits do not reign absolutely but must be weighed against the paramount aim of achieving peace and the factual circumstances that constrain its attainment. The Framework, it should be added, remains an integral part of the Constitution and as such authorises the introduction of selection and prioritisation criteria, and a very flexible use of criminal prosecution and punishment that under certain conditions includes the possibility of suspended, reduced, or alternative forms of punishment – even for serious crimes. In this regard, the Framework is irreplaceable.

Only the punitive universalism promoted by some very influential NGOs with global agendas, such as Human Rights Watch and Amnesty International – and their unwitting local ally, the moderate and radical right articulated around the *Centro Democrático* party – still saw the Legal Framework and the final agreement's sanctions regime as insufficiently punitive. Yet, it is relatively easy to show that both the Framework and the agreement helped create the conditions – albeit intrinsically unstable – to put an end to a long history of impunity.

Explaining the Shift from the Framework to D-75

We have noted that the Legal Framework for Peace narrowed case selection criteria in order to avoid an impunity-inducing collapse of the legal system, given the magnitude of the wartime violations. We have also observed that the Framework was comparatively disdainful of the interest of the presumptive accused – whether FARC leaders or military leaders – in a dignifying judicial scenario. But what ultimately explains the dramatic shift in the balance between dignity and legal security, so tilted toward the latter in the input document (the Framework) and toward the former in the output document (D-75)? To put it succinctly, the shift is explained above all by the temporary replacement of the plenipotentiaries (vis-à-vis the issue of justice) with the members of the ad hoc legal committee agreed between President Santos and the guerrilla leadership.

Obviously, it is normal in the case of a negotiation to move constantly between two extremes: that of confrontation and that of consensus-seeking. And indeed, both courses of action were present throughout the first year of the negotiation of Point 5, regardless of who held the leadership of the government team in the discussions with the FARC. However, there was a decisive shift of emphasis toward consensus-seeking with the guerrillas when the government appointees to the ad hoc legal committee (Misters Cepeda, Henao, and Cassel) entered the fray. In part, this had to do with the different marching orders given to the trio. Speed in reaching a deal on justice was their number-one assigned priority, and all other goals were secondary. But it also had to do with a larger set of variables, including a change in negotiation methodology in which the FARC and government appointees to the ad hoc legal committee met outside of the formal negotiation table, and placed greater emphasis on the importance of rapprochement and establishing an interpersonal rapport with each other.

On the Vision of the Other and the Government's Negotiating Strategy

Unlike past negotiations – such as those at El Caguán during Andrés Pastrana's government, where the FARC appeared to have arrived unwilling to make peace – in Havana the guerrillas always showed a strong willingness to end the war. Yet, the inertia of war was very powerful and the distrust between the parties very deep. This explains in part why, at least until the end of Point 5, the headline teams experienced the negotiation as 'the continuation of war by other means' and thus as a confrontation between enemies who aren't looking to become friends.

That the matter on the agenda was as divisive as that of justice did little to assuage the situation. Even in the face of the danger posed to the negotiation by the opposition of the *Centro Democrático* and the broader political right in the country, the government and the FARC were unable to construct a minimum shared narrative. But even if one had existed, it would not have been easy for Santos's centre-right government to project it, as the cost of doing so would have been very high in terms of legitimacy and popularity. As such, it was only during the so-called 'conclave' agreed by President Santos and the FARC's Timochenko (to accelerate the negotiations during the last days prior to reaching the pre-plebiscite final deal) that the parties were able to interact more fluidly and cooperate more openly in the defence of the common cause of a negotiated peace.

The only real precursor to this fluidity appears to have been the process inside the ad hoc legal committee, in which, by all accounts, the three government representatives arrived with a more empathetic view of the 'other': less confrontational and more oriented toward trust-building. After all, the other with whom they negotiated was not the FARC, but its trusted legal counsel. Thus, whereas the government's headline team generally did not separate the public enemy (*hostis*) from the private one (*inimicus*), making it very difficult to have a fluid dialogue with the counterpart at the negotiating table, the government's trio in the legal committee took the opposite approach. This was significantly aided by the fact that, seemingly, they were not hired in a decision-making capacity, and thus did not bear the same burden of responsibility and public accountability as the plenipotentiaries.

In addition, it helped that some of the necessary ground work for reaching a justice deal with the FARC had been assisted, through separate meetings, by what came to be known as 'the New York group' (an informal collection of local and international justice experts, created by Norway, that had periodic offsite meetings with the FARC's legal team).

A few anecdotes can illustrate what has been said in relation to the more confrontational attitudes and methodology of the government's headline negotiating team. For example, the chief negotiators often had bilateral meetings, both formal and informal, with each other. These could be used to discuss off-the-record matters of substance, as well as personal issues; things that would not have been viable for discussion at the larger negotiating table with everyone, including the guarantors, present. Most other plenipotentiaries, however, did not have this option, as the established rule within the government delegation was strictly against socialising and informality. The two important exceptions were the larger official ceremonies and the periodic social events organised by the guarantors which, though infrequent, facilitated more informal conversation and trust-building opportunities between the members of both delegations. Other than that, whoever wanted to talk about a specific topic or idly converse with the other party had to take advantage of chance meetings in the kitchen, corridors, or bathrooms of the meeting centre and hotel where the talks took place; or alternatively in and around El Laguito, where both delegations were housed and took regular strolls.

Because of these norms against informality and socialising, it was difficult to get a more nuanced and complete understanding of the 'other', including its expectations on issues as crucial as legal security and dignity. In fact, even within the government delegation, the subject of dignity was not always welcome. In response to a concern on this issue, raised early in the negotiations on Point 5 by Professor Orozco, he was told, 'We defend legal security. Let them defend their dignity'. Similarly, towards the end of the negotiations, when the agreement on reparations was being worked out, Professor Orozco suggested that the FARC be told that they should demonstrate that they were different from drug traffickers and narco-paramilitaries by creating a 'joint fund' with at least part of their assets, and that it be given to the state's existing Reparations Fund. This would send a clear signal that they had a political and proto-state vocation and were more than common criminals. The first reaction of some colleagues within the government team was to say, 'It is not a good idea to offer our advice to the counterpart about what we think is good for them'. Using the other's internal rationale to model and present ideas was often seen not as putting oneself in the other's shoes, but as inappropriate lecturing.

It should be noted, however, that the fact that the FARC repeatedly said they did not accept 'unilateral' government initiatives such as the Legal Framework for Peace may be an indicator that the government plenipotentiaries were right about not presenting initiatives built from the perspective of the other. It is possible that the JEP model was accepted by the FARC precisely because they perceived it as their own shared achievement. In any case, the FARC delegation did not appreciate Professor Orozco's proposal regarding the benefit for their public image of pooling assets together to repair the victims. They reacted to it with irony and with apparent indignation; though of course it is likely that this was less because of offended dignity, and more because of a self-interest on their part in financing a private life and a solvent political project at the end of the war.

In short, the operative logic was to distrust the counterpart and to keep one's distance as much as possible. There was simply no talk of empathy with the FARC delegation. Anticipating their next moves, yes; but putting ourselves in their shoes, not at all. Within the government team, this attitude was of course more marked in some delegates than in others. After all, some saw the FARC as political adversaries while others saw them as mere criminal bandits. But overall, the consequence was that, although the government's documents and vision of justice preserved an apparent balance between legal security and dignity, in practice the government team fought very much in the spirit of the Legal Framework for Peace to arrive at formulas that provided the greatest legal security as understood by the government, dealing little with the problem of dignity in terms understood by the guerrillas.

Frustration on the part of the government team was another obstacle. The FARC was unwilling to make significant concessions in the area of justice and punishment, balking at the idea of any model premised on leadership-level responsibility, despite numerous government undertakings made in the previous points on land and on political reform. Often, one heard phrases uttered internally along the lines that 'if the government made an extra effort on land reform and political participation, the time has come for the FARC to give back'. Many found it difficult to understand that the FARC believed that they owed nothing to the government and, even more so, that the guerrillas could feel that it was they who had been making the biggest gestures up to that point. For the FARC – convinced as they were that the greatest responsibility in the war belonged to the state and its organised supporters, and burdened with renouncing the ideal of revolution to assume the existential risks of demobilising and reintegrating into civilian life – they felt they deserved important concessions in exchange for making such a big sacrifice. As such, with each viewing the other as the one owing the greater debt, the climate and the progress of the negotiation of Point 5 suffered.

Cumulative delays exacted an especially heavy price. That is because, in a democracy, leaders are prisoners of short-term concerns, since public opinion usually demands quick solutions. The FARC were also under time pressure, yet theirs was associated with more distant matters, such as the need to reach agreements before the end of the Obama administration in the United States. Thus, the slow march of time was the greater enemy of the government than the guerrillas, disproving the initial premise that the combination of military superiority and the absence of a bilateral ceasefire would enable the government to force the guerrillas to negotiate quickly, even on the issue of justice. Eventually, in order to avoid crises induced by dramatic military encounters, it became necessary to appeal to unilateral ceasefires by the FARC and reciprocal measures by the government, thus easing the pressure on the FARC to negotiate in a hurry. Apparently, the premise that neither party had been defeated worked in favour of making the talks even slower.

The perception of whether time works in one's favour is, of course, very subjective. For example, after one year of negotiations on Point 5, and with hardly any in-depth conversations having taken place in Havana on the topic of criminal accountability, the legal committee – or some equivalent thereof – had become a political necessity for an unpopular President back in Bogota. Yet, several members of the government delegation were not convinced of the urgency or the need to change the approach. It was said of the FARC that after mourning the illusion that their crimes would go unpunished, they would eventually give in and accept the government's basic vision on the issue. This conviction was bolstered by the fact that the same had happened in the negotiation of the previous agenda items. The perception was that, sooner or later, the FARC always ended up folding to the wording and the positions put forward by the government team.

But as fatigue set in when the discussions on justice failed to move forward, a plenipotentiary of the government delegation privately – and prophetically – said to Professor Orozco, 'We can't continue negotiating this point as if in an arm-wrestling match in which our goal is to break the other's arm'. It seems President Santos overheard him, as just a few days later, the creation of the ad hoc legal committee was announced to the government team.

On the Jesus Christ Strategy

Before describing the events that followed the establishment of the ad hoc legal committee, it is important to understand what the government delegation had attempted immediately prior. It believed, with good reason, that the most dignified thing for the FARC – and also the best outcome for the process – would be that the leadership, or at least part of it, assume its responsibilities on behalf of the whole and, by voluntarily recognising its terrible sins, enable the bulk of guerrilla fighters to be exonerated of criminal responsibility. There was, in this sense, amused talk of a 'Jesus Christ strategy'. Like Christ, the leadership of the FARC could accept as their own the sins of their flock, in order to set it free.

The underlying idea seemed reasonable to the government team because, among other things, it was understood as allowing for a harmonisation of the interest in legal security and the interest in dignity. The thinking was that the international community and Colombian society would see their thirst for justice satisfied through punishment of the 'most responsible' (namely, the guerrilla leadership together with some members of the military hierarchy); and, what is equally important, both would recognise the 'altruism' embodied in the leadership's voluntary acceptance of responsibility. It was even suggested that this course of action might benefit the FARC in the polls when the time came for them to take to the public squares and run for office.

Yet, both internally and in discussions with the FARC, the Jesus Christ model never fully took hold – especially on the part of the guerrilla commanders in Havana. This is despite the fact that, on the margins of the main negotiating table, some members of the FARC Secretariat would privately say that they wouldn't mind going to prison (or some equivalent thereof) for a couple of years. Pablo Catatumbo, for example, said a number of times in informal conversations that confinement would give him time to delve into everything he couldn't read in the heat of the armed struggle. Yet the outcome of the negotiations revealed that his position didn't prevail among the guerrilla leaders. To this day, some involved in the Havana talks wonder if a little more generosity on this issue on the part of the guerrillas would have saved the process enormous difficulties and would have better paved the way towards their participation in politics, and a less adversarial stance by the military. In any case, the government's eventual Plan A on justice didn't really get a full and fair test. Close to a year went by between the beginning of negotiations on Point 5 and the FARC's receipt from the government delegation of its comprehensive, Legal Framework–inspired vision on the question of criminal justice.

Dignity and the Jesus Christ Strategy

It is difficult if not impossible to access the innermost secrets of the human heart. As such, it may be that the Jesus Christ analogy was, even if never presented as such, intuitively repellent. Christ had decided to bear the sins of the whole world as his own because he himself had committed no sin; he was literally a holy man. By contrast, great sinners – i.e., those whose hands are stained with blood – usually have much more difficulty recognising themselves in this manner.

Christ's was clearly an act of love, recognisable as such. For those most responsible for serious criminal acts, it would have rather been an exercise in self-incrimination and controlled humiliation. For such persons, repentance might imply a brutal fracture of their own moral identity and ego. And precisely such a fracture, it turns out, was more than what could be reasonably expected of the FARC leadership, who in most cases viewed themselves not as repentant sinners but as die-hard believers in the justness of their cause.

This is why Professor Orozco frequently defended, albeit without much success, the idea of establishing a very broad connectedness with political crime, including international crimes. This would be done not in order to facilitate a broad amnesty for the guerrillas but to make it psychologically and morally easier for those who were willing voluntarily to acknowledge their responsibility in very serious crimes to do so. In turn, this would allow them to undertake other acts of recognition that could be more easily grounded in their political and moral identity, rather than looking like greedy villains and nothing more.

Yet, one could say that this dignity-sensitive approach – involving more attention to their individual and political self-identities – did end up prevailing, just under a different guise. The voluntary acknowledgement of truth and responsibility, consecrated in D-75, brought to life the possibility of a judicial arena in which representatives of the FARC could, at least in principle, preface their statements with a contextualisation of their actions embedded in the revolutionary struggle. It would then be up to the JEP magistrates of the relevant receiving chamber to put limits on any unacceptable framing by the accused. In that regard, it could be instructive for Colombia's transitional justice community to revisit the experience and lessons of the Justice and Peace confessions and trials. It would likely show how implausible it is to expect Pauline 'conversions' on the witness stand, especially by group leaders.

In any case, under the premise that the perpetrator's interest is always to escape justice, or at least to receive the most benign punishment possible, a peace negotiation was always going to be a setting dominated by distrust between the parties. Being the ones who best fit the description of 'most responsible', it was ineludibly a stretch to convince at-risk rebel leaders to negotiate a system involving accountability, and possibly jail, especially if the core trade-off of a peace negotiation is to exchange arms for opportunities to participate in political life. For a guerrilla organisation aspiring to lay down its weapons and become a political movement or party, it is highly counter-intuitive, to say the least, to allow its historical and more charismatic leaders to go to jail. This is especially so, knowing that, without them, both the demobilisation process and the transformation into a party will be orphaned of the leaders required to maintain troop unity, avoid the fragmentation and recycling of ex-combatants back into war and crime, and mobilise the rank-and-file around a new political project. Leadership, especially the 'quasi-paternal' type that is common within guerrillas, cannot be improvised; it must instead be accepted as it is found.

As such, the FARC negotiating team constantly reminded the government, 'We were never defeated and we didn't come here to negotiate our way to jail'. Indeed, to get them out of that posture, the government would first have had to defeat them militarily. Not having done so, all that was left was mistrust in the face of a perceived existential threat. As such, it is more likely than not that the FARC believed that the real aim of the government was to side-line the guerrilla cause politically, and that the purifying shower promised them by entering through the court door marked 'most responsible' would instead prove to be a – political – death sentence.

The Internal Discussion on Legal Security

The FARC shared much of the government's conviction about the importance of legal security, and the idea that it could be satisfied only through respect for existing domestic and international standards, particularly in relation to international crimes. And yet it would be nonsense to infer that both parties understood legal security in the same way, or that the degree of interest in legal security was the same for both parties.

On the few occasions when the matter was broached, advisers Freeman and Orozco, especially the latter, contended that the FARC's aversion to the risk of legal uncertainty wasn't as strong as the military's. After all, while the former had spent a lifetime as outlaws, fighting against the constitutional order and the rule of law, the latter was accustomed to being seen as the representative of constitutional order and the rule of law.

For the FARC, legal security was more of a political problem than a legal one. It was understood as something that depended above all on the power of states and international institutions to enforce, and not so much on a set of unsettled and uncertain international standards. Such ideas were frequently expressed by FARC delegates in long tirades inside the negotiating room in Havana. As a result, the guerrillas were, by all appearances, willing to take higher risks of legal uncertainty in order to claim greater amounts of dignity.

Yet, it would be mistaken to say that the FARC's viewpoint implied that they did not aspire (once they'd laid down their arms and placed themselves under the protection of the Constitution and the rule of law) to the greatest possible legal security the state could provide through all the political and legal means at its disposal.

What is less well understood, or commented upon, is the perspective that reigned within the Armed Forces. Early on, their advisers and their representatives in the Technical Committee recognised the greater responsibility of the military in terms of human rights (i.e., as guarantors of the rights of citizens and the constitutional order), noting that, if convicted for serious war violations, they would be willing to go to jail – even if the guerrillas received a more benign treatment. It seems that the military was convinced that advocating for an equal or more favourable treatment vis-à-vis the guerrillas would leave state agents with enormous legal uncertainty, at the mercy of a community of human rights defenders and victims of state crimes that would close ranks around the argument that the military always bears greater responsibility than any non-state actor.

At the end of the discussions of the Technical Committee, however, pragmatism prevailed. It was decided that the military should be entitled to receive symmetrical but differential treatment to the guerrillas, meaning that state agents should be entitled to no-worse benefits or entitlements than the FARC, but under a different scheme.

Here, it is worth noting how different the political calculus of the military was, as compared to the guerrillas. While for the Armed Forces the goal was to 'preserve' their dignity by ensuring that they were not deprived of their presumption of legality, for the guerrillas the goal was the exact opposite: 'obtaining' dignity by creating the conditions to establish the good name they lacked. Indeed, not without reason, the military are generally well regarded among Colombians. By contrast, the guerrillas – especially as of the onset of the eight years of President Uribe's democratic security policy – sunk to extreme lows in public opinion. This matters because it helps explain, in part, why for a long period the guerrillas remained willing to sacrifice the promise of more legal security in exchange for securing more dignity.

The Path to the Government's 'Plan A'

We have already noted how the Legal Framework for Peace epitomised the government delegation's vision of how to tackle questions of transitional justice. To understand the full depth of thought the government had put into the matter, it is worth recalling that the Framework was debated in Congress at a time when the country was still unaware that secret exploratory talks between the government and the FARC were even taking place. In that regard, the intra-parliamentary negotiations that produced the Framework were, fundamentally, and despite the presence of the opposition, talks among political friends about a scenario that, for most participants, was more hypothetical than real.

Of course, there were many lively debates in Congress on issues such as the principles of prosecutorial case selection vis-à-vis international crimes; but they took place without being able to take into account the expectations and interests of the discredited guerrillas, who remained in the shadows. As such, the government was able to impose its points of view, its convictions, its interests, and especially its concern that, in the event that a negotiated solution to the war became possible, there would be a transitional justice system that offered conditional legal security for all and that respected existing international standards. The Office of the High Commissioner for Peace led the debate in Congress, backed by a very broad political coalition with a clear legislative majority.

Negotiating the text in Congress, independently from the secret talks that were taking place with the FARC, allowed for coolheaded discussion. This avoided some of the risks that the prior Uribe government had to contend with while negotiating with the paramilitary AUC in Santafé de Ralito and simultaneously in Congress. Yet, negotiating in Congress before the public talks had begun in Cuba had the disadvantage that it didn't allow the interests of the FARC to be sufficiently reflected, as the guerrillas were not only absent but also unrepresented. As such, it was perfectly foreseeable that during the ensuing years of public negotiations – and particularly during the eighteen months dedicated to Point 5 – the FARC systematically rejected the 'unilateral' Legal Framework for Peace.

Yet, rather than a set of defined imperatives, the Framework was in fact a flexible toolbox. In its spirit, it embodied a firm but adaptable vision of how the transitional justice system should operate; sufficient, it was hoped, to keep at bay the 'bogeyman' of the ICC in The Hague and the 'super-bogeyman' of the Inter-American Court in Costa Rica. However, when the public phase of talks began in Havana in the fall of 2012, the negotiations on transitional justice were no longer going to be among colleagues in Congress, but with the 'enemy'.

More than two years into the public phase of the talks, and nearly nine months into the specific negotiation of Point 5, the issue of dignity was discussed at length, perhaps for the first time, in an internal draft document of the government delegation (and in particular within the technical team attached to High Commissioner Jaramillo). The matter of the truth commission had been discussed officially with the FARC already for some time, but the question of justice remained largely undiscussed and thus unresolved.

The draft document – prepared initially as talking points meant for a planned conversation with the FARC's legal team – was succinct but dense, and the product of long and difficult internal discussions. In the eyes of Professor Orozco, however, it was more revealing for what it concealed than for what it contained. On the one hand, it showed how the government's strategy was to recognise the FARC as a political actor in various ways; on the other, it implicitly revealed the government's lack of willingness to open broad space for the category of political crime. In particular, the talking points reflected unhesitating recognition of the crime of rebellion as a political offence, but risked confirming the guerrillas' complaint that the government kept stopping short of the next logical step after recognising rebellion as the FARC's ultimate crime: namely, some form of privileged treatment. Instead, the government risked being seen as continuing – in the spirit of the Legal Framework for Peace – to treat the constitutional tradition of political crime as an anachronism of little use, and of potentially great danger.

The 'script' for the imagined conversation that was to take place with the counterpart's lawyers began with the question 'Why are we here'? It then outlined some of the answers. It stated that the goal was to reach a negotiated end to the armed conflict; clarified that the government and the guerrillas shared the two fundamental interests of legal security and dignity; stated that the chance of meeting both interests depended on the legitimacy of the measures that were agreed; explained that legitimacy had both legal components, such as that the measures adopted be in accordance with the state's national and international obligations, and political components, in the sense of requiring acceptance by the national and international community; warned that if the strategy to increase dignity undermined legitimacy, this would cause serious risks for legal security; accepted, at the same time, that an exit with legal security but without dignity would not satisfy the interests of the FARC; and then proceeded to present all the elements that in the government's opinion were dignifying for the FARC.

In this regard, the script of talking points included reiterating that the government recognised rebellion and the political motivations of the guerrillas. It then imagined explaining that it is precisely the recognition of the FARC's political identity that allows the government to: acknowledge the existence of an internal armed conflict; agree to negotiate substantive issues; recognise the potential for political reintegration of the guerrillas' members; and define the scope of application of transitional justice measures, including an understanding of the need for special formulas on legal accountability. But the imagined conversation was also meant to encompass a couple of warnings, namely to recall that the recognition of the political identity of the guerrillas did not imply, in any way, the understanding of rebellion as a right, nor the justification of a general and unconditional amnesty; and to note that the latter, which at first sight could increase dignity, would end up erasing any legal security and thus be unacceptable.

The talking points concluded with a list of additional elements that, in the opinion of the government delegation, reflected its appreciation of the need for dignifying elements in a negotiated justice deal. For example, the draft points noted the fact that any post-conflict justice mechanism would be the fruit of consensual negotiation; the solution would apply to all conflict actors under conditions of 'symmetry'; justice would be settled through a special jurisdiction, rather than simply resorting to the ordinary courts; there would be mechanisms and incentives for voluntary recognition of responsibility, as opposed to a system limited to top-down pronouncements; the selection of cases for prosecution would be made by a specially qualified legal-political committee, following the criterion of 'essential role' and with guarantees of impartiality and due process; IHL would be used as the common legal standard for all cases; judicial penalties applied against the FARC would be re-signified, such that they could include a reparative character, favour participation in politics, and operate differently from ordinary prisons; and there would be a sequencing and separation of the truth commission and the special jurisdiction, such that the former would free itself of the risk of becoming a mere handmaiden or appendage of justice.

From the same period comes another very interesting internal working document, in which the technical team attached to the Office of the High Commissioner for Peace prepared an updated draft of the government's vision on the model of criminal justice within the comprehensive system of transitional justice. The draft began by stating that its overarching purpose was to find a balance between the demands of legal security and those of dignity, for the benefit of all parties, and proceeded to make the laconic statement that peace is being negotiated with the FARC because they are rebels. It explained, however, that while amnesty for the act of rebellion is acceptable, there can be none for a long list of crimes characterised by the guerrillas as necessary means to pursue their rebellious ends.

The model itself, illustrated in the document, outlined the sequence of steps that would need to be followed to resolve one's legal status, both for those deemed 'most responsible' (voluntarily or otherwise) and those not. Regarding the latter group, the document noted that, upon signature of the final agreement, criminal prosecution, sentencing, and judicial enforcement would be suspended up until the resolution of their legal status. In a second stage, upon completion of the disarmament process and the disengagement of minors, the government would present to Congress a general amnesty for the crime of rebellion. In the third and final stage, which would take place only after the designation of those most responsible, the non-selected cases would receive a definitive resolution of their legal status by a chamber of the special court created for such purpose. That resolution could include final rulings on the removal of sentences (where they already exist) and the definitive choice of non-prosecution (where they do not), with the effect of res judicata.

This internal draft, just as the previous one, was fundamentally a projection of the philosophy of the Legal Framework for Peace. At the same time, in these tortuous attempts to strike a balance between legal security and dignity that would be acceptable to the FARC, but also the Armed Forces, both documents nevertheless represented a stepping stone to the government delegation's Plan A, and eventually to the D-75 reached with the FARC.

The fundamental moral and political issue, which at times became rather heated – including at a private meeting in Hotel Portón in Bogota – was that of the factual and normative possibility of justifying, and connecting, reprehensible means with altruistic ends. An official of the Office of the High Commissioner for Peace remarked that some had been morally unwilling to accept the idea of establishing a broad connection with political crime because this implied the justification of very serious crimes in the name of altruistic purposes. Orozco and a few others, meanwhile, having exhausted their moral and legal arguments, ended up speculating that the team's unreadiness to make more room for political crime perhaps had something to do with generational differences that made the extension of political crime seem exotic, at best. If in the philosophy of the Legal Framework for Peace political crime was a useless anachronism, now political crime was seen as outright dangerous.

Delivering Plan A

The expression 'Plan A' was born from the latter discussion at the Portón Hotel. Orozco and some others requested that their proposals be put on the back burner as Plan B, in the event that the Plan A (favoured by Freeman and the majority of the High Commissioner's team) got rejected by the guerrillas. But the baton was in the hands of Sergio Jaramillo. He was present and had a key say in everything that led to the final version of Plan A, including in the separate consultations with the Technical Committee in Bogota and the government delegation in Havana. But the process of generating the position, combined with the subsequent months-long reluctance to present Plan A to the FARC delegation, led to a fair amount of impatience and internal frustration.

The FARC filled the absence of discussions on justice when, on 19 June 2015, they presented the government delegation with the lengthy 'Minimum Agreement Initiative on the Comprehensive Rights of Victims for Peace and National Reconciliation', which we analysed in detail in the preceding chapter. Timochenko, the leader of the FARC in the field, reinforced the importance of the document by reading a long statement from his hiding place somewhere in Colombia. In it, he said, among other things, that the process would all have been meaningless if it ended simply with the government imposing the terms of transitional justice; the FARC's position has been to recognise at all times the responsibility that corresponds to it from the war, but without apologising for having taken up arms; the state and the 'establishment' as a whole must likewise be frank about their wartime responsibilities; and what is required is a solution of a political nature, to which the law must adapt itself.

A few days later, the government delegation in Havana responded to the FARC's document. It noted with special concern that the issue of justice was absent from the document, stating that the guerrillas were clearly reluctant to be held accountable for the serious violations committed by their members during the armed conflict. The government delegation also told the FARC that, with the main elements of the truth commission mandate already agreed, it was necessary to begin addressing issues of justice and reparation simultaneously, in order to build the elements of a comprehensive system. Adviser Freeman, for his part, had already been stressing for months, within the delegation, that the discussion of justice had to be inserted into the conversation, and that the government delegation would risk more than it would gain with further delays in sharing its Plan A – especially since the plan had received the endorsement of the Technical Committee quite some time earlier. In Bogota as well, public opinion, and especially the opposition, demanded results.

In the end, it was not until the evening of 19 July 2015 when Jaramillo's final polish on the delegation's agreed Plan A was handed over to the FARC delegation at their house in El Laguito in a sealed envelope. The hope was that the FARC, by then, would have sufficiently 'mourned' and absorbed the fact that a custodial sentence of some sort was a precondition to reaching a final agreement and ending the war.

Unfortunately, by the time Plan A was delivered, the climate both in Bogota and in Havana was very tense. The previous months had been among the most violent ones since the beginning of the talks in Cuba. In April, the FARC had killed eleven apparently defenceless soldiers. Amidst the public outrage, there was strong retaliation by the Armed Forces in which dozens of guerrillas were killed. Thus began an escalation of attacks and counterattacks that, in addition to deaths on both sides, caused enormous environmental damage and destruction of energy infrastructure. And, for the first time in years, the negotiated solution had less favour among public opinion than a military resolution of the war.

In early June, President Santos had warned the FARC in a public address that if the escalated war and the lack of agreements on justice persisted, the whole peace process could come to an end. In early July, Humberto De La Calle had reiterated the point in a media interview, affirming that the patience of the Colombian people was running out. However, neither the President nor De La Calle had slammed the door shut on the process. Their words contained a warning, but not an ultimatum, and suggested possible solutions to the crisis. De La Calle said, in the same interview, that he greatly appreciated that the FARC had finally accepted that there needed to be a comprehensive transitional justice system.

In the depths of this crisis, the idea of 'accelerating in Havana and de-escalating in Colombia' was agreed, and with it the shift to discussing several issues simultaneously rather than sequentially, as had been done by and large up to that point. The decision also marked the softening of the rigid routine of eleven-day cycles in Cuba, separated at regular intervals by returns by the government team to Bogota. Adviser Orozco discussed with Sergio Jaramillo the opportunity nestled within the crisis: that under the pressure of imminent collapse of the talks, the issue of justice could finally move forward.

Semana, a weekly magazine that was very close to the lead government negotiators (and consequently, well informed as regards the state of the talks), published an extensive analysis a few days after the delivery of Plan A to the FARC, interpreting the spirit of the proposal quite faithfully but without referring explicitly to it. The article included a headline in huge letters asking, 'Will This Man Go to Prison'?, with a photo of Timochenko reading a document.[34] An excerpt in bold read, 'The light at the end of the tunnel of the peace process has a final stumbling block: justice. The government has said that there will be no jail with bars or striped pyjamas for the FARC. But if there is no minimum agreement on this issue by November, the peace process could break'. Another box in smaller letters read, 'At the Havana talks, they

---

[34] See www.semana.com/nacion/articulo/timochenko-ira-la-carcel/435239-3.

will have to find a middle ground between the amnesty that Timochenko and his men dream of, and the jail without bars that Humberto De La Calle announced'. Finally, it stated, 'Political crime has to be expanded to encompass the conducts typical of war. The big question is how far it can be stretched'.

The Content of Plan A

It would be inaccurate to say that Plan A expressed excessive obsession with legal security and disdain for the issue of dignity. It would be equally wrong to say that its tone was confrontational or unsympathetic. Too much time had gone by – and too many discussions had taken place in Havana and Bogotá – for too much of the spirit of the Legal Framework to dominate in the text. Instead, Plan A constituted a delicate exercise that sought to balance everything that had been learned and debated over a period of many years, inside and outside of the process.

While insisting on non-amnesty for international crimes, and citing the counterpart's own documents to support this, the government proposal clearly stated that the penalties imposed by the proposed 'special tribunal' would have to include 'deprivation of liberty' – susceptible, of course, to being modulated in the flexible terms of the Legal Framework for Peace. Regarding the idea of the tribunal, which would be independent of ordinary justice, this was a gambit that, as said earlier in this chapter, was favoured by the guerrillas and by many in the military. However, it was also one that involved a high cost, since it could increase the animosity of the defenders of ordinary justice towards the peace process and its customised form of accountability.

The government proposal moved away from the more radical selection formula reflected in the earlier 'Jesus Christ strategy'. Rather than a model focused on the 'most responsible', the emphasis was on a selection process targeting those who played a 'decisive role' in the commission of the 'most serious and representative' crimes. Deliberately, the expression implied movement towards a revised formula that was, at once, tolerable to the justice maximalists that dominate parts of civil society, and sensitive to the perspective of the top commanders on both sides of the conflict who rejected rank as the predominant criterion of criminal responsibility. As for making concessions ex ante to the issue of dignity vis-à-vis the FARC, the document stated that the punishment would be both retributive and reparative, and its execution would be made compatible with the FARC's transformation into a political party – which was, after all, a central reason why the parties were negotiating at all.

In the spirit of the Legal Framework for Peace, Plan A also echoed long-discussed proposals within the government's Technical Committee, recognising that for those not selected for criminal sanction, the final legal resolution should be provided by the special jurisdiction through what, colloquially, was called 'the diploma office'. The JEP chamber for resolving legal status issues, formalised later in D-75, was largely the heir of this. As for the crimes that had survived the judicial asphyxiation to which the ordinary courts had subjected the treatment of political crime and its related crimes, Plan A offered essentially what the Framework had envisaged: a limited form of amnesty, meant to help meet the counterpart's expectation of dignity.

But it is also worth noting the unspoken presence of the Justice and Peace process, in particular on the question of the length of sentences. As a political reality, that process had bequeathed to the negotiations in Havana a punitive standard of between five and eight years of 'alternative punishment' for those who had committed very serious crimes not eligible for amnesty. The original formula of the Justice and Peace Law, which was to involve serving sentences in country homes (*fincas*), was defeated in Congress; but the final version was adopted by former President Uribe as the necessary standard of justice that should reign over all future negotiations with the guerrillas. 'Equal sentences for equally serious crimes' was the refrain repeated by officials and politicians close to his administration, adding that the victims are indifferent as to who violated their rights and caused them harm. The argument was very convincing; it was constructed from the point of view of the victims, and, like almost all arguments based on the principle of equality, it was evocative and difficult to refute. Having been educated in Uribe's discourse of 'democratic security' for eight years, Colombian society – including many in the Santos administration – had adopted and even internalised the formula.

Yet, the Justice and Peace model had clear weaknesses in terms of the differences between paramilitaries and guerrillas, derived from the pro-system character of the former and the anti-system nature of the latter – a distinction that had been upheld by Colombia's high courts in their rulings on the Justice and Peace Law itself. In addition, for the guerrillas, standing upon the long Colombian tradition of privileged treatment for political criminals, the demand for more favourable treatment than the AUC – their sworn enemies – was a question not only of interest but also of dignity.

Thus, the government had to find a difficult balance between the need to satisfy the demands of justice of a society whose ideological centre of gravity had moved several degrees to the right and simply wanted prison sentences for the communist guerrilla leaders, and the demands of a guerrilla group that, in terms of both selfish interest and revolutionary dignity, demanded more benign and more politically oriented treatment than what the AUC paramilitaries had received. As such, some deprivation of liberty for those who had played an essential role in the commission of the most serious and representative crimes was necessary, for reasons of justice and politics alike. Plan A thus resorted to various concepts – such as the reparative component of sentences, and the use of IHL as the common standard – to bridge the competing demands.

However, none of this would have been acceptable but for the usage – very much in the logic of the Framework – of a variety of intertwined conditions for receiving any special legal treatment. In particular, the government proposed that legal benefits should be conditioned upon meeting conditions of truth, reparation, and guarantees of non-recurrence – and in the case of the FARC, of disarmament too. This better corresponded to the most recent international guidelines, making the granting of such benefits more digestible for the human rights community, while increasing legal security in the same act. It also better honoured the multipurpose nature of transitional justice in its aim of satisfying the rights of victims.

Another key element of the government proposal was that it contemplated a multi-step procedure of objective and subjective case selection. Initially conceived at the Office of the High Commissioner for Peace, the idea matured through intense discussions within the Technical Committee, fusing the high selectivity contemplated in the Legal Framework for Peace, with the countervailing interest of the warring parties that the formula avoid being excessively humiliating. As such, Plan A proposed the creation of an independent political-legal 'investigation and selection committee', which would perform the task of case selection very quickly, drawing from a 'basket of crimes' made up of the 'most serious and representative' ones – some arising through confessions, others through investigation – out of which a 'specialised prosecutor' would choose those persons who, within the limited pool of previously defined cases, would be prosecuted following the criteria of 'essential role'. In order to prevent the number of prosecutions from becoming too large (e.g., through an inflationary use of the criterion of essential role), the government proposal also contemplated that the negotiating parties could agree, if not on a fixed number, at least on a minimum and maximum number of potential defendants.

But it was understood that the key to selling any such ideas with the FARC was the need for a mechanism incentivising and allowing voluntary acknowledgments of responsibility. In this regard, Plan A picked up on the long-standing government idea that such a mechanism should figure centrally in the transitional justice model. Although the FARC and the military had initially rejected the device (in its 'Jesus Christ' form), in the end the FARC made it their own in the interest of dignity. In a radicalised version, it became the heart of their struggle during the discussions on D-75.

In the final phase of the discussions of Point 5, the FARC took the idea to the extreme: in their opinion, everything related to the JEP should be self-imposed. However, the government delegates always insisted that justice is only intelligible (and able to offer legal security) inasmuch as it is associated with the presence of an independent 'third party' who decides on everything. That is why Plan A suggested that voluntary recognitions take place in court, prior to prosecutorial case selection, by those who thought they risked being indicted. Why this remained dignifying is that self-selection, as shown by voluntary appearance, was at its core.

In summary, the government's very late but very complete proposal had begun to move away from the Legal Framework for Peace, by departing from a model that maximised legal security to the detriment of dignity. However, it was clear that the longest stretch of road was still ahead. While Plan A managed to depoliticise justice by use of the common standard of IHL, it did not take the more definitively symbolic and dignifying step of replacing the idea of a jail-like penalty with one that simply restricts freedom of movement for those who voluntarily recognise their participation in the worst crimes. Likewise, the proposal suffered from the defect of failing to confront the key issue of the connection between drug trafficking and political crime.

About the Legal Committee and D-75

In late July and early August 2015 – when President Santos went against public opinion by responding to the FARC's new unilateral ceasefire by announcing that he was going to de-escalate the state's military offensive by suspending aerial bombardment of guerrilla camps – the final chance for the Havana talks was in play. But the President had another move up his sleeve: the creation of an ad hoc legal committee, agreed with the FARC, that would be in charge of advancing – at lightning speed – the final stretch of Point 5 negotiations on justice. In the same speech in which Santos announced his commitment to de-escalate the war, he also announced that a period of four months, up until November 2015, would be given to assess the feasibility of continuing with the entire Havana process. Thus, the legal committee began its work under enormous time pressure to produce results, whatever they might be.

There were different rumours about the origin of the idea of creating the committee, but what is certain is that it triggered a mix of confusion and concern for the core government delegation in Havana. The lead negotiators didn't offer precise explanations to the rest of the team, but it is possible they lacked full explanations themselves. As such, speculation and rumour abounded.

Before long, what became clear is that the President's decision constituted a kind of coup against the key players on the 'first team' (i.e., his long-standing delegation in Havana led by Humberto De La Calle and Sergio Jaramillo). The mandate of the three lawyers he appointed as government representatives on the legal committee was left deliberately vague, and the starting team didn't know if it had been moved to the bench, if it was still part of the starting rotation, or if it had been simply moved from a forward position to a defence position. There was a feeling that the President, without dismissing his first team, had told the 'second team' (i.e., the three lawyers): 'You fix the problem'. For the first team, not knowing the exact nature and scope of the second team's mandate meant not knowing (1) the legal and political status of these new players, and (2) the binding force, or not, of the 'agreements' that the legal committee as a whole was meant to advance in its separate discussions.

During internal conversation at Ambassador Bell's official residence in Havana, the government delegation naturally viewed with dismay this profound lack of clarity. However, being professionals, they generally tried their best to collaborate with the second team, including through regular joint meetings that were used either to assist in preparing for upcoming meetings of the legal committee, or to enable the starting team to learn about the latest developments of a 'draft' mushrooming vertiginously out of the legal committee. The problem was that, in these meetings, it was often impossible to know if the first team was receiving a report for its approval, or if it was simply being informed about matters that were settled and unchangeable. Precisely this ambiguity lay at the root of a subsequent conflict that arose between the government and the FARC, around whether the first versions of what would later become D-75 were framework drafts, final drafts, or provisional agreements. It's as if President Santos had wanted to maintain ambiguity in the matter of relations between his first and second teams, so as not to hurt anyone's feelings, and trusting that things would be settled along the way.

Regrettably, in practice, it was a profound mess. There was great confusion derived from the fact that the first and second teams were given different mandates: more defined and rigid for the former and more flexible for the latter; longer term for the former and very short term for the latter. This confusion was compounded by the fact that the second team thought of itself as the new starting line-up, when in reality they were freshmen to the talks, lacking the experience, knowledge, institutional memory, and bigger-picture perspective that come from several years of prior negotiation. At the same time, one could argue that they were also, as a consequence, less closed-minded. They saw their job in very simple terms: get a deal in place fast, with the implicit logic that a topsy-turvy deal was better than no deal at all.

The initial meetings between the first and second teams were especially difficult. The reciprocal mistrust was enormous and the substantive differences around the model of justice were abysmal. Each team seemed to want to bypass the other and talk directly to the President, both to protest and to persuade. However, it would be the substitutes who would ultimately exercise the upper hand; after all, it was the government delegation that had dropped the ball of justice, failing to put in an 'A' performance on the issue for so long that the entire match had been put at risk.

The members of the second team were characterised, by almost all members and aides of the first team, as shamelessly giving in to demands by the FARC's lawyers and showing little interest or understanding in the rest of the agreements that had already been reached or advanced. Professor Orozco, who had a pre-existing relationship with a couple of the substitutes, was, at times, about to throw in the towel. Trying to find middle ground, or to bring members of the government delegation closer to the substitutes, was often a thankless task.

So toxic were the discussions between the two teams that, at times, they seemed to become a proxy for the actual negotiations with the enemy. It is perhaps for this reason that it took the President's coup against his own delegation to bring its members to their maximal state of unity. Until the arrival of the second team, the government delegation had been marked by a lack of closeness among several of its members, each of them representing different interests and ways of thinking. The arrival of the distrusted substitutes changed all that.

It was as if there were two football matches being played simultaneously: one between midfielders and their own goalkeeper and defence, and another with the real opponent on the other side. High Commissioner Jaramillo told Orozco that the government delegation would have to begin 'playing with the black pieces': an expression taken from chess to denote that the initiative had passed to the legal committee, and that the government delegation had to be on permanent alert and ready to react. Fortunately, De La Calle and Jaramillo – and the government team as a whole – were well prepared after many years of dealing with the FARC. Thus, despite some very arduous moments, the delegation's overarching mission became to support and guide the new attackers (i.e., the substitutes) so that they could play a better game against the true opponent on the other side of the pitch. But the pitch was uneven, and it was the path to the FARC's goal line, not the government's, that sloped upwards. That is because, while the FARC representatives in the committee were often present at the official negotiating table in El Palco Hotel, thus enjoying direct access to what was happening in both venues, the government representatives on the committee were never present there, and thus had less firsthand information.

Playing with the Black Pieces

Up to this point, 'playing with the white pieces' against the FARC had meant, for the first team, playing on the offensive by favouring the interest in legal security for all parties, to the detriment of the counterpart's interest in dignity. 'Playing with the black pieces' meant playing defensively against the substitute team, and protecting the process from the excesses of legal uncertainty caused – in the eyes of the first team – by the alacrity of the substitutes to give in to the interests and the proposals of the FARC.

A clear example of what playing the black pieces meant is reflected in an internal analysis of the Office of the High Commissioner for Peace regarding one of the first rough drafts produced at a meeting of the legal committee during the development of what eventually became D-75. The draft was presented by the second team to the first team in circumstances that, as already explained, made it very difficult to know the type of meeting that had taken place. Likewise, it was impossible to know if the act of presenting the draft was one of asking for the first team's green light, or simply a progress report offered by an autonomous second team. The matter was all the more obscure because, although the legal committee had already begun to operate, its existence had not yet been made public officially. This would happen only a few days later.

The Office of the High Commissioner for Peace prepared an analysis of the document that had been presented, noting its strengths and weaknesses, while also making suggestions for improvement. Although full of doubts about the basic technical quality of the work, the Office's analysis aimed constructively to support the plenipotentiaries in their upcoming discussion with the substitute team, in circumstances in which it was not at all clear whether the latter would be willing to receive any instructions.

On the positive side, it was noted that the draft that the second team had shared with the first team excluded international crimes from being amnestied; vindicated the idea that there would be a special tribunal independent of the ordinary courts; incorporated the notion of an initial extrajudicial phase for the selection of the cases for prosecution; and adopted the idea of a 'double track' system, an idea first developed by adviser Freeman, according to which persons wishing to recognise their responsibility could choose a first track of judicial accountability offering special legal treatment, knowing that silence implied the risk of being indicted on a second track that lacked such treatment.

Nevertheless, the government delegation genuinely believed that the second team could not be left to its own devices. Not knowing the history of the negotiations well enough, they could easily and inadvertently end up throwing away its achievements, producing formulas inconsistent with the whole of what had been negotiated already, or risking an excessive focus on solving the justice issue with the FARC, paying insufficient attention to state agents (and most especially, the military). There was also concern that the FARC's efforts to arrive at a more dignifying justice formula, through its representatives on the legal committee, could cause great damage to everyone's legal security.

On the specifics of the text that the second team had shared, a first major concern noted by the Office of the High Commissioner was that the legal committee seemed already to be heading toward a justice model that barely looked judicial, in an excess of accommodation of the FARC's dignity demands. Citing the phrase used repeatedly by Sergio Jaramillo, the recommendation was for the plenipotentiaries to urge the second team to ensure that 'the duck quacks', one indicator of which would be a set of penalties involving 'deprivation of liberty'.

A second major concern, already insinuated in the text, was the omission of the military. After all, the Ministry of Defence and the Armed Forces themselves had demanded to be incorporated into the Havana justice agreements, and had insisted on principles such as that: the procedure to establish individual responsibility should be judicial, not extrajudicial; there should be no incentives for false reporting against one's superiors; the system should not require acknowledgement of collective responsibility for all parties; and the persons bearing greatest responsibility should be those who had an 'essential role' and 'effective control'. The second team needed to be urged to use these points constructively, since the demands of the military should serve as an argument inside the legal committee to force a better balance between legal security and dignity, and in so doing help the duck of justice quack more persuasively in the eyes of Colombians and the international community.

A third substantive concern was the disconnect with the parts of the comprehensive transitional justice system that had already been agreed with the FARC. In particular, the second team needed to pay more careful attention to issues like victim participation and the issue of 'conditionalities', so that all parts of the transitional justice package could be joined up in a coherent and mutually reinforcing way, bearing in mind that comprehensiveness would play a key role in terms of the political and legal legitimacy of the deal, and hence of the degree of legal security.

A final major concern about the text was the room it allowed for taking account of the guerrillas' own legal norms (*juridicidad guerrillera*). It was one thing to take into account the rebels' internal justice procedures in order to better understand the kind of voluntary acknowledgements of responsibility that might arise in future; but any explicit mention of rebel standards of justice could seriously jeopardise the whole deal, bearing in mind the planned plebiscite and the widespread animosity of the population toward the FARC.

The D-75 as a Battleground

Over the ensuing weeks, many in-depth conversations took place, and most of these were agonising for the first and second teams alike. But in the end, the government delegation seemed to play its black pieces well, helping the second team – notionally, its allies against a common enemy – get a result that, though unsatisfactory in fundamental areas, overcame even worse fears based on the initial conversations that took place and the first text that the second team had presented. D-75 was now well on its way to being adopted – or so it seemed, as the legal committee concluded its work and was thanked for its diligence.

However, a new battle was in fact brewing; one directly attributable to the ambiguity built into the relation between the government's first and second teams. The former, which seemed to have regained its negotiating power after the dissolution of the legal committee, understood that although the substitute team had been appointed by the President, what it had produced through the legal committee was a final draft, not a final agreement. Meanwhile, the FARC leadership seemed to believe that the legal committee had constituted a forum of plenipotentiary decision making and that, as such, the seventy-five-point text represented a definitive agreement on the model of justice that would govern the transition. One can thus imagine the severity of the FARC's reaction when, a short time later, the government's Humberto De La Calle told Iván Márquez that it was not a definitive agreement but a 'document in progress'.

The interim climate was very odd. During fleeting encounters in the corridors of the Hotel El Palco Convention Centre, the representatives of the FARC greeted the government delegates with broad smiles, and gave optimistic speeches about their achievements. The government delegates, on the other hand, were evasive in their greetings and appeared depressed. Despite all the effort expended, they saw the document negotiated by the committee as containing deep inconsistencies and shortcomings related to key issues that would have to be resolved before it could be made known to the public. It contained formulas that, in their judgement, crossed 'red lines' of what was politically and legally allowed in the negotiation, meaning that the agreement, as it was, would be rejected by Colombian voters, by the Inter-American Court, and by the ICC.

As the government delegation believed that it had regained full powers to negotiate on the basis of the seventy-five-point text it had received, and as it understood the text to be a final draft not a final agreement, it took the liberty of proposing a number of substantive adjustments. It gave the FARC a revised version that incorporated major additions aimed among other things at (1) avoiding the collapse of the special jurisdiction under the weight of the vast remains of the Justice and Peace macro-process, which the FARC demanded be absorbed into the JEP; (2) ensuring the JEP would be concentrated on the prosecution of those most responsible for the most serious crimes; and (3) making certain that those found to commit the crime of drug trafficking after the signing of the final agreement could be extradited.

As if that were not enough, the government delegation insisted on the need for clarity about the judicial sanctions themselves. It wanted the FARC to accept an interpretation of the legal committee's text in which the sanctions would have two independent components: one restorative, and one of effective restriction of liberty. As could be expected, the FARC's response to this and everything else was immediate and fierce. The guerrillas returned the document to the government team full of their own set of substantive corrections and additions. Their message appeared to be, 'If you repudiate what was agreed in D-75, then we understand that there is no agreement at all, and we too then have the right to redo the document'. Thus it was that the initial version of D-75 became a simple draft without any binding force. The negotiation went into another crisis.

The topics introduced by the FARC that were the subject of the most arduous dispute between the two delegations were those of amnesty; political participation; the competence of the JEP to judge former presidents, paramilitaries, and third parties; the form of the criminal sanction; and the monitoring and conditionalities associated with the sanction. On the first point, the FARC re-drafted the relevant clause, proposing a broad and general amnesty, with a presumption of entitlement across the entire guerrilla membership and 'that can only be rendered ineffective by the resolutions or rulings of the JEP'. In the battlefield that had become the draft, the FARC also sought to add a clause to the effect that 'at the moment of determining the acts eligible for amnesty and pardon, the interpretation most favourable for the amnesty beneficiary shall apply whenever there is no international prohibition'.

In the midst of the 'semantic war' that had broken out between the revived headline delegations, perhaps the biggest item was the demand made by the FARC of doing away with the exclusive jurisdiction of Congress to try presidents, and giving such jurisdiction to the JEP. This would have constituted a threat to all those former presidents who governed during the armed conflict, including Betancur, Gaviria, and Santos himself; but above all it was aimed at former President Uribe. To threaten him was to threaten to set the country on fire. But the issue also had elements of the tension between legal security and dignity. For the FARC leadership, it was a matter of dignity that if its political-military leadership had to appear before the JEP, former and sitting presidents should also appear, since they were, by constitutional provision, commanders in chief of the military and ultimately responsible for the great decisions taken in the course of the war. For the guerrillas, the issue was presented as one of equality, and thus dignity. They were saying, 'what's good for the goose is good for the gander' and 'people who live in glass houses shouldn't throw stones'. But they were also fully aware that the Colombian public would never go for it.

Thus, the crisis about D-75 continued. Both parties saw clearly that, if the document was reduced to a simple draft, the significant work done by the legal committee would be lost – something the FARC, but also President Santos, were keen to avoid. As such, the parties would have to return to something closer to the original version of the document, laying a new baseline to continue negotiating without having to start from scratch. It would also be necessary for the parties to decide whether, for the outstanding negotiations on D-75 and Point 5 in general, the legal committee would be called back onto the pitch for an 'overtime' round – an option that was finally chosen.

Playing again with the black pieces, the government's first team applied tremendous pressure on the second team, so that the latter would resist the FARC's pressure to add self-serving formulas that were excessively costly in terms of political legitimacy and legal security for the entire agreement. Such was the case with presidential jurisdiction and with non-extradition for those who continued drug trafficking after the signing of the final agreement. However, other issues – such as the conditions and timing of amnesty for the rebels – continued to plague the negotiations for a long time. The positions of the FARC and the government remained very distant, even after the legal committee set generous criteria to determine the breadth of the amnesty for political crime and connected offences.

The nature of the criminal sanction was another vexing issue that lingered. The legal committee had agreed that the text of D-75 would say, expressly, that the penalty would not be a prison sentence. In response, the government's first team began to apply pressure on the second team to introduce the adjective 'effective' as a qualifier for the penalty: a term included in the publication by the parties of a ten-point summary that Sergio Jaramillo cleverly created out of the unresolved D-75 document. Given the massive demand by public opinion and many NGOs that the FARC chiefs should go to jail, the term 'effective' served to bring the sanction a little closer in appearance to 'deprivation of liberty'. Nevertheless, it remained a source of bitterness with the FARC, and became a central issue in the partisan discussions that accompanied the 'Yes' and 'No' campaigns of the 2016 plebiscite.

Epilogue

The renegotiated final agreement that followed the 'No' victory in the plebiscite was always destined to be controversial. During the Havana ceremony to announce the new 310-page deal, Humberto De La Calle announced that of the fifty-seven substantive modifications discussed during eleven days behind closed doors with the FARC, the parties had been able to reach a new consensus on fifty-six. He added that for a single point – the ban from political office for those convicted of international crimes not subject to amnesty – it was impossible to reach agreement, despite the government's insistence on its importance as the basis of a broader national pact. The FARC stood firm on their demand for a trade-off between disarming and allowing their leaders to participate actively in democratic life.

Was this a selfish decision driven by the interest of the FARC leadership in preserving its own political eligibility? Was it a decision aimed at guaranteeing the viability of their party-to-be, understanding that only the historical commanders of the guerrillas would be able to lead it safely to port through the turbulence of the transition? Or was it, rather, a decision guided by the desire to preserve their historical identity and, with it, their individual and group dignity? To defend the heart of the agreement, self-interest and dignity had to converge in an amalgam of indiscernible motives.

Whatever the motives may have been, in the March 2018 Congressional elections FARC candidates obtained only around fifty thousand votes, representing a puny 0.53 percent of the total votes cast. During the campaign, Rodrigo Londoño (Timochenko), the presidential candidate for the new political party, was very poorly received and even assaulted in public squares. It was abundantly clear that having negotiated with the

FARC did not mean surrendering the country to 'Castro-Chavism', as the political right had spuriously warned.

Subsequently, on 17 June 2018, with a vote that based on historical Colombian averages was very high, Iván Duque, candidate of the right, was elected President of the Republic for the period 2018–2022. The defeated candidate, Gustavo Petro, who presented himself during the campaign as a great defender of the final agreement with the FARC, obtained the highest vote garnered by the left in the history of Colombia (more than eight million votes).

President-Elect Duque got voted in with an explicit mandate to modify the peace agreement, including multiple changes to the JEP that, were they to pass, would accomplish the threefold result of turning the JEP into a device for the unilateral subjugation of the FARC within the ordinary justice system, humiliating its leadership in the courts, and preventing them from taking their seats in Congress; with the cumulative result of preventing the nascent political party from consolidating. However, as of this writing, trying to derail the transitional justice system that was agreed in Havana has proven difficult. There are significant forces in Congress and society that defend the agreement, along with many foreign states and international organisations. At the same time, the peace process, and especially its transitional justice components, continue to split the country down the middle.

On a final note, we return to the issue of amnesty, for what it may portend of the future of peace with the FARC in Colombia. In August 2016, in the same week when the international ceremony on the first final agreement was held in Cartagena, matters pertaining to the scope and timing of amnesty remained open for discussion. In its 21–28 August issue, *Semana* magazine published an article explaining how the government and the FARC resolved an ongoing dispute about when the amnesty would enter into force. The FARC did not want to move forward with the concentration of their members for demobilisation and disarmament purposes, without a law regulating the specific content of the amnesty. They were concerned, among other things, about the limbo in which their troops would remain in the period between the signing of the agreement and the passing of the law. The article explains how, in the end, the guerrillas accepted the government's formal commitment to present an amnesty bill immediately after the fast-track mechanism began to operate in Congress.

An ex post reading of the bill shows that domestic political-criminal law and IHL were mutually reinforced in their capacity to underpin the amnesty model agreed and finally enshrined in Law 1820 of 2017. Making use of the fast-track procedure, lawmakers created a double amnesty: one part automatic and de jure (for a long series of crimes considered inherent to the military practice of rebellion) and the other judicially assessed through case-by-case rulings of the JEP's amnesty chamber.

Reconstructing the history of the negotiation of Point 5, and also the final text of the law, leaves the impression that, although the figure of privileged treatment for political crime gave shape to the general spirit of the amnesty, IHL was the body of law that in practice allowed the difficult discussions taking place in Havana to establish, one by one, which crimes would be subject to amnesty, on the understanding that it was allowed whenever it was not expressly prohibited (i.e., in the case of international crimes).

What comes next in Colombia's journey away from war will depend on honouring the amnesty, but on so much more. In the quest for legal security that continues, it is certain that questions of dignity will remain not only central – for FARC and state actors alike – but also controversial. The balancing act will continue.

3

Conclusions

Several years into the implementation of Colombia's 2016 peace agreement, the country is experiencing scores of complications in the application of post-conflict justice mechanisms and much else.

No negotiation could have anticipated all, or even most, of these complications. Negotiation and implementation are iterative processes by their very nature. Yet, with the benefit of hindsight, there are some important lessons that are worth summarising – some of which could make a difference in the country's future, or indeed that of others.

Against the odds, Colombia achieved some remarkable things in the negotiation of peace with justice. It is worth recalling these achievements by their name, notwithstanding the challenges many of them produced in Havana as well as in Bogota:

1. *The 2011 Victims' Law:* This was an early confidence-building measure (CBM) through which the Colombian government recognised that it was at war, and made clear that the interests of victims would not be cast aside.
2. *The 2012 Legal Framework for Peace:* Years in advance, the government built the constitutional and conceptual space for the comprehensive transitional justice system that would arise out of Havana.
3. *The 2012 General Agreement:* The parties put victims on the Havana agenda by design, not by accident – and dedicated a special chapter to them as part of a compact set of negotiation issues, and a cogent set of procedural rules that the parties made public.
4. *The 2014 Guiding Principles:* At the start of Point 5, the government reached agreement with the FARC on the criteria and benchmarks for the discussion of victims, before negotiating the details. It then made those benchmarks public.

5. *Victim Delegations:* The parties didn't merely pay attention to victims. They brought delegations of them to Havana – five times – on each occasion ensuring the minimum respect of listening to their testimonies without interruption.
6. *Peacemaking during War:* Improbably, the parties negotiated all of Point 5 in the absence of a bilateral ceasefire – often putting the process at risk, but likewise making the delegations more resolute in their commitment to end the war once and for all.
7. *Interim CBMs:* In the middle of the negotiation of Point 5, the parties agreed and implemented an interim demining programme and an urgent task force on missing persons. These favoured the interests of victims and society, while increasing the parties' commitment to the negotiation.
8. *Diversity of Mechanisms:* Primarily at the government delegation's insistence, the accord includes a panoply of bodies that, in conjunction, can help to make victims' rights functional after the conflict: a special criminal jurisdiction, two truth-seeking bodies, and increased reparations.
9. *Conditionalities:* The accord tethered the parties' commitments into a virtuous legal security loop: truth and reparations were made conditions *of* every special legal benefit and *for* every party to the armed conflict (albeit in differentiated fashion).
10. *Verification:* Conditionalities and legal incentives are important, but the parties went a step further by agreeing a system with independent verification applicable to all actors.
11. *Transversals:* The accord created a value compass for the implementation phase, incorporating cross-cutting criteria of due process, transparency, impartiality, victim participation, gender sensitivity, differential treatment, and dignity.

These achievements are all the more remarkable when one considers the context. First, a large majority of Colombia's citizens expected legal vengeance against the FARC; yet any justice pact would have to be applicable to the popular Armed Forces and other state agents as well. Second, much of the public felt that the government and army were winning the war and thus questioned the very choice to negotiate, making any perceived concessions doubly unpopular. Third, the cooperation of FARC leaders would be indispensable to ensure rapid and permanent disarmament; yet that is never something they would be able or willing to do from a jail cell. Fourth, the FARC's leaders had political convictions and naturally expected a dignified exit with legal guarantees, not a highway to humiliation.

Squaring these and other circles into a coherent agreement on transitional justice was everything except plausible. Yet, it happened. And, importantly, it remains the only case of a post-conflict accountability system that (1) resulted from the direct, unmediated negotiation between the parties to an armed conflict; and (2) is one to which the parties themselves agree to be subject. This is unprecedented, and could not have happened without years of strategic reflection and planning.

Yet, the Havana experience also reminds us that the fate of wars and the fate of negotiations are not preordained. No matter how much science we seek to provide on the challenges of peace, justice, and much else, there will always be a sizable element of human agency capable of producing the best and the worst of errors as well as innovations.

What we know from our work on the Colombian peace talks and elsewhere is that it helps to ask right questions and analyse the fullest spectrum of risks and available options. For an ambition as large and noble as negotiating peace with justice, nothing less suffices.

ANNEX 1

Basic Information about the Havana Negotiation

CONTEXT

- The peace negotiation took place in Havana, Cuba.
- It was a negotiation without mediation, with Cuba and Norway acting as guarantors and Venezuela and Chile acting as accompanying countries.
- The accord was negotiated without a bilateral ceasefire.
- In total, there were thirty-nine negotiation cycles between November 2012 and August 2016, with each cycle lasting an average of eleven days.
- Victims, women, and other affected groups had the opportunity to meet the negotiating parties in Havana.
- The rule of 'nothing is agreed until everything is agreed' was adopted, following the model of Northern Ireland's peace process.
- The Colombian government estimates that around 220,000 persons died and more than 7 million were internally displaced during the armed conflict.

CHRONOLOGY

- August 2010: Juan Manuel Santos is elected President of Colombia.
- February 2012: The secret, exploratory phase between the government and the FARC begins.
- June 2012: The Colombian Congress approves the 'Legal Framework for Peace' (*Marco Jurídico para la Paz*).
- August 2012: The Colombian government and the FARC sign the 'General Agreement for the Termination of the Conflict and the Construction of a Stable and Lasting Peace'. This sets out the agenda and rules for the 'public phase' of the peace talks between the parties.

- September 2012: President Santos announces the commencement of the public phase of the peace talks between the government and the FARC.
- May 2013: An agreement is reached on Point 1 of the agenda (Comprehensive Rural Reform).
- November 2013: An agreement is reached on Point 2 of the agenda (Political Participation).
- May 2014: An agreement is reached on Point 4 of the agenda (Solution to the Problem of Illicit Drugs) and a ceasefire is agreed for the presidential election period.
- June 2014: Juan Manuel Santos is re-elected President of Colombia.
- December 2015: An agreement is reached on Point 5 of the agenda (Victims).
- June 2016: The 'Agreement on a definitive bilateral ceasefire and cessation of hostilities' is signed.
- August 2016: An agreement is reached on Point 3 of the agenda (End of Conflict), marking the end of the peace negotiations.
- September 2016: The 'Final Agreement to End the Armed Conflict and Build a Stable and Lasting Peace' is signed in Cartagena.
- October 2016: In a national plebiscite, 50.2 percent of Colombian voters reject the agreement.
- November 2016: The FARC and the government sign a new version of the final agreement.
- December 2016: Congress approves the new final agreement.
- June 2017: The disarmament of the FARC is concluded and certified.

ANNEX 2

The Legal Framework for Peace (2012)

ACTO LEGISLATIVO 01 DE 2012 (Julio 31)

Por medio del cual se establecen instrumentos jurídicos de justicia transicional en el marco del artículo 22 de la Constitución Política y se dictan otras disposiciones.

EL CONGRESO DE COLOMBIA DECRETA:

Artículo 1°. La Constitución Política tendrá un nuevo artículo transitorio que será el 66, así:

Artículo Transitorio 66. Los instrumentos de justicia transicional serán excepcionales y tendrán como finalidad prevalente facilitar la terminación del conflicto armado interno y el logro de la paz estable y duradera, con garantías de no repetición y de seguridad para todos los colombianos; y garantizarán en el mayor nivel posible, los derechos de las víctimas a la verdad, la justicia y la reparación. Una ley estatutaria podrá autorizar que, en el marco de un acuerdo de paz, se dé un tratamiento diferenciado para los distintos grupos armados al margen de la ley que hayan sido parte en el conflicto armado interno y también para los agentes del Estado, en relación con su participación en el mismo.

Mediante una ley estatutaria se establecerán instrumentos de justicia transicional de carácter judicial o extrajudicial que permitan garantizar los deberes estatales de investigación y sanción. En cualquier caso se aplicarán mecanismos de carácter extrajudicial para el esclarecimiento de la verdad y la reparación de las víctimas.

Una ley deberá crear una Comisión de la Verdad y definir su objeto, composición, atribuciones y funciones. El mandato de la comisión podrá incluir la formulación de recomendaciones para la aplicación de los instrumentos de justicia transicional, incluyendo la aplicación de los criterios de selección.

Tanto los criterios de priorización como los de selección son inherentes a los instrumentos de justicia transicional. El Fiscal General de la Nación determinará criterios de priorización para el ejercicio de la acción penal. Sin perjuicio del deber general del Estado de investigar y sancionar las graves violaciones a los Derechos Humanos y al Derecho Internacional Humanitario, en el marco de la justicia transicional, el Congreso de la República, por iniciativa del Gobierno Nacional, podrá mediante ley estatutaria determinar criterios de selección que permitan centrar los esfuerzos en la investigación penal de los máximos responsables de todos los delitos que adquieran la connotación de crímenes de lesa humanidad, genocidio, o crímenes de guerra cometidos de manera sistemática; establecer los casos, requisitos y condiciones en los que procedería la suspensión de la ejecución de la pena; establecer los casos en los que proceda la aplicación de sanciones extrajudiciales, de penas alternativas, o de modalidades especiales de ejecución y cumplimiento de la pena; y autorizar la renuncia condicionada a la persecución judicial penal de todos los casos no seleccionados. La ley estatutaria tendrá en cuenta la gravedad y representatividad de los casos para determinar los criterios de selección.

En cualquier caso, el tratamiento penal especial mediante la aplicación de instrumentos constitucionales como los anteriores estará sujeto al cumplimiento de condiciones tales como la dejación de las armas, el reconocimiento de responsabilidad, la contribución al esclarecimiento de la verdad y a la reparación integral de las víctimas, la liberación de los secuestrados, y la desvinculación de los menores de edad reclutados ilícitamente que se encuentren en poder de los grupos armados al margen de la ley.

Parágrafo 1°. En los casos de la aplicación de instrumentos de justicia transicional a grupos armados al margen de la ley que hayan participado en las hostilidades, esta se limitará a quienes se desmovilicen colectivamente en el marco de un acuerdo de paz o a quienes se desmovilicen de manera individual de conformidad con los procedimientos establecidos y con la autorización del Gobierno Nacional.

Parágrafo 2°. En ningún caso se podrán aplicar instrumentos de justicia transicional a grupos armados al margen de la ley que no hayan sido parte en el conflicto armado interno, ni a cualquier miembro de un grupo armado que una vez desmovilizado siga delinquiendo.

Artículo 2°. Transitorio. Una vez el gobierno nacional presente al Congreso de la República el primer proyecto de ley que autorice la aplicación de los instrumentos penales establecidos en el inciso 4° del artículo 1° del presente acto legislativo, el Congreso tendrá cuatro (4) años para proferir todas las leyes que regulen esta materia.

Artículo 3°. La Constitución Política tendrá un nuevo artículo transitorio que será el 67, así:

Artículo Transitorio 67. Una ley estatutaria regulará cuáles serán los delitos considerados conexos al delito político para efectos de la posibilidad de participar en política. No podrán ser considerados conexos al delito político los delitos que adquieran la connotación de crímenes de lesa humanidad y genocidio cometidos de manera sistemática, y en consecuencia no podrán participar en política ni ser elegidos quienes hayan sido condenados y seleccionados por estos delitos.

Artículo 4°. El presente acto legislativo rige a partir de su promulgación.

Index

ad hoc legal committee, 142, 185, 213–215, 218, 232–239, 242
amnesties, 4, 8, 10, 14, 16, 19, 27, 30, 33–34, 43, 46, 48, 69, 83, 102, 141–142, 158, 163–167, 171, 173, 177, 184–185, 187, 196–197, 200, 204, 207–210, 212–213, 220, 225, 229–230, 238–239, 241
Arendt, Hannah, 78–79, 83, 95
Argentina, 79–80, 100, 102, 145, 148
arrest warrants, 46, 54, 202
asymmetrical warfare, 64, 68, 84, 88–89, 99, 129, 163, 167, 196, 205–206, 225

Belfast Guidelines on Amnesty and Accountability, 14, 35
Betancur, President Belisario, 60, 85, 239

Caguán talks, 61–64, 71, 106, 121, 215
Catatumbo, Pablo, 219
Catholic Church, 60, 75, 91, 101, 107, 124–125, 127
ceasefires, 16, 29, 40–41, 46, 70, 121, 139–140, 199, 218, 232, 244, 247–248
Centro Democrático party, 62, 77, 85, 87, 91, 98, 123, 130, 177, 190, 200, 206, 214–215
Chile, 11, 39, 72, 80, 97, 100, 102–103, 146, 148, 171, 247
Cold War, 39, 59–60, 64, 76, 82, 148, 212
Colombian Retired Officers Association (ACORE), 77, 115, 123
conditionalities, 29, 35, 42, 44, 46, 49, 128, 167, 209, 223, 231, 236, 238, 244
confidence-building measures, 5, 16, 21, 34, 40–42, 243–244
confidentiality, 26, 29, 38, 62, 71, 73, 107, 117, 181

Congress, 15, 64–65, 129, 168, 173–174, 176, 180, 182–183, 187, 190, 198–202, 222–223, 226, 230, 239, 241, 247–248
Constitution of Colombia (1886), 173–175
Constitution of Colombia (1991), 64–66, 113, 141, 148, 150, 160, 172–175, 178, 180, 182–184, 187, 195, 198, 200, 205, 207–209, 214, 222
Constitutional Court of Colombia, 160, 174, 176–178, 180, 182, 190, 198, 201, 209
constructive ambiguities, 5, 15, 21, 40–41
Cuba, 39, 42, 59, 72, 103, 106–108, 116, 118–119, 135, 143, 182, 223, 228, 247

D-75, 193–197, 205, 209, 211–214, 220, 226, 230, 232–233, 235, 237–240
De La Calle, Humberto, 117, 120–121, 123, 125, 129, 132, 135, 228–229, 233–234, 237, 240
dictatorships, 3, 6–7, 11–13, 66–67, 80, 85, 95, 98–103, 167–168, 171, 174, 191
disarmament, demobilisation, and reintegration (DDR), 5, 11, 35, 39, 43, 46, 48–49, 52, 54, 66, 104, 115, 140, 160, 178, 190, 206, 221, 226, 231, 241, 244, 248
drugs, 47, 52–53, 60, 71–73, 85, 89, 98, 107, 110, 130, 150–151, 160, 183, 197, 199, 202, 210, 212–213, 216, 232, 238–239
due process, 8, 79, 113, 157, 169, 210, 225, 244
Duque, President Iván, 201, 241

Eichmann, Adolf, 79, 95, 169
El Salvador, 4, 64, 101, 147
ELN, 68, 72, 112, 114, 124, 160
Elster, Jon, 165, 169
European Union (EU), 103
extradition, 54, 184, 197, 202, 208, 213, 239

false positives, 118, 193–194
forgiveness, 74–75, 91, 102, 119, 122, 127, 141

gender, 77, 109, 244
General Agreement (2012), 61, 71, 105–106, 137, 151, 243, 247
Geneva Conventions, 23, 27–28, 166, 198, 208
good faith, 41, 44, 48, 53, 89
grey zones, 74, 82, 92–98, 103, 126

Historical Commission, 129–135, 144, 153, 159
Historical Memory Centre, 96, 112–116, 122, 149, 153
Historical Memory Group, 112
human rights standards, 3, 6, 9–10, 13, 19, 22–24, 26–27, 31, 35, 40, 57, 67, 72, 74, 77, 80–81, 88–89, 91–92, 99–103, 109–116, 125, 136, 139–143, 149, 151, 157, 159–160, 164–166, 174–175, 177, 179, 182, 188–192, 194, 196, 200, 205–206, 222, 231

Ideas for Peace Foundation (FIP), 108, 110–111
impunity, 13, 17, 60–61, 83–84, 99, 101–102, 136, 142, 165, 167, 176, 179, 189, 196, 206, 211, 214
incentives, 1, 17, 25, 36, 46, 48, 56, 97, 158, 196, 205, 225, 236, 244
Inter-American human rights system, 101, 142, 171, 178, 180, 189, 196–197, 207, 223, 238
International Committee of the Red Cross (ICRC), 70, 103, 166
International Criminal Court, 23, 69, 158, 165–166, 179–180, 183, 188, 194–195, 197, 200, 207, 210, 223, 238
international humanitarian law (IHL), 22–24, 28, 33, 35, 49, 60, 64, 68, 88, 94, 100, 128, 134, 138–139, 142, 148, 166, 184–185, 188–191, 193, 196–197, 208, 225, 231–232, 241
Israel, 70, 78–79, 95

Jaramillo, Sergio, ix, 116, 128, 144, 146, 149–150, 154, 170, 218, 224, 234
Jesus Christ strategy, 219, 229, 232
jus ad bellum, 22, 92, 99, 134, 139, 144, 159
jus in bello, 22, 92, 99, 134, 159
Justice and Peace Law (2005), 54, 62, 96, 98, 112, 114, 156, 176, 179, 185, 206, 230, 238

Legal Framework for Peace, 14, 51, 64, 141, 148, 150, 157, 167, 175–179, 186, 205–208, 211–214, 217, 222–224, 226, 229–232, 243, 247, 249
legal security, 5, 16–17, 21, 27, 53–54, 56–57, 66, 141, 168, 170, 172, 185–186, 191, 195, 203–207, 209–210, 213–214, 216–217, 219, 221–226, 229, 231–232, 235–236, 239, 242, 244
leverage, 45–46, 144

M-19 guerrillas, 118, 174–175, 192
margin of appreciation, 20, 33
Márquez, Iván, 71, 120, 123, 125, 132, 135, 146–147, 202, 237
Marulanda, Manuel, 73
media, 28, 46, 73, 90, 117, 119, 124, 126, 130–131, 144, 151, 202, 228
memory, 77–78, 80–81, 84, 96, 99–100, 108, 113–115, 135, 233
missing persons, 42–43, 116, 210, 244
Moncayo, Víctor, 133
Mora, General Jorge Enrique, 120, 123, 147–150, 194

narrative, 43, 65, 85, 93, 97, 113, 115, 130, 134–135, 144, 159, 161, 215,
narratives, 84, 96, 115, 131, 151, 159, 203
National Front, 148, 173, 181
National Reparation and Reconciliation Commission, 112
negotiation cycles, 8, 45, 125, 128, 151–152, 212, 228, 247
Negotiationland, 6, 8–12, 15
nongovernmental organisations (NGOs), 67, 88, 107, 113–115, 139, 141, 143, 149, 159, 192, 206, 214, 240
Northern Ireland, 11, 40, 43, 60, 71, 247
Norway, 39, 42, 70–72, 103, 106, 158, 216, 247
Nuremberg trials, 78–79, 99–100, 103, 134, 168

Office of the High Commissioner for Peace (OACP), 108, 110, 153, 223, 225–226, 231, 235–236
Ordoñez, Alejandro, 183–184
overlapping consensus, vii, 47

pacta sunt servanda, 103, 168
Pastrana, President Andrés, 61, 63, 106, 215
Patriotic Union (UP), 60, 85, 122, 125, 147
Pizarro, Eduardo, ix, 65, 112, 130, 133

plebiscite, 55, 64–65, 69, 75, 103, 115, 160, 167, 179–180, 182, 194, 198–199, 204–205, 215, 237, 240, 248
political participation, 5, 11, 35, 43, 46–47, 52, 71, 107, 128, 134, 160, 217, 238, 240
process design, 32, 34, 37, 39, 44, 48
Prosecutor General, 113, 143, 157, 190, 192, 201–202
public opinion, 18, 47, 53, 61–62, 71, 75, 89, 91, 106, 124, 126, 130, 133, 186–187, 195, 218, 222, 227–228, 236, 239–240, 244

rebellion, 67, 72, 77, 121, 134, 138, 142, 159, 163, 165, 183, 185, 187, 208–209, 212, 224–225, 242
reconciliation, 67, 74, 86, 92, 99–102, 116, 118, 121–122, 124, 140–141, 146–147, 152, 156, 163, 204
res judicata, 203, 210, 226
risks, controlled and uncontrolled, 5, 15, 21, 42
rituals, 75, 86, 119–120, 126, 141, 152, 209, 211
root causes, 18, 135
rural reform, 47, 52, 73, 107, 128, 134, 154

Safeland, 6, 8, 12
Santos, President Juan Manuel, 14, 45, 61–63, 66–67, 69–70, 73, 89, 91–92, 106, 110, 113, 119, 121, 129, 137–138, 140, 145, 161, 175, 186, 190, 195, 199, 205, 214–215, 218, 228, 230, 232–233, 239, 247
Santrich, Jesús, 106, 135, 146, 150–151, 202
Shoah (Holocaust), 77–80, 83, 88, 94, 169
South African Truth and Reconciliation Commission (TRC), 19, 141, 145, 185–186
Spain, 11, 60, 102, 171, 199
Special Jurisdiction for Peace (JEP), 98, 142–143, 160, 179, 186, 193–197, 199, 201–202, 205, 209–211, 213, 217, 220, 230, 232, 238, 241–242

Technical Committee, 188, 190–191, 193, 222, 226–227, 230–231
terrorism, 81, 88, 94, 163, 187, 213
Timochenko, 194, 199, 215, 227–228, 240
trade-offs, 43, 52–53
Transitionland, 6–12
Truth, Coexistence, and Non-Repetition Commission (CEV), 98
Turbay, President Julio César, 174

UN Charter, 24, 33
UN Security Council, 23, 25, 31, 103, 166
United Self-Defence Groups of Colombia (AUC), 61, 96, 156, 176, 190, 206, 223, 230
United States, 39, 63, 68–69, 73, 78, 80, 103, 138, 163, 180, 202, 218
Uribe, President Alvaro, 61–63, 69, 73, 87, 96, 112, 115, 121, 156, 181, 184, 189, 194, 199, 213, 222–223, 230, 239

Venezuela, 39, 69, 72, 75, 103, 247
Vichy regime, 80
victimhood, 18, 67, 82, 86–87, 89, 94, 125, 138
victimisation, vertical and horizontal, 66, 84, 92–93, 95, 99–102, 135
Victims and Land Restitution Law (2011), 137, 154, 243
Victims Unit, 112, 153–156